nting
titute

Family
British

Editor
Stephen A. H

D1078182

The Family and Parenting Institute researches what matters to families and parents. We use our knowledge to influence policymakers and foster public debate. We develop ideas to improve the services that families use and the environment in which children grow up.

Family and Parenting Institute is the operating name of the National Family and Parenting Institute (NFPI). NFPI is a company limited by guarantee in England and Wales.

Registered company number: 3753345
VAT registration number: 833024365
Registered charity no. 1077444

Registered office:
430 Highgate Studios
53–79 Highgate Road
London NW5 1TL

Designed by Intertype
Printed by The Lavenham Press Ltd

ISBN: 978-1-903615-84-3

Contents

Acknowledgements

The editor and authors would like to thank all those who gave their help and support in preparing *Family Trends*. Special thanks must go to Helen Barrett for providing such a solid base. Her book *UK Family Trends 1994–2004* gave the inspiration for this new study which incorporates elements of that original text. We would also like to thank Joanna Apps for her management of this project and for her inspiring comments at all stages of this work; Clem Henricson for her encouragement; Alison Hill at Parenting UK; and Sarah Roberts for getting the work into print.

Preface

I am extremely pleased to be able to introduce *Family Trends*. It comes some years after the Institute's first study by Helen Barrett, *UK Family Trends 1994–2004*, which was conducted for the International Year of the Family 2004.

This new study has not been prompted by any such single event, but rather by an awareness that there have been considerable changes in the direction and momentum of family policy in recent years, and that there is now speculation as to its future. It is at this juncture that the Institute has considered that it would be useful to take stock and to conduct an overview of the family as it now stands in the UK.

Trends of course do not evolve in convenient annual or decade chunks and in order to enhance understanding of the context of family change we have taken a longer perspective in this publication – some 60 years. Covering demographics, migration and relationships, through to wellbeing and the recession, the study is intended to provide policymakers with a panoramic view as they seek to tackle one of the most fraught and habitually controversial areas of public policy – the family.

Family policy is a significant function of government and has been so historically. As the core social unit of society, behaviour within and between families, and the degree to which they flourish or the converse, have always been matters of concern for secular and religious instruments of government. Families are the stuff of human relationships and drama, with all the antagonism and succour that that implies. As such they require regulation for the protection of the vulnerable and the common good; they also need support. Government action should encompass these functions, but further than this, it needs to be responsive, recognising that families are the litmus test of change in morality and social mores. While governments do indeed have to regulate conduct, they also have to sense shifts in moral expression; they have to operate themselves as part of a process of change, and a high degree of sensitivity and knowledge of that process is critical if beneficial judgements are to be made.

Whatever verdict there may be on this balancing feat by the current government, it cannot be disputed that there has been enormous intellectual and financial investment in the development of family policy. There has been activity of such an order that it would be fair to say that one of the defining features of this administration has been its concern for personal relationships – parenting, adult couples and neighbour relations.

What the future has in store is uncertain, but points of interest and preoccupations are emerging in commentaries and debates on family issues. Significantly, the fertility rate has become a focus of attention; for example it was the theme for the 2009 Council of Europe Conference of Ministers and it features in publications such as *The power of numbers: why Europe needs to get younger* (Ehrman 2009). While the UK fertility rate is one of the highest in Europe, there are arguments in favour of maintaining current population levels, not least because of growing concerns as to how an ageing population can be financed. Issues of race and religion inevitably find their way into population debates and there will be a need to be alert to obvious dangers here. Broadly speaking, however, the population debate may come to inform the way in which work–life balance and childcare issues are addressed; the need to provide a congenial environment for having children will be high on the agenda.

A further interesting issue is the degree to which the socially liberal society that has embraced same-sex partners with the introduction of the Civil Partnership Act 2004 may continue. There are no contra-indicators, although the issues of marriage, cohabitation and single parents may provide an ongoing source of tension in public policy.

What does appear to be the case is that the high level of government concern with personal relationships is set to continue. For example, there is cross-party commitment to providing increased support for adult couple relationships. While in parenting there may be changes in emphasis possibly from early years to teens, by and large the state's substantial role in the upbringing of children is also likely to remain.

The recession may have an impact on the level of services provided, and a sensible point of debate here will be the relatively critical nature of different service requirements. One of the major areas of assessment emerging is the division of the economic cake across the generations. While children have been the focus of attention, there appears to be a growing tendency to focus more on the family and the interplay of need and support across the life span. The current parliamentary *Inquiry into intergenerational fairness and employment* is an example of these shifting preoccupations.

Whatever the course of public debate, it is essential that there should be as much evidence of the reality of family life available as possible so that the conversation is an informed one. In particular, policymakers' grasp of the whole picture is critical in developing a comprehensive, balanced family policy. This study of family trends is intended to contribute to that awareness and body of knowledge. It draws together and distils information from a wide range of sources, and is intended to be a key resource in a complex and intellectually challenging area of policy thought.

Clem Henricson
Director of Research and Policy

About the authors

Stephen A. Hunt joined the Family and Parenting Institute as a Research Fellow from the Department of Early Childhood and Primary Education at the Institute of Education. He previously worked at the London Business School and the Institute of Food Research. His research interests include risk perception, communication, and trust; and national and cross national surveys research.

Claire James has worked on a range of policy areas including family and parenting support, welfare reform, housing, and family policy across Europe since joining the Family and Parenting Institute as a Policy Officer. Previously she worked at Scope as a Policy and Research Officer and focused on disability rights, independent living and direct payments. Recent publications include *Homes fit for families* (Family and Parenting Institute 2008), *Families and the credit crunch 2008* (Family and Parenting Institute 2008) and *Ten years of family policy* (Family and Parenting Institute 2009).

Martina Klett-Davies is a sociologist who has specialised in family and gender studies and modern social theories that culminated in her monograph *Going it alone? Lone motherhood in late modernity* (Ashgate 2007). She is a Research Fellow at the Family and Parenting Institute where she co-authored *Mapping and analysis of parenting services in England* (Family and Parenting Institute 2009) as well as editing *Putting sibling relationships on the map* (Family and Parenting Institute 2008) and *Is parenting a class issue?* (Family and Parenting Institute forthcoming). She previously worked at the London School of Economics where she continues to be a visiting Lecturer. Martina's focus is on family dynamics and the interplay between social identities, social policies and social capital.

Eleni Skaliotis is currently working as an Operational Research Analyst for the Home Office. Prior to this she was a Research Fellow at the Family and Parenting Institute where she specialised in quantitative analysis of longitudinal datasets. She has worked on a variety of research projects in the fields of parental involvement and education. She recently operationalised Sen's capability approach to investigate children's physical wellbeing and examined the characteristics of parents of teenagers that change levels of involvement in schooling over time (forthcoming). Eleni has also conducted a study on the mapping and analysis of parenting services in England (Family and Parenting Institute 2008).

Introduction

The 1960s and 1970s marked a turning point throughout western Europe in the pace of change in almost every demographic series, particularly those concerning fertility, extramarital childbearing, marriage, cohabitation, divorce and family structure. Haskey (2001) has pointed out that these changes have amounted to a structural shift in societal norms and individuals' demographic behaviour, and have been termed 'the second demographic transition'. Chapter 1 examines these demographic changes, particularly since the 1970s.

The shift in societal norms can be attributed to the western world entering a 'late modern' epoch, characterised by 'individualisation' and 'de-traditionalisation' (Beck 1992). This has been identified as the product of post-war welfare reforms, universal education and economic prosperity. This epoch is allied to the 'project of self', which emphasises individual self-fulfilment and personal development, and replaces relational social aims (Duncan and Phillips 2008). Consequently, this report also examines how attitudes towards various family structures such as marriage or cohabitation have changed.

Arguably the centrepoint for the majority of UK families, mothers and motherhood is the focus in Chapter 2. The majority of mothers now have three central roles within the family: bringing up children, supporting their child's education and some choosing to work. This chapter investigates trends in how motherhood is experienced, in terms of which mothers choose to work and when, and how they balance their work and home life. A significant minority of mothers choose not to work, and their experiences of being a full-time mother are explored.

This work also reflects the growth in research relevant to the family; this is nowhere better illustrated than in the case of the research on fatherhood. Lamb and Lewis (2004, p.288) state: *"There is impressive evidence that mothers and fathers may have different effects on child development."* Chapter 3 examines the contribution of fathers to the development of their children.

Chapter 4 examines the kind of issues that parents and families face at various stages of their children's development, and how parenting might have changed over recent decades with respect to these issues. The issues examined include: how parents control their children; how parents and children perceive risks that are likely to influence parenting; whether children are growing up 'too fast'; teenage pregnancy;

the impact of technology on parenting, both established (such as TV) and more recent (such as mobile phones and the internet); and the issues faced by young adults in their attempts to establish independence.

Chapter 5 concerns a more general issue that is likely to confront families: that of economic recession. It looks at international and UK research concerning the impact of recessions both historically and in terms of the contemporary situation.

The present volume also endeavours to take into account the views and attitudes of children to the various situations and events which affect them directly, whether this is in terms of children's views about step-parents, or about issues such as parental control.

The various data sources used in the present work are referenced, and a description of each appears in the Appendix, with the exception of publicly available data maintained by the Office for National Statistics, where the appropriate dataset is referenced within the text.

Major demographic trends

Stephen A. Hunt

Key statistics

These statistics are cited from independent research, ranging from small, qualitative studies to large-scale representative surveys.

- The total fertility rate has declined from a peak of 2.95 per woman to 1.95 per woman from 1964 to 2008.

- The average household size fell from 3.1 people to 2.4 from 1961 to 2006.

- The percentage of the UK population born outside the UK has approximately doubled over the period 1951 to 2001.

- Marriage remains the most common form of partnership for both men and women: 52 per cent of men and 50 per cent of women were married in 2006.

- The proportion of children born outside marriage increased from under 10 per cent in 1971 to 45 per cent in 2008 in England and Wales.

- Registration of all births outside marriage to a single parent fell from 60 per cent to 17 per cent between 1964 and 2004.

- Fewer adults agree with the statement: *"People who want children ought to get married"* – the agreement rate fell from 70 per cent in 1989 to 54 per cent in 2000.

- The percentage of adults living in one-person households increased from 6 per cent in 1971 to 12 per cent in 2008.

- The percentage of children living in a couple relationship fell from 92 per cent in 1972 to 77 per cent in 2008.

Introduction

This chapter aims to outline the demographic profile of the UK and show the changes that it has undergone, particularly those that relate to families, in the latter part of the 20th and early 21st centuries.

Throughout the chapter data are used from the UK censuses taken from 1951 to 2001 and the statistical projections derived from them: these datasets are maintained largely by the Office for National Statistics (ONS). In addition, data are used from British, UK and Europe-wide population surveys, although these were undertaken mostly from the 1980s onwards. Specifically, this chapter examines changes in rates of fertility and immigration, both of which affect the size of the population and its composition: for example, in terms of age structure and ethnic make-up. This provides the context in which to look at changes in rates of activities critical to the family, such as marriage, cohabitation and divorce, and to examine how these have influenced family composition. The chapter also examines whether attitudes to these activities, various family forms and behaviours have changed.

The chapter is structured around five questions, each of which is addressed in turn.

1.1 How have fertility rates and family sizes changed?

1.2 How has the make-up of the UK population changed?

1.3 How have family forms changed?

1.4 How have attitudes to family forms changed?

1.5 In what kind of family do dependent children live?

1.1 How have fertility rates and family sizes changed?

This section examines the size and composition of the UK population and the components that determine these, specifically fertility rates and net immigration.

General population: census data and projections

The population of the UK has shown a steady increase since 1951, as shown in Table 1.1, an increase mirrored in each of the constituent countries with the exception of Scotland, where a declining population has been observed, specifically since the mid-1970s. However, the population of Scotland is predicted to increase, but it is still expected to maintain lower life-expectancy and fertility rates than the rest of the UK (ONS 2008a).

Table 1.1: Population of the UK, 1951–2001 with estimates until 2031*
Source: ONS (2000, 2003a, 2008a).[1]

	1951	1961	1971	1981	1991	2001	2006	2011	2021	2031
England	41.2	43.6	46.4	46.8	47.9	49.5	50.8	52.7	56.8	60.4
Wales	2.6	2.6	2.7	2.8	2.9	2.9	3.0	3.0	3.2	3.3
Scotland	5.1	5.2	5.2	5.2	5.1	5.1	5.1	5.2	5.3	5.4
Northern Ireland	1.4	1.4	1.5	1.5	1.6	1.7	1.7	1.8	1.9	2.0
UK	50.2	52.8	55.9	56.4	57.4	59.1	60.6	62.8	67.2	71.1

* Figures in millions. Data for 1951 are census enumerated; mid-year estimates from 1961 to 2006; 2006-based projections for 2011 to 2031.

Projections estimate that the UK population will grow by approximately 10 million between 2006 and 2031. Of this growth, 47 per cent is likely to be the result of net immigration: that is, the difference between people arriving in and leaving the UK (Bray 2008).

Birth rates

The birth rate has exceeded the death rate every year since 1951 to 2008, with the exception of 1976 (Jefferies 2005). While natural change (the difference between

---

1   All ONS statistics in this publication are under Crown Copyright and reproduced with kind permission under the terms of the Click-Use Licence.

birth and death rates) was the principal source of the UK's population increase over the period 1951 to 2001, between mid 2001 and mid 2007 net migration became the main driver of population change, for example accounting for over 70 per cent of the total population change between mid 2001 and mid 2002. The trend has reversed again and between mid 2007 and mid 2008, natural change has accounted for 54 per cent of total population growth. The increase in natural change is mainly attributable to a growth in the number of births, although a decrease in the numbers of deaths has also played a part (ONS 2009a).

The immediate post-war years saw a progressive increase in the UK's total fertility rate,[2] reaching a peak of 2.95 per woman in 1964. Between 1964 and 2001 the trend was downward, with the fertility rate at its lowest at 1.63 in 2001 (Dunnell 2007). However, during the early years of the 21st century there has been a marked upswing which has seen the rate steadily increasing, reaching 1.92 in 2007 and 1.95 in 2008, at least according to provisional figures; this is the highest level since 1973, when the figure stood at 2.00 (ONS 2009b).

There are specific trends associated with UK fertility rates. First, age-specific trends are observable. The last 25 years have seen fertility rates for women of younger ages decreasing, while they have been increasing for women of older ages, specifically those in their thirties and forties. This period has seen greater female participation in full-time employment and higher education, both of which are linked with delayed fertility. Indeed, women with higher educational qualifications are not only more likely to delay childbirth, but also more likely to remain childless (Rendall and Smallwood 2003). (This is examined in more detail in Chapter 2.) However, since 2001, the fertility rates for younger women, particularly those aged between 25 and 29 years, have increased. Possible reasons cited include: improved maternity leave, taxation and benefits for those with children and increased levels of international migration (Dunnell 2007).

There is a distinct impact of immigration associated with fertility rates: in 1998, 14 per cent of all UK births were to mothers born outside the UK; by 2008 the (provisional) figure had risen to approximately 24 per cent, and in 2007 the figure stood at 23 per cent (ONS 2009b). It is plausible that the expansion of the European Union (EU) to include 25 countries in total in 2004 contributed to this increase: births to mothers born in the EU but outside the UK and Republic of Ireland had increased by 87 per cent over the period 2001–06, and by 2006 accounted for 4 per cent of all UK births.

---

2   Total fertility rate (TFR) is defined as: *"The average number of children a group of women would have if they experienced the age-specific fertility rates for a particular year throughout their childbearing life … a TFR of 1.84 in 2006 means that a group of women would have an average of 1.84 children each during their lifetime based solely on 2006's age-specific fertility rates"* (Dunnell 2007, p.16).

Different rates of ageing in general and particular populations within the UK

The decline in fertility rates over the period 1964–2001 and general improvements in mortality since 1945 have resulted in population ageing, one of the most profound changes in the UK's demographic profile. Figure 1.1 shows the increase in those aged 65 and over as a percentage of the UK population, including projections from 2001 onwards.

Figure 1.1: Growth of the UK elderly population as a percentage of the total UK population, 1951–2001, with estimates until 2031*

Source: Office of Health Economics (2009)

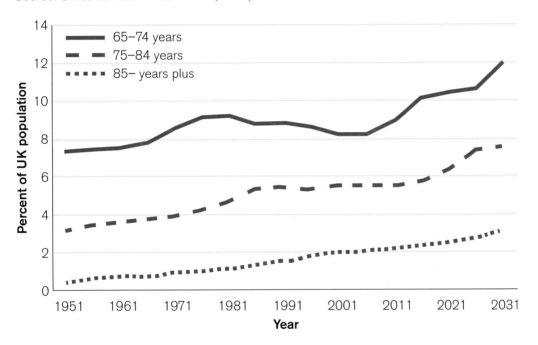

* Projections from 2001 are based on mid-year estimates.

People aged 65 or older accounted for 11 per cent of the UK population in 1951. This had risen to 16 per cent by 2001 and by 2031 it is predicted to rise to 23 per cent. The increasing concentration of the UK population in older age groups has consequences for the profile of the population as a whole. Figure 1.2 shows a clear trend throughout the late 20th century and projected into the 21st century that, in tandem with the growing elderly population, the UK population under 16 is contracting and is predicted to decline further.

Figure 1.2: UK dependent population by age, 1971–2021*
Source: ONS (2009c)

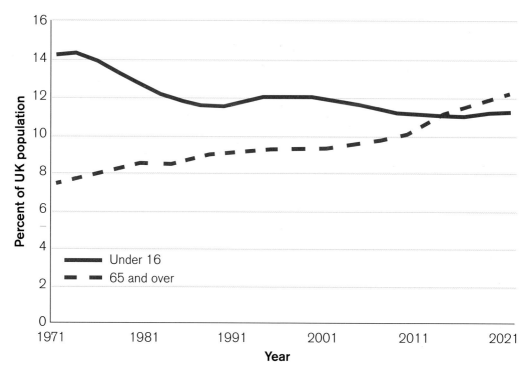

* Population estimates for 2001 and 2002 include provisional results from the Manchester matching exercise; all post-2001 estimates are predications based on 2001 data.

By 2007, the percentage of the UK population of pensionable age had become greater than that of teenagers for the first time since records began. Gray (2005) states that between 1981 and 2001, the chances of a young child having a maternal grandmother under 70 years of age increased from 46 per cent to 56 per cent, due to increased life-expectancy and the youthful age at which current grandparents became first-time mothers in the 1970s (average age somewhere between 26 and 27 years).

ONS Omnibus Survey data analysed by the School of Hygiene and Tropical Medicine found that 90 per cent of those aged 60 or over were grandparents (ONS 2003b). The effect on family forms of the ageing population, combined with decreasing family size, is to increase the prevalence of families with several generations alive at the same time, but with fewer aunts and uncles, etc., producing a so-called 'beanpole' effect with fewer family members in each 'tier' or generation of a family. Grandparents acting as surrogate parents has been estimated at only about 1 per cent (Clarke and

Cairns 2001). The percentage of UK households with resident grandparents has been estimated at 2.22 per cent over the period 1994–96 (Koslowski 2009).

However, the trend towards an ageing population is not uniform across the population: for example, age structures vary across ethnic groups, which are shown in Figure 1.3.

Figure 1.3: UK population by ethnicity and age, 2001–02*
Source: ONS (2002a)

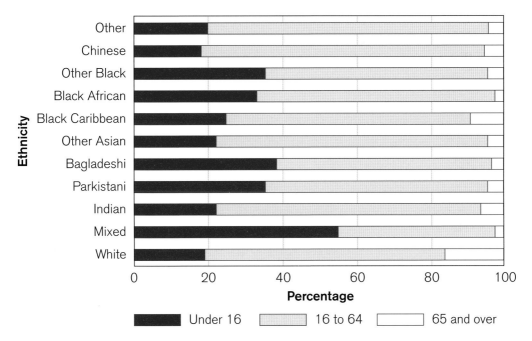

* Population living in private households. 'Other Black' sample size too small to allow '65 and over' percentage to be calculated reliably.

Figure 1.3 indicates that in 2002, 16 per cent (the white group) had the greatest proportion of people aged 65 and over; in comparison, other ethnic groups have much younger age structures. The Bangladeshi group has double the proportion of children under 16 years of age (38 per cent) compared to the white group. Much of the difference in the ethnic groups' age distributions can be attributed to the point at which they arrived in the UK. Immigrant populations tend to be composed of those of working age and their children, hence the relatively high proportion of people aged 65 or over among residents of Caribbean origin, who first began to arrive in the 1950s.

Household and family size

Household size has shown a distinct trend since 1961,[3] with an increase in the proportion of households with small occupancy numbers and a corresponding fall in the proportion of those with larger occupancy numbers. This has resulted in the average household size falling from 3.1 in 1961 to 2.4 in 2006. Figure 1.4 shows the change in more detail.

Figure 1.4: Households by size, Great Britain only, 1961–2006
Source: ONS (2008b, 2009d)

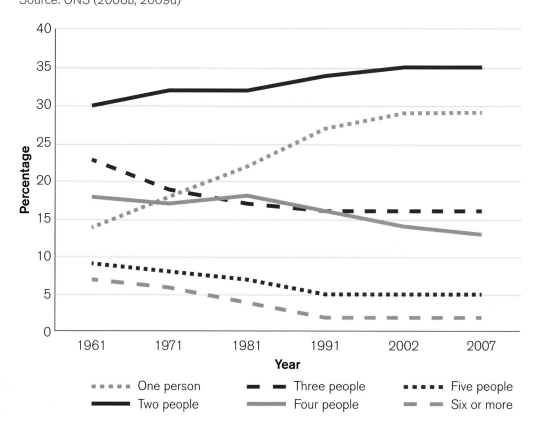

The decrease in the average household size since 1961 is partly the result of the increase in single-person households and due to changes in family size. As Table 1.2 indicates, there has been a discernible trend since 1961 towards generally smaller families. The proportion of couples with three or more children had halved by 2001, while the proportion of lone parents with dependent children had increased 3.5 times by 2007.

---

3   Prior to 1961, censuses did not distinguish adequately between households and families.

Table 1.2: Households by type of household and family in percentages, Great Britain only, 1961–2007

Source: ONS (2002b, 2008b)

Household composition	1961	1971	1981	1991	2001	2007
One person:						
under state pension age	4	6	8	11	14	14
over state pension age	7	12	14	16	15	14
One-family households:						
couple						
no children	26	27	26	28	29	28
1–2 dependent children	30	26	25	20	19	18
3 or more dependent	8	9	6	5	4	4
non-dependent children only	10	8	8	8	6	7
lone parent:						
dependent children	2	3	5	6	7	7
non-dependent children only	4	4	4	4	3	3
Two or more unrelated adults	–	4	5	3	3	3
Multi-family households	3	1	1	1	1	1
All households	16.3	18.6	20.6	22.4	23.8	24.2

The ONS estimates that family sizes peaked for women born in 1934 at 2.46 children – the 1960s 'baby boom' – for women born in 1920 the figure was 2.07. Since the 1960s family size has declined: it is projected that for women born in the mid-1980s, the figure will be approximately 1.74 children. The explanation for the trend since the mid-1960s is fewer women having large families and an increase in women remaining childless (ONS 2004a). As noted earlier, one result of reduced family size is that people will have fewer relatives such as uncles and aunts; the consequences of this for parenting, and particularly the role that grandparents play in childcare, are considered later.

As with the population age profile, the trend towards smaller families is not uniform across ethnic groups. Penn and Lambert (2002) argue that preferences concerning family size vary across ethnic communities. They found that more than 50 per cent of Indian and more than 60 per cent of Pakistani respondents said that they preferred to have three or more children, compared with only one-third of other British respondents. Differences in household size by ethnicity, which are not identical to family size but give some indication of their likely differences, appear in Figure 1.5.

Figure 1.5: UK household size by ethnic group, 2002
Source: ONS (2009e)

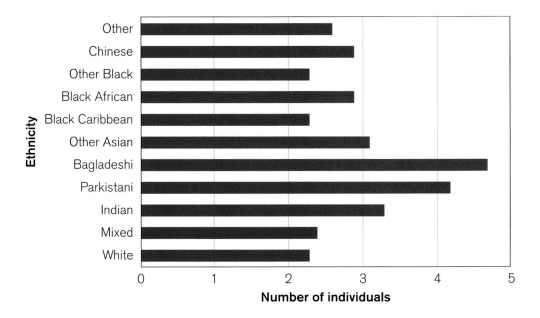

Bangladeshi and Pakistani families tended to be larger than those of all other ethnic groups. Of these families, 40 per cent had three or more dependent children in 2001; this was the case for only 28 per cent of black African families, 20 per cent of Indian families and 17 per cent of white families in Great Britain (ONS 2005a).

1.2 How has the make-up of the UK population changed?

The data on ethnic group membership are relatively limited. Questions relating to ethnic group membership were used first in the 1991 census, with revisions in 2001 to include a 'mixed ethnicity' category. Before 1991, respondents were asked only their country of birth. Figure 1.6 shows that the percentage of the UK population born outside the UK has increased steadily since 1951 and approximately doubled over the period 1951–2001 (Rendall and Salt 2005).

Figure 1.6: Percentage of population born outside the UK, 1951–2001
Source: Rendall and Salt (2005)

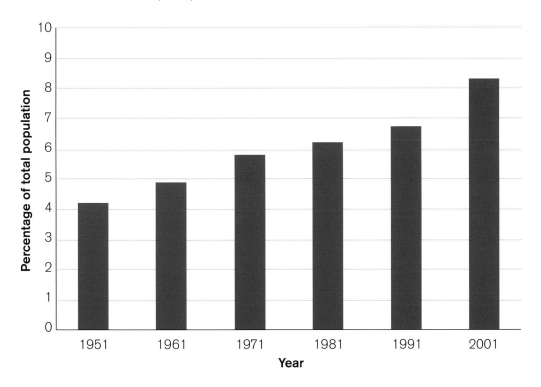

Clearly, country of birth has a limited utility as a measure of 'ethnicity', particularly when second-generation children of original immigrants are born. The introduction of the census 'ethnicity' question allows further detail concerning members of the UK population identified as being born outside the UK, and this is presented in Figure 1.7.

Figure 1.7: Distribution of population born outside the UK, 2001
Source: Rendall and Salt (2005)

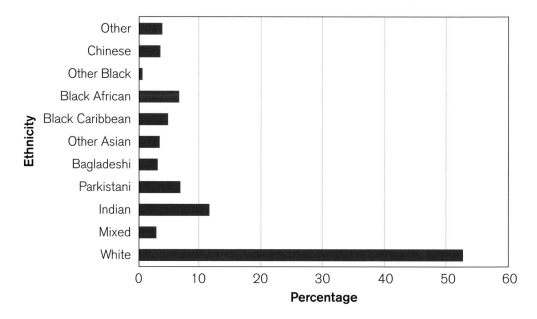

The white ethnic group, which is by far the largest, is composed principally of individuals from Europe, North America or Oceana. This is a group which typically experiences a high degree of 'replacement' – the numbers remain relatively stable but the individual members are being continually replaced: 50 per cent leave within four years (Rendall and Salt 2005).

The data in Table 1.3 give some indication of the ethnic composition of the UK – currently, if not historically – in terms of both the proportion of the UK population accounted for by minority ethnic groups and the ethnic diversity of the current UK population.

Table 1.3: Population by ethnic group, 2001
Source: ONS (2009f)

Ethnicity	UK	England	Wales	Scotland	Northern Ireland
			2001		
White	92.1	90.9	97.9	98.0	99.3
Mixed	1.2	1.3	0.6	0.3	0.2
Indian	1.8	2.1	0.3	0.3	0.1
Pakistani	1.3	1.4	0.3	0.6	0.0
Bangladeshi	0.5	0.6	0.2	0.0	0.0
Other Asian	0.4	0.5	0.1	0.1	0.0
Caribbean	1.0	1.1	0.1	0.0	0.0
African	0.8	1.0	0.1	0.1	0.0
Other Black	0.2	0.2	0.0	0.0	0.0
Chinese	0.4	0.5	0.2	0.3	0.3
Other	0.4	0.4	0.2	0.2	0.1

As Table 1.3 indicates, approximately 8 per cent of the UK population identify themselves as belonging to a minority ethnic group. The remainder of this section examines current attitudes to minority ethnic groups and the issue of immigration.

Attitudes to ethnicity and immigration

Using data from successive waves of the British Social Attitudes Survey (most years between 1983 and 1996), Ford (2008) argues that prejudice towards minority ethnic groups – specifically of white Britons towards black and Asian Britons – is in decline. The actual questions from the survey concerned respondents' estimates of general and personal tolerance of a black or Asian boss at work, and of a member of the respondent's family marrying a member of a minority ethnic group.

The decline in prejudice is explained not in terms of individuals revising their own attitudes, which appear to be stubbornly held in the manner of core values, but rather the effective replacement of one generation with another, with the younger generation being markedly less prejudiced than their predecessors (Ford 2008).

This intergenerational difference itself is explained in terms of the social context in which each generation spent their formative years: the younger the individual, the more likely they were to have grown up in an ethnically diverse community. Given the generational basis of the trend, Ford (2008) predicts that the diminution of prejudice throughout the British population is likely to continue.

Immigration, the driving force behind recent growth in the UK population and likely to influence its future composition, is also an issue which is often embroiled in controversy (ONS 2008c). Figure 1.8 indicates the levels of immigration to the UK since 1991 by point of origin. It is worth noting the steep rise of EU immigrants from between 2003 and 2004, corresponding to the period when the EU was enlarged from 15 to 25 nations, although figures for the first quarter of 2009 indicated that the number of East Europeans seeking work in the UK had fallen by 47 per cent, a presumed response to the prevailing economic conditions (Travis 2009).

Figure 1.8: Estimated levels of migration, by citizenship,* 1996–2006
Source: ONS (2008a)

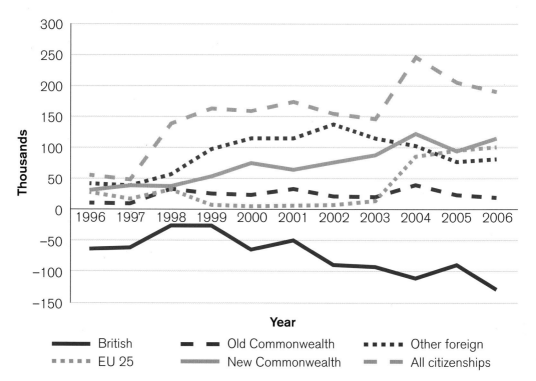

* Old Commonwealth: Australia, Canada, New Zealand and South Africa. New Commonwealth is the rest of the Commonwealth. Up to and including 2003, estimates are for the EU 15. From 2004 onwards, estimates are for the EU 25.

Table 1.4 shows attitudes to future levels of immigration and records a 9 per cent increase in respondents claiming that immigration should be reduced between 1995 and 2003.

Table 1.4: Attitudes to immigration, 1995–2003
Source: McLaren and Johnson (2007)

	1995	2003
The number of immigrants to Britain nowadays should:		
Be increased a lot or little	3	5
Remain as it is	26	15
Be reduced a little	24	23
Be reduced a lot	41	51
N	970	793

Dustmann and Preston (2007) examined the data from the question featured in Table 1.4 over successive waves of the British Social Attitudes Survey (from 1983 to 1990, excluding 1989). They identify two *"channels of concern"* as important in explaining opposition to further immigration: the additional demands that immigration is perceived to place on the welfare system; and the possible dilution or eradication of the indigenous culture, with the attendant problem of social tensions resulting from large cultural differences between groups. Labour market concerns, such as increased competition for jobs, were not found to be important.

In addition, McLaren and Johnson (2007) used the data from the question in Table 1.4, specifically from the 2003 wave of the survey, and identified attitudes to immigration as largely hostile. They found that this hostility stemmed from concerns about immigrants threatening "*in* group *resources*", particularly the jobs of British workers in general, rather than individual respondents feeling that their own interests were directly threatened. McLaren and Johnson (2007) also found hostility associated with the perceived threat that immigration posed to 'national symbols', non-economic elements such as values, customs and traditions and, to a lesser extent, a possible increase in crime.

Research concerning Northern Irish attitudes to immigration, derived from the European Social Survey, found no evidence of economic self-interest; rather that experience of social marginalisation or oppression and social contact with persons from minority ethnic groups predicted greater tolerance for immigration (Hayes and Dowds 2006).

Using 2003 British Social Attitudes Survey data and summarising their own research findings on British national identity and attitudes towards immigration, Heath and Tilley state:

> *On the whole Britain is not particularly welcoming to immigrants ... However, once immigrants have arrived the British public appear to be rather more tolerant. Most people do not have strong views on questions of assimilation and multiculturalism and most are in favour of laws outlawing discrimination.* (2005, p.131)

Heath and Tilley (2005) tentatively suggest that hostile attitudes might give way to greater tolerance, as younger people move through their life cycle and as older generations pass away. However, the financial crisis of 2008 and global recession of 2009 (International Monetary Fund 2009) may yet see the appearance (or reappearance) of economic self-interest as a source of hostility to immigration.

Effects of internal migration

Internal migration, essentially people and families moving house, is a far less contentious issue than international migration, but it may have profound implications for the family. Geographic proximity among family members might *appear* to be a requisite for family cohesion. The relationships between family members, particularly between parents and children experiencing geographic dispersion, might be at risk of dilution or even dissolution. However, the relocation of one or more family members is not something that all families experience to the same degree: some social groups are more likely to experience greater levels of family member mobility than others. Often, mobility is related to employment and some minority ethnic groups: in particular, those that maintain family ties across countries or continents also experience higher levels of mobility, although consideration of this lies outside the scope of this publication.

Mobility in relation to the pursuit of employment opportunities is experienced often by those with higher educational qualifications, and particularly young people. The main advantages to be gained from employment-initiated mobility are increased income and career advancement, although there is evidence of couples experiencing some disadvantages from such mobility. This is particularly the case with respect to dual-earner families, where moving to improve one partner's job effectively means that the other has to abandon theirs. More generally, in using longitudinal data featuring retrospective accounts from individuals in Austria, Boyle et al. (2006) found that couples that moved frequently faced a higher likelihood of separation or divorce. The authors identified the risks to a couple as stemming from greater stress introduced into the union by moving, and hence greater instability in the relationship.

Green and Canny (2003) explored some of the consequences of family relocation, focusing on the disruption that moving introduces into the lives of those involved and the differing impacts that these moves have at different life stages. They found that while younger parents were willing to endure the inconvenience, older parents found the disruption more demanding. Furthermore, while parents were concerned about any disruption to the education of any school-age children, adolescents or young people were concerned about disruption to their relationships with their peers, and older people were concerned about losing contact with established social networks.

However, despite these concerns, the impact of mobility on actual wellbeing is not always straightforward. The impact of mobility on children was examined by Verropoulou et al. (2002). Using National Child Development Study data, they did not find any detrimental effect of moving house or geographic location on children's wellbeing. Apparently, the association between children's development and families' living arrangements were mediated by human, financial and social capital.

Moreover, there is evidence that once the move is made, geographical distance between family members does not invariably lead to family dissolution. Using the ONS Omnibus Survey, Grundy et al. (1999) looked at four generations of the same families and the extent to which they were in touch with each other. Of those who had a parent or (eldest) child separated geographically from them, half made contact at least once a week, and although the distances concerned were small, half of these lived within half an hour's journey. There was also evidence of a high degree of reciprocity between parents and children: two-thirds of mothers and nearly half of fathers both provided and received help.

US-based research is consistent with these findings, that despite the geographical distance, parents and their adult children maintain contact and exchange social support (Lye 1996). Further research has indicated that intergenerational family support occurs on the basis of need rather than distance or closeness, and as such does not depend on co-residency or even geographical proximity (Bengston 2001; Silverstein and Bengston 1997). Riley and Riley (1993) conceive of family relationships in terms of a 'latent kin matrix'. Relationships effectively lie dormant in extended families when there is no necessity for support, but become activated when they are needed, such as when a family member is in crisis.

The greater dispersion of family members may be responsible for some changes in family dynamics, particularly the frequency of contact, but does not in itself operate so as to dissolve families' bonds

1.3 How have family forms changed?

This section considers a number of different trends related to the composition of the family: marriage, divorce and cohabitation.

The composition of the UK population by marital status has changed steadily throughout the latter period of the 20th century: the proportion of single to married individuals has increased, as has the proportion of divorced individuals (see Figures 1.9a and 1.9b for England and Wales). By 2031, in Great Britain, the numbers of single – more specifically 'never married' – are projected to become greater than the married. The number of 'married' and 'never married' women in particular is predicted to reach approximate parity by 2031 (ONS 2009g).

Figure 1.9a: Marital status of male adults aged 16 and over, England and Wales, 1971–2007

Source: ONS (2009h)

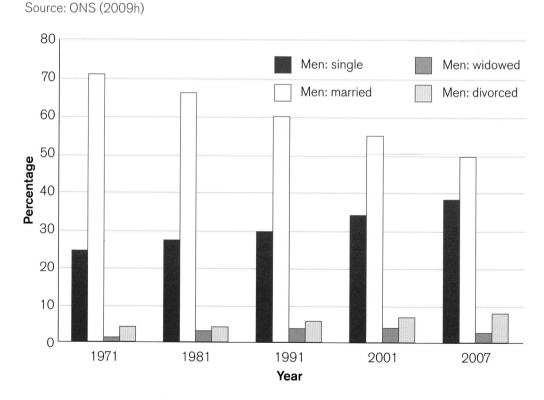

Figure 1.9b: Marital status of female adults aged 16 and over, England and Wales, 1971–2007
Source: ONS (2009h)

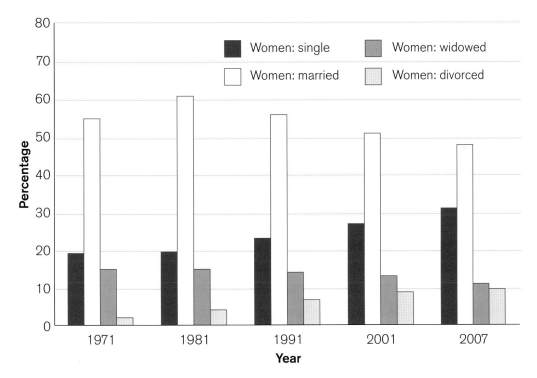

Marriage remains the most common form of partnership for both men and women; in Great Britain in 2006, 52 per cent of men and 50 per cent of women were married. However, marriage in the UK is less common now than it has ever been: by 2005 the annual marriage rate was the lowest since 1862, the year that the statistics were first compiled (ONS 2008d). Although the marriage rate has fluctuated, the general trend is downwards. For example, first marriages have dropped by almost 10 per cent between 1976 and 2006, as shown in Figure 1.10.

Figure 1.10: Frequency of marriage, divorce and remarriage, UK, 1956–2006
Source: ONS (2008d)

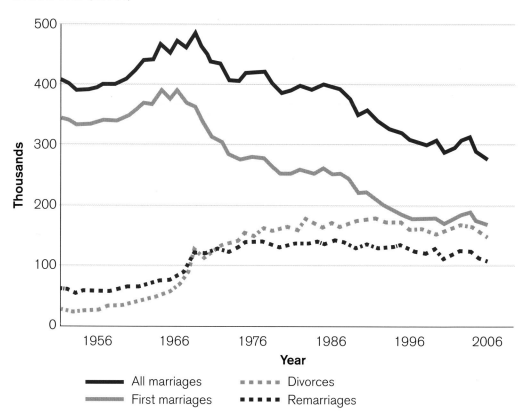

As the rate of marriage has decreased, the age at which both men and women get married has increased. Additionally, there has been an associated increase in the age at which individuals are divorced. This is shown in Figure 1.11.

Figure 1.11: Average age (in years) at marriage and divorce, England and Wales, 1971–2007
Source: ONS (2004b, 2009i)

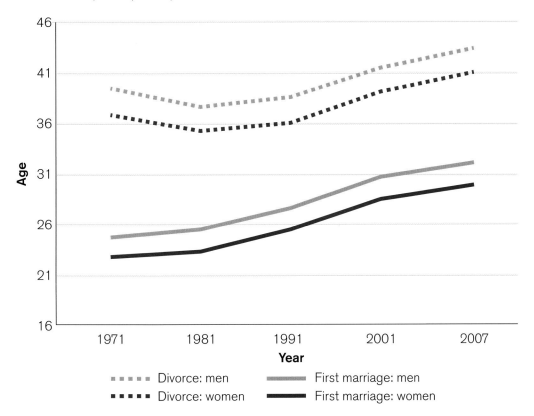

As Figure 1.10 indicates, the divorce rate rose steadily throughout the latter part of the 20th century, stabilised in the mid-1980s and then showed a distinct decline; in 2007, it reached its lowest level since 1981. The divorce rate in 2006 was 12.2 per 1,000 married population; in 2007, the provisional divorce rate in England and Wales fell to 11.9.

Econometric analysis has identified two principal predictors of divorce, both of which effectively lead individuals to reconsider their commitment to the union: age – the younger the individual is at first marriage, the greater the risk of marital dissolution; and unexpected changes in marital economic circumstance (Becker et al. 1977; Weiss and Willis 2007).

In analysing cross-sectional General Household Survey data from 1989 to 2000, Chan and Halpin (2008) were able to separate the sample into marriage cohorts divided by decade from the 1950s to the 1990s, and examine whether the risk factors associated with divorce have changed over time.

They found that the negative influence of premarital cohabitation had reduced over time, as had the similarly negative influence of marriage to a divorcee. Both these changes might be simply a result of the increasing prevalence of cohabitation and divorce, effectively diluting their impact. Furthermore, Chan and Halpin (2008) found that women with higher educational attainment, specifically graduates, were less likely to divorce in the more recent marriage cohorts, which marked not just a change but a reversal: these women had been the most likely to divorce in the 1960s, while those most likely to divorce in the most recent marriage cohort were identified as women without any educational qualifications. This reversal is possibly the result of divorce becoming easier to realise both socially and financially, and so becoming less dependent on resources, access to which is typically signalled by educational attainment.

Further, Chan and Halpin (2008) found the presence of children in a marriage ceased to operate as a disincentive to divorce, as had been the case with earlier marriage cohorts. Of the couples most recently married, those with children were more likely to divorce than equivalent couples without children, and the destabilising influence of children increased with the number of children in a family. Further analysis of the destabilising effect of children found that premarital births predicted a greater rate of dissolution. However, increasingly those experiencing premarital births tend to be women with low or no educational attainment, which is also associated with higher rates of divorce. It is the children of these mothers who are more likely to experience parental divorce.

In analysing data covering the subsequent decade, specifically successive waves of the British Household Panel Study gathered over the 1990s, Boheim and Ermisch (2001) found both age and unexpected improvements or reversals in family finances to be predictive of union dissolution, including both married and cohabiting couples. Additionally, improvements in employed women's income were found to be associated with increased risk of dissolution, whereas similar increases for men resulted in greater union stability. They also identified the destabilising influence of children: specifically, that the likelihood of union dissolution increases with the number of children, which is consistent with Chan and Halpin (2008). Furthermore, they found that cohabiting couples were twice as likely to separate as married couples, indicating that while the negative influence of cohabitation on union stability may be waning, it is still strong.

The following section examines the prevalence of, and issues specifically associated with, cohabitation.

Births outside marriage

The years since the Second World War have shown a huge increase in the proportion of children being born outside marriage: for the UK, the average in 1951 stood at 4.2 per cent; by 1998, it had reached 38 per cent. The change in proportion for England and Wales rose from under 10 per cent in 1971 to approximately 45 per cent by 2008. However, this trend is not unique to the UK – as Figure 1.12 indicates, it is Europe-wide.

Figure 1.12: Births outside marriage, European countries, 1997–2007*
Source: Eurostat (2009a)

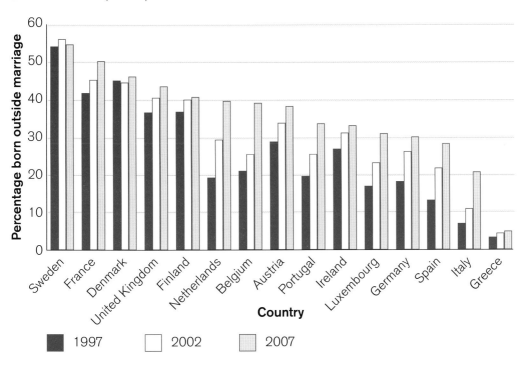

* Data for France 1997 imputed 1998 value; data for Belgium 2002 imputed 1999 value; data for France, UK, Ireland and Spain 2007 imputed 2006 values.

The data across the European countries for the period 1997 to 2007, presented in Figure 1.12, show a consistent increase in the proportion of children being born outside marriage in all countries, with the exception of Sweden, which historically has the highest rate – more than 50 per cent since 1997. It is also worth noting that countries which have experienced the steepest rates of increase (typically, although not exclusively, those in southern Europe), are now all, with the exception of Greece, at levels found a decade previously only in northern European countries. Since the trend of increased births outside marriage is a Europe-wide phenomenon, any consequences associated with it are also likely to be found Europe-wide. However, countrywide aggregations may not represent trends in family life accurately for specific minority ethnic groups: for example, it is likely that far fewer children than the national average are born outside marriage to those of Pakistani or Bangladeshi heritage, although the same overall upward trend still might be evident.

In the UK, births outside marriage have been typically attributed to single mothers rather than cohabiting couples. In 1964, 60 per cent of all births outside marriage were registered to a single parent; however, by 2004 this had fallen to 17 per cent, the remainder being registered jointly. Figure 1.13 shows this UK trend from 1964 to 2004.

Figure 1.13: Proportion of children born outside marriage by registration, 1964–2004

Source: ONS (2009j)

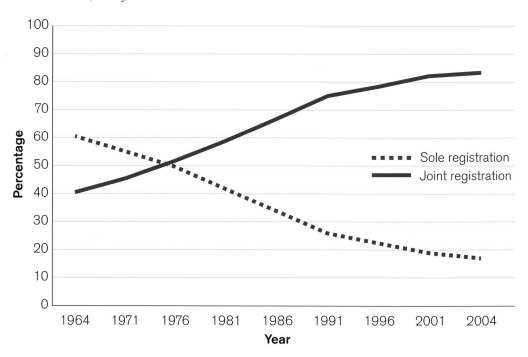

The pattern of registration of births outside marriage since 1986 is shown in Figure 1.14. An important distinction is introduced between jointly registered births for parents who live at different addresses and those who share the same address, whom (it is reasonable to assume) are cohabiting. This inference indicates the difficulty associated with estimating levels of cohabitation. Cohabitation is an informal arrangement and, unlike the legal union of marriage, is not subject to official record, therefore estimating its prevalence is more difficult. Furthermore, Haskey (2001) makes the point that, due to attendant social stigma, it was often difficult for voluntary surveys, such as the innovative Family Formation Survey conducted in 1976,[4] to obtain accurate estimates of cohabitation, as cohabiting respondents, perhaps in an act of evasion, often claimed to be married. However, long running surveys provide the best means of estimating both incidence of cohabitation and attitudes in the general population towards it.

Figure 1.14: Patterns of birth registration for births outside marriage, England and Wales,* 1986–2008

Source: ONS (2009k)

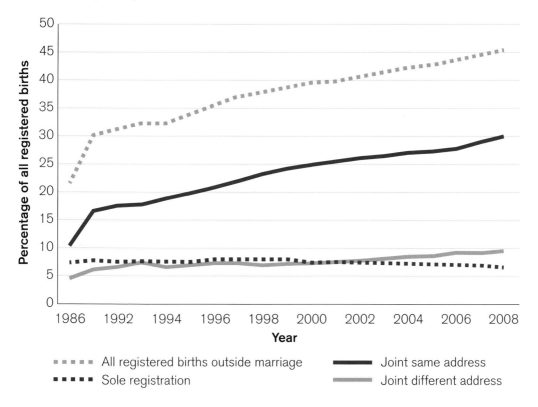

* Estimates for 2008 are average of three quartiles' prediction.

4   The Family Formation Survey of 1976 was not only one of the first social surveys to include items concerning cohabitation specifically, but was also constructed to address the issue of respondent reluctance to answer questions about cohabitation. It included a number of ingenious supplementary questions which allowed more accurate estimates to be drawn (Haskey 2001).

Figure 1.14 indicates that the proportion of jointly registered births to cohabiting couples in 2008 stood at approximately 30 per cent, with the remainder, approximately 15 per cent, being solely registered.

Despite the difficulties associated with making precise estimates of the prevalence of cohabitation – Murphy (2000) points out that historically, these have been profound – there is little doubt that its prevalence in the population has shown a dramatic increase.

Wilson (2009) estimates that in 1992, 6 per cent of the population of England and Wales aged 16 or more were cohabiting; by 2007, this had risen to 10 per cent. Haskey (2001) estimates that by 2021, the figure will have reached 22 per cent. Non-married women aged 18 to 49, for which there are 1976 data from the Family Formation Survey, showed a rise from 9 per cent to 33 per cent by 2007 as estimated using General Household Survey data (Ali et al. 2009; Haskey 2001).

There is also evidence that cohabitation has not only increased but undergone a qualitative shift in recent years. While the prevalence of cohabitation increased throughout the 1970s and much of the 1980s, its characteristics, such as duration and ages of the participants, remained relatively unchanged. However, latterly the average length of cohabitation has increased. The median duration of current cohabitation for women aged 18 to 49 increased from 20.3 months in 1979 to 23.3 months in 1989, but by 1995 it had increased to 33.9 months (Murphy 2000).

Whatever the motivation for its initiation or expectations of its participants, cohabitation can be either transitory or permanent. One important facet of the former is cohabitation as a precursor to marriage; in the case of the latter, cohabitation becomes a replacement or alternative to marriage itself.

Cohabitation as a precursor to marriage has established itself as a standard part of the process of marriage itself: the prevalence of cohabitation before first marriage has risen from little more than 2 per cent at the end of the 1950s to 77 per cent by 1996 and the figures for cohabiting prior to second marriage are even higher (Haskey 2001).

In addition, cohabitation as an alternative to marriage has increased. Rates of marriage have decreased to a record low in 2005. Moreover, evidence from the British Social Attitudes Survey indicated that the proportion of cohabiting relationships ending in marriage has shown a reduction, down from 59 per cent in 2000 to 56 per cent in 2006, while cohabitation rates, as cited above, have shown an increase and are expected go on climbing (Barlow et al. 2008).

Summarising analyses of British Household Panel Study data, Ermisch (2001) estimated the break-up rate for cohabiting relationships into which children are born at 65 per cent. Children of cohabiting parents are twice as likely to see them separate as children of married couples. Combined with the growing prevalence of cohabitation, this means that there is an increasing population of children who are more likely to experience new parental partnerships, live with a lone parent or a step-family than hitherto has been the case (Haskey 2001).

A consequence of the greater fragility of cohabiting relationships is that children born to cohabiting couples spend on average 4.7 years living with one parent, compared to 1.6 years for those born to married couples. Analysis of British Household Panel Study data for individuals born in the 1970s indicated long-term negative consequences for those children who grew up in lone-parent families, particularly if this occurred during the pre-school period. These children tended to have poorer educational attainment and poorer employment and health outcomes as young adults (Ermisch and Francesconi 2001). Therefore, the children of cohabiting parents are more likely to be socially disadvantaged than those of married couples (Ermisch 2001).

There is also evidence that children of cohabiting couples may be subject to disadvantage, not just because of the increased likelihood of relationship dissolution, but due to the features inherent in cohabiting relationships. Using data from the Millennium Cohort Study, Kiernan and Smith (2003) found evidence of distinct differences *within* the childrearing environment provided by cohabiting and married unions. Compared to married women, women in cohabiting relationships were more likely to be socially disadvantaged. Additionally, compared to married women, cohabiting women were also more likely to smoke and less likely to breastfeed or attend ante-natal classes. However, in some respects the childrearing environment in cohabiting relationships was equivalent to that found in married relationships: for example, the male partner was likely to be as involved in childcare as the husbands of married women. Furthermore, both married and cohabiting women scored higher on all health and social indices than lone mothers (Kiernan and Pickett 2006).

The following section examines attitudes to marriage, divorce and cohabitation.

1.4 How have attitudes to family forms changed?

The British Social Attitudes Survey has been tracking attitudes towards marriage and related social and sexual behaviour over several decades. The results of two questions asked in selective years since 1984, concerning approval of premarital and extramarital sex, are shown in Figure 1.15. These show a distinct increase in tolerance or acceptance of premarital sex over time, which has clear implications concerning attitudes to cohabitation, but a practically unchanged level of disapproval of extramarital sex, which has remained high throughout (Duncan and Phillips 2008). This disjunction is important as it indicates a change in a particular attitude, rather than a general change in, or perhaps collapse of, moral attitudes, which would predict an increase in approval of, or indifference to, both types of behaviour.

Figure 1.15: Attitudes to premarital and extramarital sex, 1984–2006
Source: Duncan and Phillips (2008)

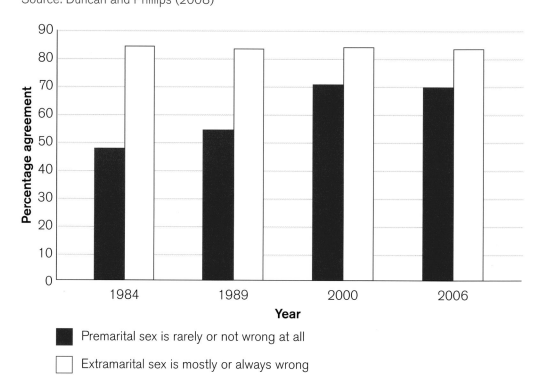

Premarital sex is rarely or not wrong at all

Extramarital sex is mostly or always wrong

Further indication of changes in attitude towards cohabitation are identifiable in the responses to the question: *"People who want children ought to get married"*, which was included in the 1989 and 2000 versions of the survey. The agreement rate for the question dropped from 70 per cent in 1989 to 54 per cent in 2000. Further examination of the responses to this question shows generational divisions, specifically that tolerance decreases as age increases, but over time all age groups are less intolerant (see Figure 1.16).

Figure 1.16: Agreement with the proposition: *"People who want children ought to get married"* **by age, 1989 and 2000**

Source: Barlow et al. (2001)

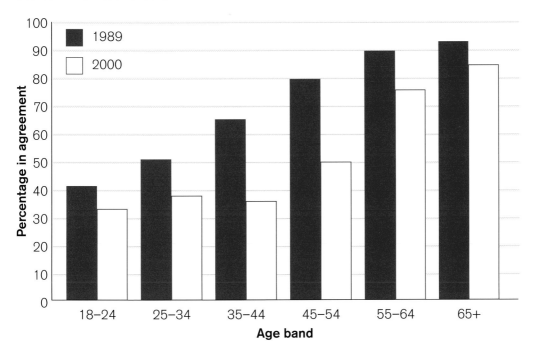

There are clear reductions in the numbers agreeing for each age group, although the numbers in the groups are quite low.

More recently, the 2006 British Social Attitudes Survey specifically examined whether cohabitation was perceived as equivalent to marriage (Duncan and Phillips 2008). The responses to the four questions used to examine this are presented in Table 1.5.

Table 1.5: The equivalence of unmarried cohabitation and marriage, 2006
Source: Duncan and Phillips (2008)

	Response		
	Agree	Neither	Disagree
There is little difference socially between being married and living together	66	12	19
A wedding is more about a celebration than lifelong commitment	53	16	28
Living with a partner shows just as much commitment as getting married	48	13	35
Married couples make better parents than unmarried ones	28	28	40

There was a clear majority agreeing that there is little difference socially between marriage and cohabitation, and a majority expressing scepticism about the 'traditional' significance of marriage. Further, half of the respondents felt that cohabitation showed as much commitment as marriage. The greatest resistance to cohabitation – that is, those holding more traditional views concerning marriage – was found among those who were older, practised religion, were from a professional background or were married themselves.

Interestingly, an identifiable 'knowledge gap' exists concerning cohabitation: there is a widespread misapprehension that the simple act of cohabitation bestows similar or comparable legal rights on couples or common law spouses as marriage: 53 per cent of cohabiting couples wrongly believed that 'common law marriage' exists, and only 39 per cent of people knew that it does not (Barlow et al. 2008).

The dilution of the perceived significance of marriage is mirrored by a current acceptance of divorce as a standard social practice. The 2006 British Social Attitudes Survey explored the different conditions under which divorce might be considered an acceptable option (see Table 1.6). Attitudes to divorce show not just an acknowledgement of its utility *in extremis*, as addressed by the first statement, but an almost equal approval of its pragmatic application – that is, divorce as a lifestyle choice, as addressed by the second statement: *"Divorce can be a positive first step towards a new life"* (Barlow et al. 2008).

Table 1.6: The normality of divorce, 2006
Source: Barlow et al. (2008)

	Response		
	Agree	Neither	Disagree
If either partner is at all violent, then divorce is the only option	64	18	14
Divorce can be a positive first step towards a new life	63	26	7
It is not divorce that harms children, but conflict between their parents	78	12	7

The third statement in Table 1.6 addresses the possible negative effects on children of divorce itself rather than a troubled relationship: the responses indicate that there is little support for the view that divorce is damaging; rather it is the context which results in divorce.

Nevertheless, the introduction of parenting issues reveals an interesting distinction in people's attitudes. When presented with the statement: *"It should be harder than it is now for couples with children under 16 to get divorced",* 30 per cent agreed and a further 26 per cent were undecided. Furthermore, in terms of responses to questions dealing with lone parenting, only 42 per cent agreed that lone parents are as good as two parents at bringing up children (Barlow et al. 2008).

The doubts concerning lone parenting are mirrored perhaps in more positive attitudes to two-parent but non-traditional family forms, such as 'reconstituted' families: families featuring step-parents and step-children. Of the respondents, 78 per cent thought that a family featuring a stepfather could bring up children under 12 just as well as families containing both biological parents (Barlow et al. 2008).

In summary, while it is not seen as irrelevant, marriage is perceived as a *version* of a union between co-residential couples, with cohabitation widely seen as its equivalent. Furthermore, 'reconstituted' family units, themselves often the outcome of prior failed marriages, are seen as equally valid environments in which to bring up children, perhaps being the consequence of a more generally tolerant attitude to divorce. However, each of these unions embodies the typically heterosexual, co-residential couple. These can be contrasted with further alternatives, particularly in terms of people's attitudes, specifically towards individuals living alone, couples that 'live apart together' (LATs) and same-sex couples.

Alternative family forms

Single-person households

About 6 per cent of adults aged 16 or over were in one-person households in 1971, but by 2007 this figure had risen to 12 per cent (ONS 2008b). While frequently associated with the elderly, solo living also owes its rise to an increased prevalence among those aged 25 to 44 years, precisely the age group most likely to be married and/or parents, within which age group the rise was from 2 per cent in 1971 to 12 per cent in 2005 (Roseneil 2006). In 2006, the British Social Attitudes Survey examined attitudes to solo living. The responses to the following two statements indicated that attitudes towards living alone were largely positive.

- You do not need a partner to be happy and fulfilled in life.

- People who choose to live alone just aren't good at relationships with others.

Almost 70 per cent agreed with the first statement and 60 per cent disagreed with the second (Barlow et al. 2008).

Couples living apart

A recently identified, if not recently occurring, social phenomenon involves those who are in a relationship but not co-residential. Haskey (2005) estimates that there are about 4 million individuals in Great Britain who can be classified as belonging to LATs – that is, non-married and non-cohabiting individuals with partners. These individuals tend to be young (16 to 24) and living with their parents, LATs typically being the product of circumstance rather than choice. However, using British Social Attitudes Survey data, Barlow et al. (2008) found distinct approval of non-residential partnering: 54 per cent agreed that *"A couple do not need to live together to have a strong relationship"* and only 25 per cent disagreed, although attitudes were less positive when single living was presented as lone parenting.

Same-sex partnerships

The 2001 census found, throughout most of Britain, fewer than 0.3 per cent of co-resident couples identified themselves as same sex, although this figure is likely to have been subject to underreporting because it was based on self-definition. The figure also excludes those in a relationship but living apart (Duncan and Smith 2006). Until 2005, same-sex partnerships were entirely informal and so estimating their prevalence presents the same difficulties as estimating levels of cohabitation generally. However, civil partnerships were introduced in 2005; by the end of 2008 the ONS estimated that there had been a total of 33,956 (ONS 2009l). There is a fairly even split between the proportion of men and women forming civil partnerships: men made up 53 per cent in 2008, and 55 per cent in 2007. The total number of civil partnerships in the UK for 2008 was 7,169, a drop of 18 per cent from 2007. Approximately half of the current total of civil partnerships were formed in the first year that they were introduced. In 2008, 180 civil partnership dissolutions were granted (ONS 2009l).

Attitudes towards same-sex partnerships show a marked degree of tolerance or acceptance when the relationship is presented as between two consenting adults. Of the 2006 British Social Attitudes Survey respondents, 58 per cent agreed that *"Civil partnerships should have the same rights as married couples"*. Furthermore, 63 per cent agreed with the statement *"A same-sex couple can be just as committed to each other as a man and a woman"*. However, much greater disapproval was apparent when a same-sex partnership was presented as primarily parental. Only 36 per cent agreed with the statement that *"A lesbian couple are just as capable of being good parents as a man and a woman"*, and only 31 per cent agreed that a male or gay couple are just as capable of being good parents (Duncan and Phillips 2008). The issue of dependent children and the kind of family that they are likely to be brought up in is the subject of the next section.

1.5 In what kind of family do dependent children live?

The changes in the rate of marriage, divorce and cohabitation have resulted in changes in the kind of environment in which children grow up. Of dependent children,[5] 92 per cent lived in a couple relationship in 1972; by 2008 this had dropped to 77 per cent. Much of this change can be explained in terms of the increase in lone parents. One in four dependent children lived in a lone-parent family in 2008, an increase from 1 in 14 in 1972. These changes over time are depicted in Figure 1.17.

---

5   Dependent children are those living with their parent(s) and aged under 16 or up to 18 if in full-time education, excluding all children who have a spouse, partner or child living in the household.

Figure 1.17: Dependent children by family type, UK, 1972–2008*
Source: ONS (2009m, 2009n)

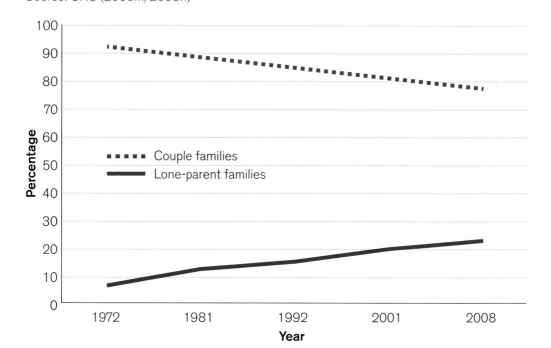

* Years 1991, 2002 data taken at spring. These estimates are not seasonally adjusted and have not been adjusted to take account of the census 2001 results. Also excludes cases where the dependent child is a family unit: for example, a foster child.

More specifically, by 2008 64 per cent of children were living in families with married couples, 13 per cent with cohabiting couples and 23 per cent with a lone parent (ONS 2009n). Married couple families were generally larger than other family types, with an average of 1.8 children in 2006, compared with 1.6 in cohabiting couples, 1.7 in lone-mother families and 1.4 in lone-father families. In the following section the result of divorce will be examined (ONS 2007).

Lone parents and families after divorce or separation

Lone parenthood

Of all households, 11 per cent were comprised of a lone parent and their dependent children by the second quarter (April–June) of 2008; in 1971, this figure stood at 4 per cent. Between 1997 and 2008 the proportion of dependent children living with lone mothers increased from 19 to 22 per cent. The proportion of those living with lone fathers has remained at around 2 per cent. (The issue of lone fatherhood is considered separately in Chapter 3.) The prevalence of lone parents by ethnicity is shown in Figure 1.18.

Figure 1.18: Lone parents with dependent children by ethnicity, 2008*
Source: ONS (2009o)

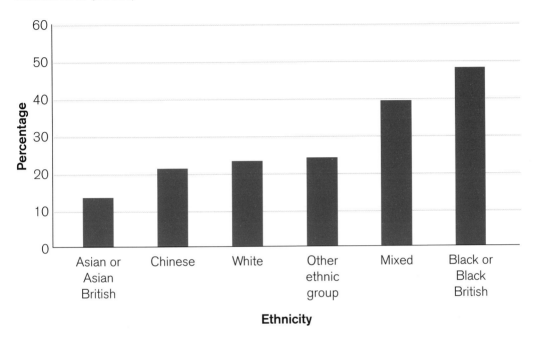

* Dependent children aged under 16 or 16–18 if never married and are in full-time education. For further specification of ethnic groups, see ONS (2006, Appendix, part 1). For data collected in the second quarter and not seasonally adjusted, see ONS (2006, Appendix, part 4).

The economic consequences relating to ethnicity and lone parenthood are considered in the section below, 'Families in poverty'. Generally, 37 per cent of lone-parent families live in households below the poverty line: that is, with a combined income 60 per cent below the median income (Yeo 2007). These low income levels are partly the result of relatively high rates of unemployment among lone parents. During the period April–June 2008 the employment rate for lone parents with dependent children stood at 56.3 per cent: this was a fall of 0.5 per cent from a year earlier, but an increase of 3.4 per cent from five years earlier (ONS 2008e).

Research cited earlier indicates that lone mothers are likely to fair worse on social and health indices than comparable individuals who are either married or cohabiting (Kiernan and Pickett 2006); furthermore, the children of lone parents are more likely to be disadvantaged in terms of lower educational attainment, and poorer labour market and health outcomes as young adults (Ermisch 2001).

Step-families

Historical data concerning step-families, a family unit that by definition must include children, are severely limited. For example, information on step-families was not gathered by the national census until 2001. The results of that census indicated that there were 0.7 million step-families with dependent children living in households in the UK or 10 per cent of all families with dependent children, 0.4 million of which were married couple step-families and 0.3 million were cohabiting (ONS 2005b).

Typically, step-families tend to be larger and the children older than in other family forms. The 2001 census results indicated that 27 per cent of step-families had three or more children, compared with 18 per cent of non-step-families. Furthermore, 38 per cent of cohabiting couples with dependent children were step-families, as opposed to only 8 per cent of married couple families with dependent children. However, step-families composed of married couples were more likely to have natural children in the family as well as step-children than cohabiting couple step-families: a figure of 57 per cent, as opposed to 35 per cent (ONS 2005b).

Questions concerning step-families have featured in the General Household Survey since 1991. Table 1.7 presents data from this survey, including the most recent available (McConnell and Wilson 2007).

Table 1.7: Step-families with dependent children,* Great Britain, 1991–2006
Source: McConnell and Wilson (2007); ONS (2004b)

	Year				
Family type	1991–02	1996–97	2000–01	2001–02	2006
Children from the woman's previous marriage or cohabitation	86	84	88	83	84
Children from the man's previous marriage or cohabitation	6	12	9	9	10
Children from both partners' previous marriage or cohabitation	6	4	3	8	6
Lone parent with children from a former partner's previous marriage	1	–	–	–	–

* Family head aged 16 to 59.

Table 1.7 indicates that the majority of children under 16 who were living in step-families during the period under review had been born within their mothers' previous relationship. The data indicate very little change, it always having been relatively uncommon for children to live either with their parents' new partner's children or with their biological father.

There is evidence that step-families are more stressful environments than first families (Pryor and Rodgers 2001). Feijten et al. (2009) found that step-parents and their partners are at greater risk of having poor mental health than their equivalents in first families. These risks are compounded if the step-parents constitute a couple who are step-parents to each other's children. Using National Child Development Study data – a longitudinal dataset – Feijten et al. (2009) were able to explain this partly in terms of a prior disposition to poor mental health on the part of individuals who eventually became step-parents. This prior disposition was accounted for in terms of a greater proneness to behavioural problems at age 16. The authors surmise that the stresses peculiar to step-parenting have a particular effect on those who had behavioural problems in adolescence. Those step-parents who did not have such adolescent behavioural problems are only at greater risk of mental health problems if they are also the partner of a step-parent or are lone parents. Additionally, having non-resident children, being younger, not working or working part time and having an adolescent step-child in the household all added to the risk of mental health problems, although these also increased the risk for parents in non-step-families.

Children's views of step-families

Dunn and Deater-Deckard (2001) found that children expressed a greater sense of closeness to birth parents than step-parents. Dunn and Deater-Deckard (2001) applied an innovative method, 'four-field maps', to elicit younger children's (four- to seven- or eight-year-olds) perceptions of their families. The maps are concentric circles with the child placed at the centre: the child locates the rest of their family or acquaintances nearer or further away, depending on their sense of emotional distance. From a sample of 258 children, the results indicated that 57 per cent of children in stepfather families placed their stepfather in an outer circle (not emotionally close), compared to 29 per cent of children in two-parent non-step-families, and 38 per cent of children in stepmother families' placements of their fathers. Children in step-families were also less likely to group their current parents as being close to each other than children related to both parents. The results for older children aged eight years old and over who were interviewed were similar: furthermore, parental estimates of closeness were consistent with the children's.

However, serious issues such as conflict and hostility were not linked to family form. These tended to be subject to individual differences in terms of adjustment[6] problems, so children with poor relationships with their father or mother tended to have behavioural or psychological issues, such as aggression or anxiety.

Families in poverty

The material wealth of families is not distributed evenly, and this is clearly apparent with respect to ethnicity: Figure 1.19 indicates that there are clear differences in the proportion of each ethnic group in the lowest income group.

Figure 1.19: Percentage of those in the lowest income group by ethnicity of head of household, after housing costs,[7] Great Britain, 2006–07*
Source: Department for Work and Pensions (2009a)

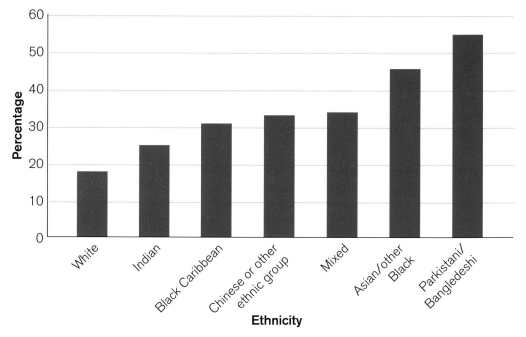

* Equivalised household disposable income after deduction of housing costs has been used to rank individuals into quintile groups.

---

6   Adjustment includes externalising or behavioural measures such as conduct disorder or aggression and internalising or psychological measures such as anxiety and depression. The instrument used in the study was the Child Behavior Checklist, cited by Dunn and Deater-Deckard (2001).

7   The different 'Mixed' ethnic groups have some things in common. The populations are generally young, the majority of people were born in the UK and many have one white parent.

In analysing data from the Government's Households Below Average Income dataset, which is derived from the Family Resources Survey, Kenway and Palmer (2007) found that 32 per cent of couples from minority ethnic groups with children were identified as experiencing low income levels, compared with only 16 per cent of white British couples with children.

Kenway and Palmer (2007) argue that differences between ethnic groups' poverty levels can be explained partially in terms of differences in household family and age structure and employment status. For example, lone parents and those of working age living alone are much more likely to experience low income levels and, across ethnic groups, the rate of lone parents experiencing low income levels is similar: 58 per cent of lone parents from minority ethnic groups were identified as experiencing low income levels, compared to 46 per cent white British.

The detrimental economic effects associated with lone parents and those of working age who live alone are likely to be more pronounced for black African and Caribbean families, as they have a greater prevalence among black African and Caribbean households: 15 to 20 per cent of black African and Caribbean households are lone parents, and 25 to 30 per cent are of working age who live alone.

However, family structure does not explain the low income levels experienced by the Pakistani or Bangladeshi group. In the case of this group, the levels of lone parents and those of working age who live alone are similar to white British. However, the Pakistani or Bangladeshi group is quite distinct in terms of age structure: 40 per cent of Bangladeshis and 35 per cent of Pakistanis in the UK are children, and only 5 per cent are of pensionable age. This contrasts with white British, where 20 per cent are children and 20 per cent are of pensionable age. Yet despite these differences, age structure actually explains very little of the difference in income distribution. A more important factor is the high proportion of Pakistani or Bangladeshi households that are workless – approximately 30 to 35 per cent – which is double the rate for white British households. Moreover, Kenway and Palmer (2007) claim that differences in pay rates by ethnicity provide an additional explanatory factor concerning differences in income levels.

Mothers, childcare and the work–life balance

2

Martina Klett-Davies and Eleni Skaliotis

Key statistics

These statistics are cited from independent research, ranging from small qualitative studies to large-scale representative surveys.

- The average age for women to have their first child increased from 23.7 years to 27.5 years between 1971 and 2007.

- The number of babies born following *in-vitro* fertilisation (IVF) and Intra-Cytoplasmic Sperm Injection (ICSI) treatment more than quadrupled between 1992 and 2006.

- Mothers now spend more time with their children and are more involved in their education than three decades ago.

- Mothers' employment has tripled since 1951.

- Many more mothers with higher qualifications work than mothers with lower qualifications. The employment gap between mothers with high educational qualifications and those with no educational qualifications rose from 13 per cent to 50 per cent between 1981 and 2008.

- The percentage increase in employment was largest for lone mothers at 39 per cent, compared to 15 per cent for married and cohabiting mothers between 1992 and 2008.

- The employment rate of lone mothers drops sharply after the second child, while married and cohabiting mothers are more likely to drop out of employment after the third child.

- White mothers have had the greatest increase in employment rates compared to other ethnic groups since the 1980s. ▶

- Black mothers are more likely to be in full-time employment than other ethnic groups.

- The percentage of women managers has quadrupled since 1990.

- The gap between women's and men's pay reduced by a quarter between 1994 and 2006, but remains an issue, particularly for part-time workers.

- The number of three- and four-year-olds in schools and school-based nurseries has tripled since 1970.

- Grandparents were cited as the most common source of informal childcare by about one-third of working mothers in 2006.

- Of working mothers with children under five, 54 per cent chose formal childcare in 2006.

- Children are more likely to attend formal care settings if they have a parent in the top education, occupation and family income groups.

Introduction

Becoming a mother always has been a profound moment of personal change. This chapter looks at how the experience of motherhood has changed over time for working and non-working mothers. Over the last four decades family composition has altered considerably, with family living arrangements and personal relationships becoming more complex and varied. Chapter 1 highlighted that mothers are more likely to cohabit, separate or divorce. Besides the nuclear family – two parents living with their children – there are more lone mothers and 'patchwork' families with step-parents and step-children due to divorce or remarriage. Although the general trend of marriage is declining, in 2006 52 per cent of men and 50 per cent of women were married in Great Britain (Chapter 1).

Key changes

Since the 1970s, women's lives have undergone major changes which have had an effect on the age at which women give birth, as well as the birth rate. The average age for women to have their first child in England and Wales was 23.7 years in 1971, 26.1 years in 1997 and 27.5 years by 2007 (ONS 2009p). Three key contributing factors can be identified.

First, the availability of the contraceptive pill since the mid-1960s and the legalisation of abortion enabled women to gain more control over their fertility so that, if they chose to do so, they could delay child-rearing and limit the number of children that they conceived (Barrett 2004). Deliberate planning of pregnancies has been the case especially for older mothers. According to the Millennium Cohort Study, 87 per cent of mothers aged 18 and under indicated that their pregnancy was a surprise, in comparison to only 23 per cent of mothers aged 31 and over, who were more likely to have planned it (Joshi 2008).

Second, the number of women participating in higher education increased dramatically, particularly from 1970 onwards. This was helped by the creation of the new universities of the 1960s, which offered innovative broad-based curricula that proved particularly attractive to women students (Dyhouse 2008). These more highly educated women tended to delay having their first child longer than the previous generation, or those without the same levels of education. One study found that in the early 1990s, the mean age at first birth among British mothers who were highly educated was five years older than that of mothers with low education. The authors suggest that mothers with higher qualifications are delaying childbirth due to increased participation in the labour force (Gustaffon et al. 2002 cited by Sigle-Rushton 2008; Joshi 2008).

Third, a rising number of women were able to enter the labour market (Dyhouse 2008). Changes occurred in the workplace, the kinds of work available and conditions of employment. The government tried to make paid employment a more equal place for women and men through the Equal Pay Act 1970, the Sex Discrimination Act 1975 and the abolition of the 'married women's option' in 1975, which ended the unequal treatment of women in the social security system (Hantrais 1994; Sainsbury 1996).

Paid employment and the welfare state

During the last four decades, the British welfare state has transformed itself. While the post-war welfare state was designed on the assumption that men went out to work and women stayed at home, the welfare system in the UK – as in other European Union (EU) countries – has moved towards an 'adult worker model', where men and women expect, and are expected, to be paid workers (Lewis and Giullari 2005). The UK social policy agenda of the Labour Government considers the adult worker model as the best way out of poverty for mothers and their children.

In line with the UK policy context, European employment policy has promoted paid employment for mothers. The Lisbon Strategy set targets for increasing the employment rate of women to 60 per cent by 2010. By 2008, the UK had surpassed the target already, with 73 per cent of women without dependent children in employment, and 68 per cent of mothers in employment. In comparison, there has been less change in other European countries (European Trade Union Confederation 2006; ONS 2008f). For example, Italy and Greece had female participation rates of 47 per cent and 49 per cent respectively in 2008 (Eurostat 2009b).

Inequality

Smart (2007) has argued prominently that motherhood is the remaking of inequality and privilege, creating both gender divisions and inequalities that women without children do not experience to the same degree, and that impact particularly on those in circumstances of disadvantage. This chapter will investigate this thesis by drawing attention to the intersection of motherhood, gender, socio-economic background, education and age.

Hawkes (2008) gives supporting evidence from the Millennium Cohort Study that shows how motherhood perpetuates inequality. For example, children born to younger parents are more likely to be exposed to the disadvantages from their mothers' background, which includes the disadvantages incurred by living in a more deprived area. Those who enter motherhood later are less likely to have experienced the separation of their own parents, have experienced life in care, have left school without educational qualifications or be from a minority ethnic group (Hawkes 2008).

Infertility

Arguably, the way that infertility has become treatable is another major trend in motherhood. Louise Brown, the first 'test-tube baby', was born in the UK in 1978, and now babies born following IVF or ICSI account for slightly more than 1.5 per cent of all babies born in the UK each year. About one in six couples are affected by infertility and the number of babies born following these two treatments more than quadrupled between 1992 and 2006 (Human Fertilisation Embryology Authority 2007).[1] Two-thirds of cycles are conducted privately, but at an average cost of about £2,000 per cycle, this is not an affordable option for all couples (Henderson 2008).

This chapter will address the following questions:

2.1   How is motherhood experienced?

2.2   Which mothers work?

2.3   What kinds of jobs do mothers have?

2.4   How many hours do mothers work and when do they work?

---

1   In this timeframe the number of IVF and ICSI babies increased from 3,113 to 12,589 in the UK.

2.1 How is motherhood experienced?

There is a cultural assumption that women want to become mothers, and this shapes the experience of all women, whether they become mothers or remain childless (Phoenix et al. 1991). Even at the beginning of the 21st century, women continue to be defined in terms of their biological function, their ability to give birth. Motherhood is socially constructed as valued and important, particularly if it happens within the 'right' circumstances and age. Such powerful ideologies override individual experiences and fail to accommodate the diverse experiences of mothering. Academics have argued that through these social constructions, the old myth of motherhood perpetuates and retains its sacred aura (Miller 2005). By looking into the characteristics of women who remain childless and their reasons for not having children, we can gain insight into how women anticipate the experience of motherhood.

Childlessness

Despite the enduring cultural assumption that women want to become mothers, the proportion of childless women by the age of 35 has more than doubled (Berrington 2004). One in 10 women born in 1945 remained childless, compared to around one in five born in 1960. National population projections estimate that this figure will increase to about 22 per cent of women born in 1990, although certain subgroups are likely to experience a sharper increase in childlessness (Berrington 2004).

We can distinguish between women who do not have children and are voluntarily childless (i.e. childless by choice), those who are involuntarily childless (due to infertility or lack of opportunity) and those who are a mixture of both. A qualitative study found that while many voluntarily childless women were involved with other children in their families, e.g. nieces and nephews, or were caring for their elderly parents, the respondents felt that it would be undesirable, difficult or impossible to make parenthood part of their own lives. The study also established that although highly qualified women are more likely to remain childless, careers were not a particular priority. Indeed, early retirement emerged as a popular goal among many of those interviewed (McAllister and Clarke 1998).

A recent quantitative study found that cohabiting women were less likely than married women to become mothers. Also, compared to mothers, childless women were significantly more likely to be qualified to degree level or above (26.8 per cent and 19.2 per cent, respectively). In addition, childless women were more often in paid employment (up to 90 per cent) as well as employed in professional and managerial or technical occupations (Portanti and Whitworth 2009). This could indicate a new trend, with some childless women today prioritising their career over combining a career with being a mother.

Trends in the experience of motherhood

Motherhood is a complex experience that differs from individual to individual and is associated with a range of negative and positive aspects. What do we know about motherhood now, as an experience that makes it different from the experience of motherhood in previous decades?

Thomson et al. (2008) interviewed women who gave birth in the 1950s and 1970s. The mothers in the older cohort felt that motherhood then was taken for granted more and that they did not rely on experts as much as new mothers do now. These earlier cohort mothers also mentioned that they did not have as many material goods or choices in how to live their lives. They lamented the increased materialism of the 2000s and the pressure on young mothers today to combine paid work with parenting young children.

Moreover, motherhood has become more 'professionalised' and more demands are placed on parents now. Motherhood has been claimed by 'experts' in terms of a response to children's needs (Lawler 1999). For example, new mothers are encouraged by many authorities and experts to breastfeed on demand for as long as possible, and to submit their daily schedule to that of their newborns.

The explosion in parenting programmes – such as *Supernanny, Nanny 911* and *Wife Swap* – combined with a bewildering array of books, magazines and gurus offering advice, suggests that parents are working harder than ever to become 'professional' parents who know more about what good child-rearing is. For some parents this means greater focus on both their children's education and leisure time. For example, one British study found that in affluent two-children families, parents are coordinating an average of 8 to 10 extracurricular activities a week for their offspring (Bunting 2004). Increasingly, parents are making time to spend with their children and often marriage is being transformed from being partnership-centred to being children-centred (Nave-Herz 1992).

2.2 Which mothers work?

While the employment rate of all women has increased over the last six decades, for mothers it has increased at a particularly high rate, more than tripling between 1951 and 2008. In 1951 around one in six mothers were employed; in 2008, around four in six were employed (Joshi 1985, cited by Hansen et al. 2006; ONS 2008f).[2] Figure 2.1 shows that between 1951 and 1991 there was a fairly constant increase in mothers' employment of approximately 11 per cent per decade. Only as the rate of mothers' employment neared the rate of employment of women without dependent children did the increase in the rate of mothers' employment slow down (ONS 2008f). In fact, during the 1990s, including the 1991–92 recession, mothers' employment grew by only 2 per cent, while it grew by 4 per cent between 2001 and 2008 when Britain experienced an economic upturn.

Figure 2.1: Mothers' employment rate, 1951–2008

Source: Census and Labour Force Survey, 1951–81. Census data from Joshi (1985, cited by Hansen et al. 2006); 1981 Labour Force Survey data from Harrop and Moss (1994); 1991–2001 Labour Force Survey data from Twomey (2002); 2008 Labour Force Survey data from ONS (2008f)

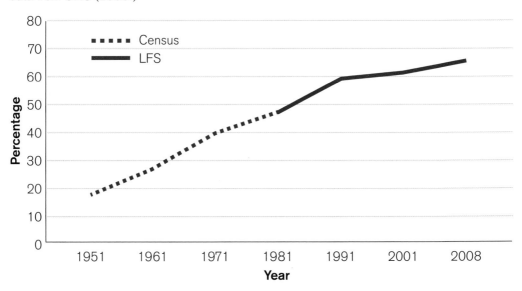

While the average employment rate for all mothers has increased, there are certain groups of mothers that are more likely to be employed than others. In the 2000s, mothers are more likely to be employed if they:

---

2 Women with dependent children under 16 and children aged 16 to 18 who have never married and are in full-time education. Employment rates for men aged 16 to 64 and women aged 16–59.

- are married or cohabiting mothers

- own a property

- have fewer children

- have older children

- have higher academic qualifications

- are white.

The following sections will explain the trends in more detail.

Marital status

In the late 1970s, the employment rates of married mothers and lone parents were broadly similar, at 52 per cent for lone parents and marginally higher for married mothers. However, while the employment rate for married mothers grew steadily from 1984, so that by the mid-1990s it was broadly similar to women without dependent children, the employment rate of lone parents fell in the 1980s and then stagnated until the late 1990s, when it began to increase again (Gregg and Harkness 2003).

Figure 2.2 illustrates the employment rate of married or cohabiting mothers and fathers, lone parents and working-age people without dependent children since 1992 (data which looked separately at lone mothers and lone fathers were not available for this timespan). There has been great change in employment rates during this period, with the greatest increases among lone mothers. The percentage increase for working-age people without dependent children over the 16-year period was 3 per cent; the equivalent was 15 per cent for married or cohabiting mothers, and 39 per cent for lone mothers.

Married fathers were most likely to be in paid employment (91 per cent) in 2008. The next largest working group was married and cohabiting mothers, 72 per cent of whom were working in 2008. This means that employment rates for married and cohabiting mothers are now very close to the rates for working-age people who have no dependent children (74 per cent).

Despite rapid increases in the number of lone parents in employment, they are the least likely to be in paid employment (56 per cent). However, the gap between married or cohabiting mothers and lone mothers is narrowing, from 24 per cent in 1997 to 15 per cent in 2008. The effect may stem from increased government pressure on lone parents to return to work. In addition to the policies mentioned earlier, the New Deal for lone parents, which was launched in 1997, introduced a range of measures to help mothers into work, including a guaranteed job interview for every lone parent who was looking for and ready to start work, a childcare fund pilot as financial support for childcare, and an in-work emergency discretionary fund to help lone parents overcome any financial barriers which might prevent them from remaining in a new job (Department for Work and Pensions 2009b).

Figure 2.2: Employment by marital and parental status, 1992–2008

Source: Labour Force Survey (spring percentages). 1992–2006 data from ONS (2009q); 2006–2008 data from ONS (2009r)

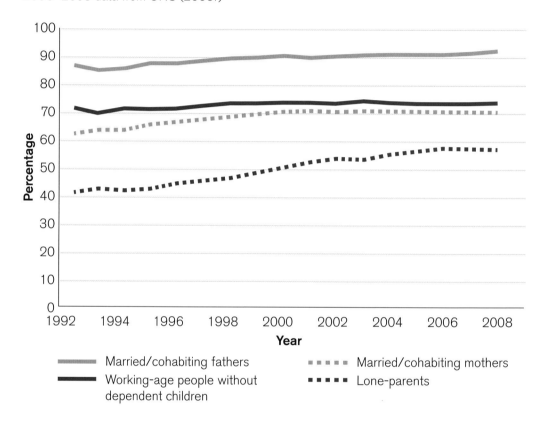

Housing tenure

Analysis of the seventh wave (2005) of the Family and Children's Study has indicated that families were most likely to be in work if they owned their house or flat. Of all couple families, 80 per cent were owner-occupiers, with 79 per cent of mothers in couple families working. Only 32 per cent of lone parents were owner-occupiers, but among these mothers the employment rate was 91 per cent. Employment rates were greatly reduced for mothers in social housing. Of married or cohabiting mothers in social housing, 40 per cent worked, compared to 44 per cent of lone mothers living in social housing (Hales et al. 2007).

Number of dependent children in family

Labour Force Survey statistics over the last three decades have shown consistently that as the number of children in a family increases, the employment rate of mothers decreases (Harrop and Moss 1994; Kent 2009; Walling 2005).[3]

Figure 2.3 illustrates the clear correlation between mothers' employment and number of children for both married or cohabiting and lone mothers. Based on data from 2007, the employment rate drops sharply with the third child for all mothers. For married or cohabiting mothers with two children, the employment rate was 73 per cent. It dropped to 58 per cent for mothers with three children and to only 40 per cent for mothers with four or more children. It is possible to see that the difference in employment rates for mothers was greatest between having three and four children for married or cohabiting mothers (58 per cent and 40 per cent respectively), and two and three children for lone mothers (54 per cent and 37 per cent respectively).

Figure 2.3: Mothers' employment by marital status and number of children, 2007
Source: Labour Force Survey (Kent 2009)

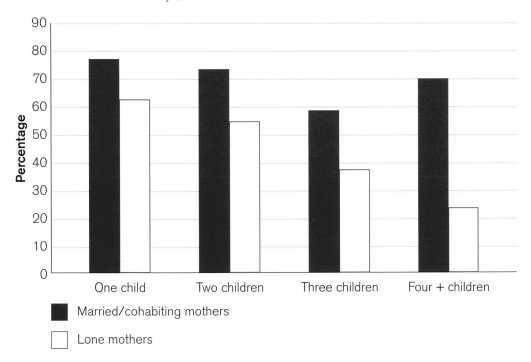

3   Analysis of the Labour Force Survey from 1981, 1989, 2004 and 2007.

The biggest differences were seen between those with one child and those with what is now considered to be a large family of four or more children, especially in families headed by a lone parent. For example, in 2007, almost twice as many couple mothers with one child were employed as couple mothers with at least four children (77 per cent and 40 per cent respectively). The corresponding percentages for lone mothers were 62 per cent and 23 per cent.

Age of dependent children in family

Figure 2.4 illustrates that the employment rate for mothers with children of all ages has increased over time. Mothers with a child aged under five consistently have the lowest rates of employment, particularly lone mothers (35 per cent, compared to 63 per cent of couple mothers in 2008). In fact, lone mothers with children under the age of five are the least likely to be in paid employment. The largest employment gap between couple and lone mothers according to the age group of their youngest child is for mothers with children under five. These mothers may choose to be with their children or find it difficult to be the only earner in the household, and to command a high enough wage to pay for flexible childcare. Only when lone mothers' children reach compulsory school age does their employment rate increase markedly. For example, in 2008 the difference between lone and couple mothers' employment with children under five was 28 per cent, whereas the difference between lone and couple mothers' employment with children aged 11 to 18 was 11 per cent.

As Figure 2.4 demonstrates, as the age of the youngest child increases, the difference in rates between lone mothers and partnered mothers decreases, so that for mothers whose youngest dependent child is aged 16 to 18, 76 per cent of lone mothers worked in 2008, only 6 per cent lower than for mothers with a partner (82 per cent).

Since the mid-1990s, the biggest increase in employment has been seen for lone mothers with children under 11, particularly aged five to 10 years. The employment rate for partnered mothers with children under five has seen the most significant increase, while it has plateaued for partnered mothers with older children.

Figure 2.4: Rate of women's employment by age of youngest child, 1996–2008*
Source: Labour Force Survey. 1996–2004 data from Walling (2005); 2008 data from ONS (2008g)

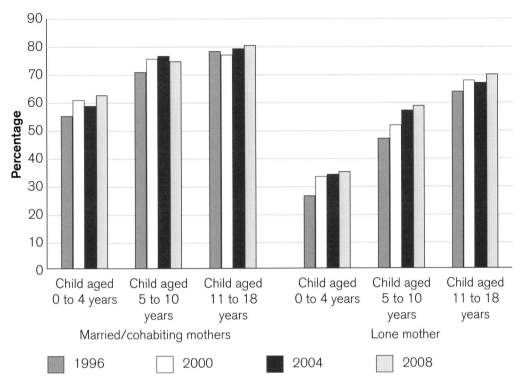

* Figures in 2008 are for children aged 11 to 15 and not 11 to 18 years. The employment rate of mothers with children aged 16 to 18 in full-time education was 82 per cent for couple mothers and 76 per cent for lone mothers.

Kent (2009) asserts that data on age of the youngest child are linked to data on the number of dependent children, as the more children mothers have, the more likely it will be that one is in the youngest group.

Mothers' qualifications

As mentioned previously, mothers with higher educational qualifications tend to have a higher employment rate than other mothers. Analysis of Labour Force Survey statistics between 1981 and 1994 has indicated that not only did the employment rate vary by qualifications, but also that the increase in the employment rate over the period was largest for the most educated mothers (Brannen et al. 1997; Harrop and Moss 1994). For example, between 1981 and 1989 the employment rate for mothers with higher education or degrees increased by 21 per cent to 78 per cent. On the other hand, the employment rate for mothers without any qualifications increased by only 5 per cent to 49 per cent (Table 2.1). In other words, the increase in the employment rate during the 1980s was four times larger for mothers with higher qualifications.

Table 2.1: Mothers' employment by highest qualification, 1981–2008*

Source: Labour Force Survey. 1980s data from Harrop and Moss (1994); 1993 data from Sly (1994)[4]

	1981	1989	1993	1997	2001	2008
Degree or equivalent	57	78	79	80	82	83
Higher education				84	83	82
GCE A Level or equivalent	43	59		67	72	75
GCSE grades A–C or equivalent	45	59	59	65	69	69
Other qualifications	44	54		59	60	55
No qualification	44	49	42	42	41	33

* Figures given in percentages.

On the one hand, the employment rate of mothers with the highest qualifications continued to rise in the 1990s to 83 per cent in 2008, while the employment rate of mothers with no qualifications decreased by 25 per cent between 1981 and 2008 to 33 per cent. On the other hand, the employment rate for mothers with higher qualifications or a degree increased by approximately 26 per cent over the same time period. Thus, the employment rate gap between mothers with higher education and mothers with no qualifications has increased from 13 per cent to an incredible 50 per cent in the last 17 years.

Alongside an increasing demand for highly skilled employees, women are now more likely to gain higher educational qualifications. Between 1970–71 and 2006–07 the proportion of female higher education students increased from 33 per cent to 57 per cent, and there has been a higher proportion of female higher education students than males each year since 1995–96 (ONS 2009p). The *Leitch Review of Skills* (HM Treasury 2005), reported that the proportion of employment requiring at least a Level 4 qualification (degree) rose from 23 per cent to 30 per cent between 1994

---

4   Data for 1997–2008 obtained via personal communication with ONS Household, Labour Market and Social Well-being Division, 23 June 2009.

and 2004, and the proportion of employment requiring no qualifications fell from approximately 18 per cent to 11 per cent over the same 10-year period. The *Leitch Review* analysis suggests that by 2020, 42 per cent of jobs will be filled by those with at least a Level 4 qualification, and potentially only 2 per cent of jobs will be filled by those with no qualifications (HM Treasury 2005).

Interestingly, in 2007, lone mothers with a degree were slightly more likely to be in employment than couple mothers with a degree. Kent (2009) reports Annual Population Survey data from 2007, which showed that 83 per cent of lone mothers with a degree were in employment, compared to 81 per cent of couple mothers. Annual Population Survey data has shown that the gap between mothers with the highest and lowest education levels has risen to 43 per cent for couple mothers and 57 per cent for lone mothers in 2007, compared to Labour Force Survey data in 1981 that showed a difference of 13 per cent for all mothers.

Mothers' ethnicity

In 1981, Harrop and Moss (1994) reported that black African and Caribbean mothers had the highest employment rate at 56 per cent, compared to 47 per cent of white mothers and 31 per cent of South-Asian mothers. However, eight years later the rate of employment had grown for white and South-Asian mothers, but contracted by 2 per cent for black mothers.

Figure 2.5 illustrates the data spanning 30 years from the Labour Force Survey. After a slight contraction in the employment rate for black mothers in the 1980s, the employment rate increased to 59 per cent in 2008. White mothers saw the biggest increase in employment of 24 per cent to 71 per cent in 2008. Asian (all Asian and South-Asian) mothers saw a modest increase of 7 per cent over the period to 38 per cent in 2008.

Figure 2.5: Mothers' employment by ethnicity, 1981–2008*

Source: Labour Force Survey; 1980s data from Harrop and Moss (1994)[5]

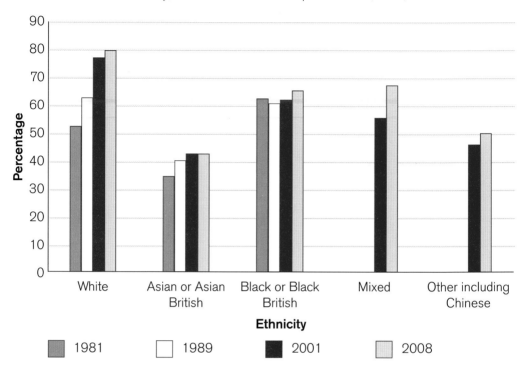

* In 1981 and 1989 the Labour Force Survey defined black people of African and Caribbean descent and Asian people of Indian, Pakistani and Bangladeshi descent.

Over the same period, the percentage of employed white mothers working full time has increased from 34 per cent to 43 per cent (Figure 2.6). However, as Figure 2.6 clearly illustrates, the majority of employed black mothers work full time and always have done so (73 per cent in 1981 and 69 per cent in 2008). In 2008, employed black mothers were more than 1.5 times more likely to be working full time than employed white mothers. Employed Asian mothers are now less likely to be working full time than two decades ago (77 per cent in 1981 and 55 per cent in 2008).[6]

5   Data for 2000s obtained via personal communication with ONS Household, Labour Market and Social Well-being Division, 16 June 2009.

6   Small sample sizes for 'Mixed race' and 'Other including Chinese' prevented reliable estimates for detailed analysis on full-time employment. Data were unavailable for these groups in 1981 and 1989.

Figure 2.6: Percentage of employed mothers working full time by ethnicity, 1981–2008*

Source: Labour Force Survey; 1980s data from Harrop and Moss (1994)[7]

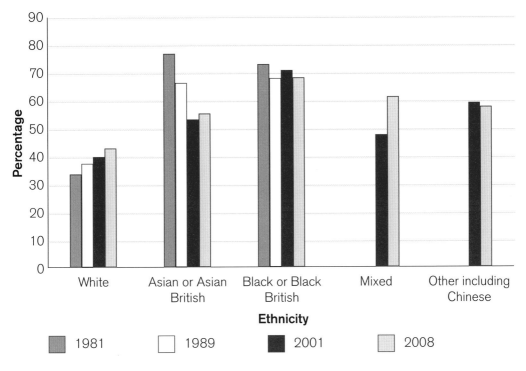

* In 1981 and 1989 the Labour Force Survey defined black people of African and Caribbean descent and South Asian people of Indian, Pakistani and Bangladeshi descent.

Dale et al. (2008) pooled data from the Quarterly Labour Force Survey to form an early time cohort (1992–96) and a later cohort (2001–05), in order to investigate the economic activity of different ethnic groups. They also found major differences between ethnic groups over the life stages.

Black Caribbean women had higher rates of economic activity across the lifecourse than white women, and were more likely to remain economically active when they had children. It is argued that *"in a culture where paid work is the 'norm' we see only limited reduction in activity for black mothers with the presence of children and across levels of qualification"* (Dale et al. 2008, p.92). A 2003 study carried out by One Parent Families (cited in Barrett 2004) suggested that black lone mothers emphasised the

---

7   Data for 2000s obtained via personal communication with ONS Household, Labour Market and Social Well-being Division, 16 June 2009.

importance of providing good, strong maternal role models for their children, and in particular saw employment as the best way to provide for their children.

Levels of economic activity among Pakistani and Bangladeshi women fell substantially once they had a partner, and again when they had children (Lindley and Dale 2004). The findings of the Labour Force Survey *"provide strong support for the ideal of children and maternal care of children among Pakistani and Bangladeshi mothers"* (Dale et al. 2008, p.93). Since the Bangladeshi and Pakistani communities tend to be among the most recent immigrants, Lindley and Dale (2004) suggest that as this community evolves, these patterns may be expected to change. In fact, among younger and highly qualified women there is evidence of change, with a delay in marriage and childbearing (Dale et al. 2008).

In summary, qualifications and dependent children have an effect on women's employment for all groups, but have the largest effect for Pakistani and Bangladeshi women, and the smallest for black Caribbean women (Dale et al. 2008).

2.3 What kinds of jobs do mothers have?

It is not always easy to obtain information about the exact nature of work undertaken by mothers, as data are collected and presented often on the basis of gender rather than parental status. Therefore, while information is available about the kind of work undertaken by women compared to men (Table 2.2), more precise details about the kinds of jobs that parents take on compared to non-parents are not currently available.

The Labour Force Survey offers us information from 1978 on the sectors in which men and women are employed. In 1978, the three key sectors that women worked in were education, health and public administration; distribution, hotels and restaurants; and manufacturing. Manufacturing has been in decline since the late 1970s; instead, the financial and business sector has grown rapidly in the last three decades and has become the third largest industry to employ women. Education, health and public administration has remained the sector which employs the most women, with almost two-fifths of women working in this sector in 2008. Very few women work in energy and water supply, agriculture, construction and transport and communication.

In addition, the decline of the manufacturing industry and growth of financial services has had an impact on male employment choices in the last 30 years. Thus, while there has been a slight decline in women working in distribution, hotels and restaurants, there has been an increase in men working in this industry during this time period.

Table 2.2: Employee jobs by gender and industry, UK, 1978–2008*

Source: ONS (2009s),[8] seasonally adjusted

	Females				Males			
	1978	1988	1998	2008	1978	1988	1998	2008
Education, health and public administration	32	34	34	38	13	15	13	14
Distribution, hotels and restaurants	26	26	26	24	16	18	20	21
Manufacturing	20	14	10	5	31	23	21	14
Finance and business services	11	15	18	20	10	14	18	22
Other services	6	7	6	7	3	4	5	6
Transport and communication	2	2	3	3	9	9	8	8
Construction	1	2	2	2	11	12	10	12
Agriculture and fishing	1	1	1	1	3	3	3	2
Mining, electricity, gas and water	1	1	0	0	4	2	1	1
All employee jobs (in millions)	10.8	12.4	13.5	14.8	16.1	15.6	15.3	16.9

* Figures given as a percentage.

Moreover, the difference in men's and women's occupation choices is reflected in their higher education choices. In 2006, new entrant females dominated the social sciences, business and law category and education and the health and welfare category, while new entrant males heavily dominated the engineering, manufacturing and construction category and the science category (Higher Education Authority 2008).

---

8   Data for 2000s obtained via personal communication with ONS Household, Labour Market and Social Well-being Division, 16 June 2009.

Occupational status

Dex et al. (2006) used two data sources, the Women and Employment Survey and National Childhood Development Survey, to examine how women's occupational status and mobility have changed between 1980 and 2000. Their analysis showed that downward occupational mobility after the birth of a first child has declined, compared to earlier generations in the Women and Employment Survey: that is, women are now less likely to return to lower status jobs after their first child is born. However, Dex et al. (2008) found that downward occupational mobility varied by occupation, and was higher for mothers who had a longer duration out of employment after having children and for those who returned to a part-time job.

The Chartered Management Institute (2009) reported a steep increase in women managers over a 12-year period from its survey of more than 22,000 managers. In 1990, 8 per cent of managers were women, compared to 29 per cent in 2002. Data from the Labour Force Survey indicated a slightly higher rate of 32 per cent female managers in 2002, and has shown that the proportion of women as managers has increased fairly slowly since, to 34.5 per cent in 2008 (Figure 2.7).

Figure 2.7: Proportion of female managers, UK, 1990–08
Source: 1990–2002 data from Chartered Management Institute (2009), 2002–08 data from ONS (2009t), spring quarter, not seasonally adjusted

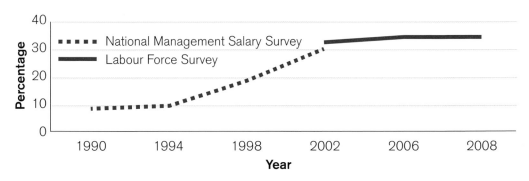

Full-time working mothers are more likely to have higher status jobs than part-time working mothers. In 1981, only 3 per cent of part-time working mothers indicated they had a high-status professional or managerial job, compared to 11 per cent of mothers working full time (Harrop and Moss 1994). In the following eight years, the percentage of working mothers in managerial or professional positions nearly doubled to 5.5 per cent for part-time working mothers and 21 per cent for full-time working mothers.

2.4 How many hours do mothers work and when do they work?

The full-time breadwinner and female part-time worker have become the most common arrangements in the UK (Lewis et al. 2008). Couple mothers are most likely to work part time (41 per cent), compared to 31 per cent working full time (Table 2.3). However, lone mothers are split fairly evenly between part-time and full-time work – 27 per cent and 28 per cent respectively. Since 1996, it has been clear that the rise in mothers' employment stems from an increase in couple mothers working full time and lone mothers entering full- and part-time employment.

Table 2.3: Full-time and part-time employment for mothers, 1996–2008*
Source: Labour Force Survey. Walling (2005) for 1996–2004; ONS (2008g) for 2008 from second quarter

	Full time		Part time	
	Married or cohabiting mothers	Lone mothers*	Married or cohabiting mothers	Lone mothers*
1996	25	22	42	22
2000	28	25	42	26
2004	28	28	42	26
2008	31	27	41	28

* Figures given as a percentage. Data for 1996–2004 is for all lone parents, including fathers.

The percentage of UK residents working more than a 48-hour week decreased from 22 per cent in 1999 to 18 per cent in 2008 (ONS 2000, 2009p). A representative survey found that 30 per cent of fathers and 6 per cent of mothers work more than the 48-hour week, above the limit of the Working Time Directive: 12 per cent of fathers and 3 per cent of mothers work more than 60 hours a week (La Valle et al. 2002).

When do mothers work?

The pattern of work varies greatly among employed parents. While professional parents are more likely to work long hours, parents who regularly work at weekends are more likely to have no qualifications and be on a lower income (Barnes and Bryson 2004; Brannen et al. 1997; Lyonette and Clark 2009). La Valle et al.'s (2002) survey found that more than one-half of mothers and four-fifths of fathers frequently worked at atypical times of day, outside nine to five. In addition, one-quarter of mothers and just under one-third of fathers worked once a month or more on Sundays. Couple parents where at least one of the parents reported frequently working atypical hours were dissatisfied with the amount of time that they or their partner spent with their children (24 per cent and 33 per cent respectively). However, some families, particularly two-parent families, viewed atypical work as beneficial, as it enables parents to spend more time with their children and enjoy more time for themselves, as well as decreasing their reliance on formal childcare. However, it is a consequence of both parents frequently working atypical hours that many report being dissatisfied with their time spent as a couple (41 per cent).

Recent research by the Relationships Foundation finds that parents working atypical hours are more vulnerable to psychological distress and lower self-esteem, which can have an impact on children. In particular, Sunday working appears to affect time spent with children more than other atypical work. Finally, parental satisfaction regarding time spent with children is lower for parents working atypical hours than it is for parents working standard hours, even when those working hours are relatively low (Lyonette and Clark 2009).

2.5 What are the reasons for mothers to move back into employment?

This section will discuss how mothers negotiate the relationship between motherhood and paid work. One often-cited reason for moving back into paid work is economic necessity: this may mean being able to pay the household bills and the mortgage, or being able to afford holidays and little extras (Thomson et al. 2008). For Dex (2003a), women's increased participation in the labour force is viewed very much as a consequence of the decline in men's wages and the growing insecurity of men's earnings throughout the 1990s, which has affected not only traditional male sector occupations such as manufacturing, but also professional and managerial positions.

Preferences

Hakim (2000) distinguishes between types of mothers and their attitudinal preferences to paid work: there is the full-time work-oriented mother, the stay-at-home-oriented mother and the part-time work-oriented mother. Kan (2007) responded to Hakim's 'preference theory' by using work–life history data from the British Household Panel Survey (1991–2001), in order to examine the work trajectories of married or cohabiting women. The author found both supportive and opposing evidence for Hakim's theory.

In support of Hakim's argument, Kan (2007) found that women with work-centred attitudes were more likely to engage in full-time work over a long period, and the presence of dependent children for these mothers was less of an influence on the likelihood of full-time work. However, contrary to Hakim's theory, Kan (2007) found that gender role preference can be changed according to employment experience and may not remain fixed over time.

McRae (2003) has critiqued Hakim's preference theory by conceptualising two kinds of constraint that women are facing in their balance of employment and family. Normative constraints include women's own identities as well as gender relations in the family, while structural constraints encompass job availability and the cost and availability of childcare. Social class is a key underlying factor, which explains why some women have greater choices and can overcome constraints more easily (McRae 2003).

Duncan (2005) interviewed 50 mothers and also found class-based differences. However, the divisions are more subtle social identities rather than just structural divisions between working-class and middle-class mothers. Most strikingly, the suburban middle-class wives in the sample showed a strong primarily mother identity and had almost identical understandings as those of the poor 'peripheral' working-class group, despite huge class differences in income, status, education and housing. Therefore, Duncan (2005) suggests that mothers' situations are down to neither purely preference nor structural constraints. Instead, the reasons for how mothers combine caring and employment are socially and culturally created. More precisely, negotiations are influenced by their social context, such as their own biographical experience, relationships with their partner, neighbourhood and friends, and family history and background. In this way they become 'social moralities' (Duncan 2005).

However, economic necessity – or at least mothers' perception of necessity – cannot be sidelined, and the time at which women return to work or take up work has been changing over the last three decades. For example, in 1996 two-thirds of mothers were taking up or returning to work within a year of their child's birth, compared to only one-quarter in 1979 (Callender et al. 1997). In 2005, a nationally representative survey of more than 2,500 mothers found that nearly half of mothers took exactly six months' paid maternity leave, and a further 14 per cent took their full 52-week entitlement. The duration of maternity pay was the single most important factor explaining the duration of maternity leave (Smeaton and Marsh 2006).

Hence, economic factors must be a larger part of 'social moralities' than the credit which Duncan (2005) gives them. Additionally, the economic recession which began in 2008 is having an effect. A recent YouGov survey of 1,148 adults revealed that 70 per cent of mothers were re-entering the job market earlier than originally intended because of money concerns, such as a shortfall in the family budget and fears about household income (Pykett 2009) (see Chapter 5 for the impact of recession on families).

Choosing part-time employment

A recent British study asked more directly why mothers were either not in paid employment, or were in 'mini-jobs' for fewer than 16 hours a week. The predominant answer given was that the mother wanted to spend time with her child (or children), and it was felt to be the right decision for the sake of the child (or children). This was mentioned by 54 per cent of couple mothers doing mini-jobs and 53 per cent of those not working at all (Hales et al. 2007). Lone mothers also felt that their child's need for their mother's presence was still the dominant barrier to work, but were slightly less likely to mention it (40 per cent of those working in mini-jobs or not working at all). Among those not working at all, three of the main constraints were the same as those cited by non-working couple mothers: their own illness (17 per cent), a child's illness (7 per cent) and the cost of childcare (14 per cent) (Hales et al. 2007).

For many mothers the preferred employment option is part-time working. According to the Labour Force Survey in 2004, the reasons given most frequently by women for working part time relate to their family or domestic situation (Equal Opportunities Commission 2005c). In total, 53 per cent of female part-time employees said that they wanted to spend more time with their family, had domestic commitments which prevented them from working full time, or felt that there were insufficient childcare facilities available. By contrast, only 6 per cent of male part-time employees stated that their reason for working part time related to their family or domestic situation. Instead, the most common response, accounting for 40 per cent of male part-time employees, was that they worked part time because they were a student or at school. Although more than four-fifths (81 per cent) of part-time employees were women, almost all (97 per cent) of those citing family or domestic reasons were women.

Motivations for being in paid employment

Survey results have suggested that women differ in their motivations for paid employment. Hinds and Jarvis (2000) found that women were more likely to say that their main reason for working was related to social or personal preference (e.g. to earn money of their own, to earn money to buy extras, for the company of other people, for a change from their children or housework). In this study, almost one-third of women (30 per cent) gave these kinds of reasons as their main ones for working, as opposed to only 8 per cent of men.

According to the British Social Attitudes Survey, working women and men have different main motivations to be in paid employment (Figure 2.8). While the majority of men report working for basic essentials (59 per cent in 2007), women were split fairly evenly between working for basic essentials and working for social or personal preference, with a slight divergence in 1984 and 2007. Figure 2.8 indicates that there is no clear upward or downward trend over time for women, although there is a slight downward trend for the percentage of men who say that their main motivation to work is to earn money for basic essentials. This is likely to reflect the increase of women working in recent years.

Figure 2.8: Main motivation for working, 1984–2007*
Source: British Social Attitudes Information System (2009)

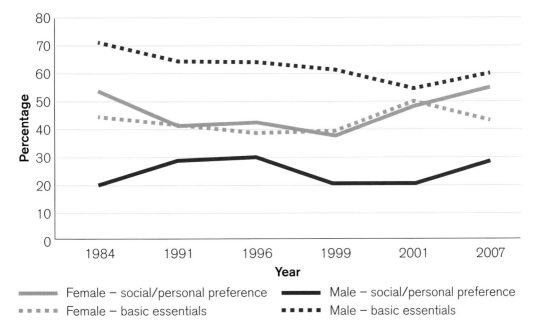

* Social/personal preference includes: to earn money to buy extras, to earn money of my own, for the company of other people, I enjoy working, to follow my career, for a change from my children or housework.

2.6 Have employment conditions improved?

Since the 1970s, a number of developments have taken place which have been designed to improve employment conditions for men and women in the UK. These include changes in conditions of pay, length of working hours, the availability of parental and maternity leave entitlements and the right to request flexible working. Clearly, working mothers have benefited from some of these policies, although they remain disadvantaged in the labour market.

As the number of women in paid employment is increasing, they can become financially independent in the workplace and are no longer assumed to be economically dependent on a male breadwinner (Klett-Davies 2007).

The right to request flexible working

The British welfare state has been very active in supporting women's employment. The right to request flexible working was introduced in 2003 for working parents with children aged up to six and the right was extended to include working parents with children aged up to 16 in 2009. The Women and Work Commission (2009) estimates that 10.5 million people can now make this request. It reports research by the Chartered Institute of Personnel Development showing that businesses that use flexible working successfully are at a recruitment advantage, due to factors such as higher employee retention.

However, the right to flexible working does not translate automatically into the uptake of this law. An online survey found that some parents were unaware of the right to ask for flexible working (20 per cent) (Government Equalities Office 2009). Two-thirds of parents (66 per cent) expressed some concern about making a request to work flexibly to their current employer, and that this concern might prevent them from doing so. Around one-third (32 per cent) thought that if they made such a request, it might mark them out as being uncommitted to their job, and slightly fewer than one-quarter (23 per cent) thought that such a request might affect their promotion prospects (Government Equalities Office 2009). This is despite the fact that slightly more than half (51 per cent) of working parents feel that their relationship with their children would improve if they could work flexibly. Mothers who work full time are more likely than fathers who work full time to agree that their job prevents them from spending the amount of time that they would like to spend with their children (72 per cent and 59 per cent respectively) (Government Equalities Office 2009).

One rare study which consulted children who had lone working mothers found that many younger children wanted to have more time with their mothers. They wanted their mothers to be in employment, but only to work during school hours and term time (Miller and Ridge 2008).

The right to request flexible working has not promoted equality. In practice, even for those who qualify to apply for flexible work arrangements, their ability to achieve the flexibility that they want rests on their bargaining power (Dean 2008). Those with the skills to negotiate the working patterns that suit their lives outside of work are likely to be those who have the most desirable skills for employers – that is, they are more likely to be highly skilled professionals in higher paid occupations.

It is also significant that notions of flexible working are highly gendered. Fewer men than women make requests to work flexibly, fewer have their requests granted, and fewer who take their cases to tribunals are successful (Working Families 2006). A report from the Equal Opportunities Commission (2005a) found that fewer fathers than mothers are aware that they have a right to ask for flexible working. A working culture that contains an implicit notion that flexible working is aimed primarily at women with caring responsibilities will only reinforce the expectation that it is women who should take on caring roles. It also reinforces that it is women's career opportunities that are curtailed and their pension contributions that are disrupted (Lewis, Gambles and Rapoport 2007). Social policies might encourage fathers to take parental leave, and managers are often sympathetic to this in principle, but workplace strategies to facilitate and encourage men actually to take leave can be lacking (Lewis, Gambles and Rapoport 2007).

The homecare allowance of paying parents to stay at home with their young children has been put forward as a possible policy initiative by the Conservative Party (Hall 2004). However, evidence from other countries such as Finland and Germany shows that cash payments in the form of parental leave promotes female labour market exit, rather than leading to the reallocation of domestic labour and childcare towards men (Lewis and Giullari 2005; Klett-Davies 2007).

Maternity leave

Maternity leave entitlements have greatly improved over time. As mentioned previously, British women can take up to 52 weeks' maternity leave, with statutory maternity pay for up to 39 weeks. If entitled, a woman can receive 90 per cent of her average weekly earnings for the first six weeks, then up to £117.18 per week for the remaining 33 weeks. The last 13 weeks, if taken, are unpaid. Many employers' provisions go beyond the statutory minimum, providing either more pay or extra-statutory maternity leave. On top of maternity and paternity leave, each parent is entitled to 13 weeks' unpaid leave per child up to their fifth birthday, with a maximum of four weeks' leave to be taken in any one calendar year (O'Brien and Moss 2008).

Of the 21 European countries compared in Moss and Korintus's (2008, cited by James and Henricson 2009) international review of leave policies, the UK is the only country providing fewer than two months of earnings-related leave. However, many countries such as Ireland have ceilings on earnings-related payments, and therefore these ceilings should be taken into account when making comparisons.

Most countries allow leave to be taken by mothers or fathers after the first few months. The UK and Hungary currently reserve the first year of leave for mothers, although the UK is intending to make the second six months of maternity leave transferable to fathers (James and Henricson 2009). In addition, there is a goal of extending maternity pay to one year by 2010 (Department for Business Enterprise and Regulatory Reform 2009).

Gender pay gap

The gender pay gap has been narrowing in the last 30 years, partly due to an increase in women's educational qualifications and partly due to legislation, although it has not been eliminated yet. The Equal Pay Act was introduced in 1970 and implemented in 1975, and in 2004 the prime minister set up the Women and Work Commission (Yeandle 2006). In addition, the Equalities Bill 2009 will require businesses with more than 250 employees to report information on the differences in pay between male and female employees (Women and Work Commission 2009).

The TUC (2008) has highlighted two key reasons why action should be taken on gender pay gaps besides their injustice: first, there are links between women's low pay and poverty (both adult and child); second, undervaluing women's work leads to economic inefficiency. It is estimated that the underutilisation of women's skills costs the economy £11 billion a year.

Historically, the gender pay gap has been less for full-time workers and has narrowed more than for part-timers over the last three decades (Table 2.4). The percentage change in the gender pay gap was 41 per cent for full-time workers and 14 per cent for part-time workers between 1975 and 2007, despite part-time workers experiencing a larger gap. For full-time workers the actual gap decreased from 29 per cent to 17 per cent. In contrast, part-time workers' pay gap decreased slightly from 42 per cent to 36 per cent over the same time period.

Table 2.4: Mean gender pay gap in per cent, 1975–2007

Source: New Earnings Survey and Annual Survey of Hours and Earnings; 1975 data taken from Department of Employment (1975, cited by Equal Opportunities Commission, 2005b); 1997 and 2008 data from TUC (2008) using the Annual Survey of Hours and Earnings

	1975	1997	2007	Percentage change
Full-time workers	29	21	17	-41
Part-time workers	42	42	36	-14

Analysis using the New Earnings Survey has shown that when comparing the hourly earnings of men and women, the gender pay gap becomes visible at a later age. While in 1975 the gap was visible at 18 years, in 2006 it was visible at 34 years (ONS 2009p). This could be explained by the increase in women's qualifications and delayed childbearing.

The gender pay gap peaks for adults in their forties for both full- and part-time workers, and is higher in the southern regions of the UK (Leaker 2008; TUC 2008). The gap varies with people's circumstances, such as the number of dependent children, company size and type of occupation and company (Leaker 2008; TUC 2008; Yeandle 2006). For example, the Women and Work Commission (2009) reported a gender pay gap of 11 per cent in the public sector and 20 per cent in the private sector. The gap also varies with educational level, although it still exists for those who are the most educated (Yeandle 2006).

The underlying causes of the gender pay gap include undervaluation of women's work – a persistent employment penalty for mothers through lower wages and discriminatory treatment in the workplace (TUC 2008). According to a recent analysis of ONS data, full-time working mothers with two children earn about 22 per cent less than their male colleagues with two children. Women without dependent children earn 9 per cent less than men on average (Woodroffe 2009). The Women and Work Commission (2009) also reported research by the Equalities Review, which found that employment penalties were greatest for lone mothers with a child under 11 years, and partnered women with children under 11 years.

In addition, women's employment continues to be concentrated in poorly paid sectors. Bellamy and Rake (2005) found a low value associated with the occupations that women hold because the skills are seen as natural rather than acquired, due to women traditionally doing the jobs on an unpaid basis in the home. The jobs are often flexible and local and fit in with caring responsibilities.

EU comparisons of the gender pay gap in 1994 and 2006 demonstrated that the UK had the highest gap in 1994 of 28 per cent, and the second highest in 2006 of 21 per cent. The two countries with the smallest gap between men and women's pay, at one-third of the UK gap, were Italy (taken at 1998 value) and Belgium. The UK has made considerable progress in narrowing the gender pay gap by 25 per cent, although it is mainly full-time workers who have seen the gap narrow (Eurostat 2009c).

2.7 What do mothers feel about their ability to balance work and family life?

The term 'work–life balance' is a relatively recent one, as before the 1990s the widely used term 'working mothers' showed a disregard for the conflict that mothers face in combining work and family life. The term 'work–life balance' is a more inclusive approach that widens the debate to engage men as well as women, both with and without children (Lewis, Gambles and Rapoport 2007).

Clearly, the Labour Government has put paid work at the top of its agenda. It wants to *"help people to achieve their potential through employment, so that they are able to provide for their children and to work and save for secure retirement"* (Department for Work and Pensions 2009c). Much has been invested in getting people into work and it is promoted as the best form of welfare, particularly to reduce child poverty, which the Government aims to halve by 2010, and end by 2020.

A number of policies have been introduced to support parents in employment, including the right to ask for flexible working, increasing the number of childcare places, extending maternity leave and pay, introducing paternity leave and enhanced rights for part-time workers.

The tax system was reformed in 2003 to introduce Child Tax Credit as the main form of financial support for families with children, and Working Tax Credit for people on low incomes who are working more than 16 hours a week. There is a particular focus on supporting lone parents back to work, with new obligations for lone parents to claim Jobseeker's Allowance instead of Income Support if their youngest child is seven or older (from 2010), and they are able to work. In addition, lone parents with children aged three to six will have obligations to work with an adviser to plan their route into work (Department for Work and Pensions 2009b).

Besides the Government's policies which help mothers go back to work, there are increased expectations on mothers as carers, hence mothers experience a dilemma. 'Good mothering' is based on the idea of being with the children and is premised on intensive nurturing, while at the same time it involves taking up paid work and providing financially for a child, being a good role model to one's children and in paid employment. In other words: is motherhood about staying at home and looking after children, or is it about paid work and financial security? (This chapter will return to the life experiences of being a full-time mother later.)

While some mothers who are working full time feel that they are losing out, some who are staying at home with their children think that their children are losing out. However, some mothers in part-time paid employment feel that they are not doing very well (Gimson 2008). Ideals of 'good' mothering and workplace norms are conflicting requirements, placing irreconcilable demands on women and constraining their choices.

Spending time with children

Parents may hold modern values, but the arrangements put in place to care for children tend to be along traditional lines (Duncan 2005). For example, in a large-scale survey, more than three-quarters of mothers stated that in day-to-day life they have the primary responsibility for childcare in the home (Ellison et al. 2009).

It cannot be assumed that because mothers are more likely to be in paid employment, they spend less time with their children. In fact, parents are spending longer on child-rearing activities each day than ever before. The time spent by working mothers with their children has grown over the last two decades, from fewer than 40 minutes per day in 1974–75 to more than 90 minutes in 1999. Indeed, working mothers spend more time with their children now than non-working mothers did in 1981 (Gershuny 2000). According to ONS data, parents reported spending three times as much time with their children per day in 2002 than in 1972 (Williams 2005).

Mothers continue to devote more time to childcare than fathers, although more fathers are involved in childcare now and spend a greater amount of time on this than they used to previously. It would appear that parents are reducing their time devoted to personal and leisure activities in order to preserve time with their children (Gauthier et al. 2004). Moreover, the time that is saved on household activities with the introduction of convenience products and time-saving devices such as disposable nappies, dishwashers and washing machines is spent increasingly on improving children's educational development through parental involvement (Thomson et al. 2008).

Recent nationally representative surveys have shown that over time, parents have become more involved in their children's education, with the majority of parents now more likely to see a child's education as mainly or wholly their responsibility. In the past, they were more likely to see it as the school's responsibility. The Parental Involvement in Children's Education 2007 survey found that 51 per cent of parents felt very involved in their child's school life, compared to 29 per cent just six years previously (Peters et al. 2008). It is widely accepted now that parental involvement is a positive influence on children's attainment (Department for Children, Schools and Families 2008a; Desforges and Abouchaar 2003). Research literature has characterised 'involved' parents as more likely to be women and parents with young children (Peters et al. 2008), although recent research on parental involvement in secondary schools has shown that involvement levels can vary greatly from one year to the next (Skaliotis submitted).

What determines the division of domestic labour?

The definition of domestic labour is difficult to disentangle from child-rearing, as the two often go hand-in-hand. However, domestic labour is thought to be the unpaid work carried out in and around the home such as cooking, cleaning and shopping.

While women now spend less time on housework, they are still more likely to do the housework than men. Men's share of domestic work rose from the 1960s onwards, but this increase appears to have reached a plateau since the middle of the 1990s (Crompton and Lyonette 2009). Sullivan (2000) found that wives performed 60 per cent of housework in 1997, compared to 62 per cent in 1987 and 68 per cent in 1975 (Sullivan 2000). According to the British Social Attitudes Survey in 1994, 2002 and 2006, women still do the washing and ironing, and while food shopping is more likely to be shared, women still do more of it (Crompton and Lyonette 2009).

The most recent Time Use Survey shows that on weekdays, mothers spent three times as much time on everyday household tasks as fathers, and twice as much time at the weekend. Women were more than 3.5 times more likely than men to say they did the majority of household tasks, and more than 12 times as likely to strongly agree that they did most of the childcare. They also reported that they were more likely to manage everyday activities such as bathing children, vacuuming, cooking and washing (Green and Parker 2006).

Some studies point out that the change to the unequal share of domestic work between men and women has been slow because it is driven primarily by women's reduction in their domestic work time, in the wake of increases in their participation in labour market work, rather than by men's increases in housework time (Bianchi et al. 2000; Gershuny 2000). In fact, the reduction in women's housework time does not compensate for the increase in their paid work time. Hence women's total work time (for paid work and unpaid domestic work) has increased over the years (Bianchi et al. 2000; Gershuny 2000).

By far the most significant factor in the division of domestic labour is whether or not the woman is employed and the extent of her earnings. Women's full-time employment is associated most with a less traditional division of domestic labour. For example, when women work full time or earn more than men, men do more routine work. It also seems that women with more education do less housework, and better-educated men do more. Social class also matters, as men from both the professional or managerial and manual classes and women from the professional or managerial class have a less traditional attitude towards housework (Crompton and Lyonette 2009).

This links in with British Household Panel Survey data, which show that relative economic resources influence significantly the distribution of housework between husbands and wives. Kan (2008) found that attitudes towards family roles matter, and hence the domestic division of labour is likely to be the outcome of both bargaining and individuals' gender role preference.

However, the British Social Attitudes Survey from 2006 found that women who are not in paid employment reported that they do as much housework as women who are in part-time paid employment. In other words, women's part-time work seems to have very little impact on the gendered division of labour (Crompton and Lyonette 2009). It is important to remember that British men work among the longest hours in Europe, reducing the actual time available in the home. It could be argued that gender equality cannot become a reality unless women and men have shorter hours in paid work. Lewis, Sarre and Burton (2007) argue that the full adult worker model is limited, as caring would have to be outsourced – this is not considered desirable, as it lowers quality of life. This model also underestimates the importance of social reproduction for national economies, as arguably it would lead to a further decline in birth rates (Lewis, Gambles and Rapoport 2007).

2.8 What are mothers' experiences of being a full-time mother?

During the past decades, the role of women in society has changed significantly, but it is doubtful that full-time mothers will become obsolete. Despite the shift toward paid work, about 23 per cent of wives with dependent children and a working resident partner were economically inactive in 2005 (34 per cent with children under five) (Walling 2005).

It has been suggested that mothers who care for their children full time and do not work outside the home are not sufficiently valued in societies such as the UK, which has become focused increasingly on defining citizens through their roles in paid employment while at the same time upholding traditional gender role expectations. Put another way, women remain constrained by a persisting ideology of 'domesticity' (Crompton and Lyonette 2005).[9]

Contemporary social values and policies emphasise the significance of paid work, and by implication marginalise homemaking as a career. However, there are indications that families are increasingly conscious of the negative pressures brought about

---

9   For the purpose of this chapter, mothers who are not participating in paid employment will be defined as either 'stay-at-home mothers' or 'full-time mothers', even if their children are in childcare or at school for some of the time, and even if these mothers engage in other activities such as voluntary work.

by women's employment (Crompton and Lyonette 2005). There is also talk of 'new emergent femininities' – of women who no longer want the struggle of combining paid and unpaid work, but do not perceive themselves to be unequal to their partner (Hall 2004).

There is evidence for this idea in the British Social Attitudes Survey. Men and women are increasingly less likely to strongly agree with the statement: *"A working woman can establish just as warm and secure a relationship with her children as a mother who does not work."* In 2002, 25 per cent of women and 15 per cent of men strongly agreed with the statement; in 2006 the number had decreased to 13 per cent of women and 10 per cent of men (British Social Attitudes Information System 2009). This is a far cry from Ann Oakley's milestone study from the 1970s, which found that being a housewife as well as conducting housework was perceived as unsatisfactory, repetitive, demeaning and a source of subjugation and inequality (Oakley 1974a). Oakley also concluded that the housewife role played a major part in hampering progress towards gender equality (Oakley 1974b).

Why do mothers choose to stay at home?

A recent large-scale survey of mothers who were not in paid employment showed that most wanted to provide childcare at home, as they considered this to have a positive influence on their child's development. Of mothers of pre-school age children, 60 per cent stated a preference to look after their children. These were the key reasons for not working, although 25 per cent of non-working mothers with pre-school children mentioned the affordability of childcare and lack of family support (Ellison et al. 2009).

This can be supported by data from the Millennium Cohort Study. Here, a similar percentage of full-time mothers who were not seeking work at the time or who were studying said that they preferred to look after their children themselves (58 per cent), while 11 per cent felt unable to earn enough to meet childcare costs (Ward and Dex 2007).

According to the Labour Force Survey, in 2008, looking after the family or home was the most common reason for inactivity among women aged 25 to 34 (72 per cent) and for those aged 35 to 49 (61 per cent). This is in stark contrast to the figures for men. Only 9 per cent aged 25 to 34 and 16 per cent aged 35 to 49 were likely to look after the family. For men, long-term sickness or disability was the main reason for economic inactivity among working-age men aged 25 and over, particularly for those aged 35 to 49 (62 per cent) (ONS 2009p).

Motherhood is embedded in a social context and it can be an opportunity for change in a woman's life. A qualitative study with lone mothers who received state benefits found that some mothers resigned themselves to mothering because they could not find suitable employment. Others professionalised it in a desire to further the development of their child. In particular, lone mothers who lacked educational qualifications and work experience perceived full-time mothering as an 'alternative career' and preferred it to a low-skilled and low-paid job that would give less satisfaction. Women with a long work history welcomed full-time mothering as a career break and time away from their former identity as a worker, or as time to reconsider personal and professional goals (Klett-Davies 2007). Some lone mothers perceived state benefits as a form of unofficial 'carer's allowance', which enabled them to care for their children at home (Klett-Davies 2002).

Full-time mothers demonstrate that motherhood is actively negotiated and not only based on a financial cost–benefit analysis. Full-time mothers do not add to the household income and even tend to have unequal access to the household income besides their lower pension entitlement (Bellamy and Rake 2005). The pension gap is caused by a combination of career breaks, lower earnings and savings and a rise in the number of divorced women without a husband's pension to support them. As a consequence, their pension contributions reduce significantly and their state pensions often take a hit as well. For example, women who retire in 2009 will receive an average of £6,642 less a year from their pension than men (Pykett 2009).

The next section shows that support for full-time mothers is diminishing, as fewer adults think that a mother with a young child should stay at home.

Attitudinal trends towards full-time mothers

In the last 20 years there has been a clear downward trend in adults agreeing that women with a child under school age should stay at home, from 64 per cent in 1989 to 40 per cent in 2006 (British Social Attitudes Information System 2009). This trend holds for both genders and all education levels. Figure 2.9 illustrates that there is a clear distinction in opinion according to the adult's highest qualification. In 2006, 27 per cent of adults with a degree strongly agreed with the statement, compared to 47 per cent of adults with low or no qualifications. This is in line with the earlier finding of the present study, that more educated mothers are more likely to be in work.

Figure 2.9: Percentage strongly agreeing with the statement *"Do you think that women should ... not [work] at all ... when there is a child under school age?"* **by highest qualification, 1989–2006**

Source: British Social Attitudes Information System (2009)

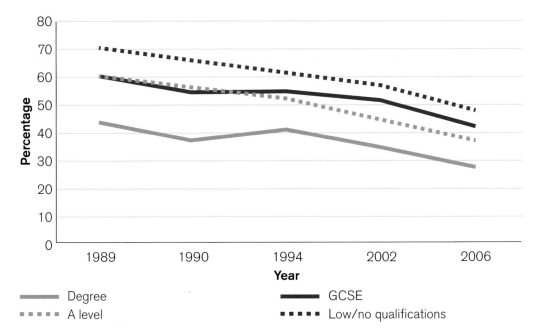

In line with a downward trend over time of men and women who strongly agree with the statement that a mother with a child under school age should not work, there has been an upward trend of adults who strongly agree that lone mothers with a child under school age should work. Over the 10-year period to 2003, more than three times as many adults with a degree strongly agreed that lone mothers with a child under school age should work (11 per cent in 2004, 3 per cent in 1994). Similarly, almost twice as many adults with low or no qualifications strongly agreed with the statement (21 per cent in 2004, 12 per cent in 1994) (British Social Attitudes Information System 2009).

2.9 What are the trends in childcare?

In 1998 the New Labour Government launched the National Childcare Strategy, which aimed to ensure good-quality, affordable childcare for all children aged 0 to 14, in order to promote the wellbeing of children and support parents in balancing work and family life (Department for Education and Employment 1998). The government believed that high-quality childcare is good for the child, parents, community and the national economy

(Prime Minister's Office 2003). The assumption was that the more mothers work, the less likely the chances of their children living in poverty and becoming disadvantaged adults. An added factor was that a high proportion of working-age adults who were not in employment would rely heavily on benefits (Ermisch et al. 2001). However, the commitment to free nursery places for three- and four-year-olds for just 2.5 hours per day may not be enough to enable mothers to be in paid employment.

In their summary of the Organisation for Economic Cooperation and Development (OECD 2006) report on early childhood education, James and Henricson (2009) highlight the distinction between two approaches to early childhood services. The UK, Ireland, France and the Netherlands focus primarily on preparing children for school, which could result in approaches that are poorly suited to the psychology and natural learning strategies of young children. On the other hand, the Central European and Nordic countries adopt a social pedagogy approach, where children are expected to learn through play, and this is seen to be a foundation for lifelong learning and a broad preparation for life.

What types of childcare are used?

Childcare provision takes a range of forms, and education has become part of the provider's duty of care (George and Hansen 2007). Childcare can be provided formally by nurseries or crèches, playgroups, registered childminders, after-school clubs or breakfast clubs and holiday schemes, and informally (i.e. usually unregistered or unregulated) by grandparents, other relatives, older siblings, partners, ex-partners and friends.

Since the 1970s there has been an increase in the use of formal registered childcare (nurseries, daycare, childminders) and an increase in informal childcare, such as the use of grandparents or other relatives (Gray 2005).[10] Using the Women and Employment Survey, Hansen et al. (2006) reported an increase in the use of grandparents from 34 per cent in 1980 to 47 per cent, and using the Millennium Cohort Study, at age nine months in 2001.

National statistics also indicate that over the last 40 years, there has been an increase in the proportion of three- and four-year-olds in schools, from 21 per cent in 1970 to 64 per cent in 2007 (ONS 2009p), as illustrated in Figure 2.10. The latest increase has been due to the increase in uptake of free childcare places in nurseries and schools for children aged three and four.

---

10 Several data sources, including birth cohort studies dating from 1958, the Women and Employment Survey in 1980 and the British Household Panel Study, have indicated this increase.

Figure 2.10: Proportion of under-fives in schools, 1970–2006
Source: ONS (2009p)

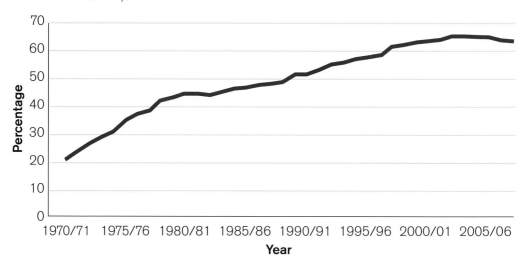

Who accesses what type of childcare?

In 2006, two-fifths (40 per cent) of all working mothers relied on informal childcare, with grandparents being the most common source at 32 per cent for couples and 31 per cent for lone parents (ONS 2009p). In fact, the use of formal care decreased as the child grew older, as 54 per cent of working mothers with children under five chose formal care, compared to 33 per cent of working mothers with children of primary school age and 6 per cent of working mothers with children of secondary school age.

The Millennium Cohort Study identified differences in the types of childcare favoured by working and non-working mothers. Non-working mothers were more likely to choose a nursery, crèche, nursery school or playgroup (56 per cent), compared to working mothers (29 per cent of full-time working mothers and 24 per cent of part-timers). Instead, working mothers (both full and part time) were more likely to cite grandparents as their main form of childcare, perhaps due to flexibility and reduced cost (George and Hansen 2007). In fact, 90 per cent of grandparents in the Millennium Cohort Study had provided some form of financial support such as buying gifts or essentials for the child or contributing to other household costs (Hawkes and Joshi 2007b). In addition, the differences may be due to the consideration that mothers have to give to the length of time that their children have to spend in care. For example, children attended on average 12 hours a week of care if their mother did not work, and 21 hours a week if their mother did.

The type of childcare that parents choose for their children not only depends on whether mothers are in paid work or not. There is evidence that children were more likely to attend formal care settings if they had at least one parent in the top education, occupation and family income groups (George and Hansen 2007; Kazimirski et al. 2008; Philo et al. 2009). This may reflect mothers' greater ability to pay, but also the non-availability of informal care on a full-time basis (Hansen et al. 2006). As discussed in Chapter 4 regarding the role of grandparents in family life, grandparents with lower levels of education are more likely to live nearer their grandchildren and have frequent contact with them (Clarke 2003). Other research finds that middle-class mothers are most likely to value child development through formal provision (Duncan 2005).

Bell et al. (2005) found that white and black Caribbean families were more likely to have used childcare than families from minority ethnic backgrounds. Pakistani, Bangladeshi and black African families had the lowest incidence of childcare use, which could reflect circumstances such as marital status and employment status, and preferences such as cultural or religious reasons. Black Caribbean children had on average the greatest number of hours of childcare in the past week, and their parents were most likely to be using only formal care, which is likely to be related to the aforementioned high incidence of full-time employment among black mothers. White families were most likely to use informal care and were twice as likely to use grandparents for childcare.

Childcare in the UK is a costly affair. In 2009 a typical full-time nursery place for a child under two was £167 a week, compared to average earnings of £479 per week. The highest childcare costs were reported in London and the south-east, of up to £226 a week (Office for National Statistics, cited by Daycare Trust 2009). A review of early childhood education and care in 20 OECD countries reported that parents in OECD countries paid on average 25 to 50 per cent of the costs of childcare for young children. This ranged from 10 to 15 per cent in Finland, Norway and Sweden, and was 45 per cent on average in the UK. While some low-income families were subsidised by up to 80 per cent of costs through Childcare Tax Credits for those who worked more than 16 hours a week (subject to a maximum amount), and some employees received childcare vouchers from their employers, others paid the full cost themselves (OECD 2006).

Fathers' involvement in family life

Stephen A. Hunt

Key statistics

These statistics are cited from independent research, ranging from small, qualitative studies to large-scale, representative surveys.

- There was a 200 per cent increase in the time that fathers are actively engaging with children between 1974 and 2000.

- Black Caribbean, African and mixed-race fathers reported being more involved in their child's school life than white fathers.

- Fathers' interest and involvement in their children's education and learning result in better educational outcomes.

- Of teenage fathers, 22 per cent themselves had teenage mothers, compared with only 13 per cent who had children at a later age.

- Lone fathers account for only about 10 per cent of lone parents and 2 per cent of all families with dependent children.

- Lone fathers are more likely to have been married or widowed than lone mothers.

- Children's levels of contact with non-resident fathers are closely related to background characteristics such as socio-economic status, and lifecourse decisions such as remarriage and the time since parental separation.

- The proportion of fathers taking paternity leave exclusively was 50 per cent, and a further 30 per cent incorporated additional leave entitlement in 2005.

Introduction

This chapter examines fatherhood, family forms and fathers' involvement in family life, particularly that of their children. The kinds of fathers referred to in this chapter include:

- married and unmarried biological fathers – whether co-resident or not, and whether in contact with their children or not

- social fathers – including co-resident step-fathers, cohabiting partners and other resident and non-resident father figures.

Until quite recently, fathers had been largely overlooked in developmental research. Initially attachment theory, for example, attributed the quality of attachment between mother and child to instinctive biologically prepared responses, but provided no account of father–child relationships (Bowlby 1969). The position of fathers in family research in general is encapsulated in the title of Lewis's (1975) publication "Fathers: forgotten contributors to child development".

Conceptions of fatherhood in social and developmental psychology only began to emerge in the late 1970s. Initially such research tended to be comparative, specifically comparing the role of the father with that of the mother (Lamb 1981; Lewis 1987; Lewis and O'Brien 1987). However, research on fatherhood has increased in recent years, with the accumulation of evidence showing the impact of different aspects of fathers and fathering styles on children's later outcomes (O'Brien et al. 2007). Furthermore, the demographic and societal changes already considered in this report, such as the decline of marriage, increase in divorce and increased female participation in the workforce, have had an impact on paternal involvement and fatherhood in general, and this chapter also considers these.

The following sections examine issues surrounding fatherhood in a number of family forms, and in particular focus on the issue of paternal involvement. The central questions addressed are as follows.

3.1   Have fathers become more involved in everyday childcare and household tasks?

3.2   Why is paternal involvement important?

3.3   How do diverse family forms affect fatherhood?

3.4   What happens to relationships between fathers and children when parents separate?

3.5   How do fathers perceive fatherhood?

3.6   How father-friendly is the UK?

3.1 Have fathers become more involved in everyday childcare and household tasks?

Initially, fathers' involvement with their children was characterised in terms of three childcare activities: engagement, accessibility and responsibility (Lamb et al. 1987). This distinction has informed a great deal of subsequent research. The involvement of fathers with their children is subject to a complex array of influences, which include:

- biological
- motivational
- cultural
- economic
- historical
- legal
- social policy
- relationship with the mother (Lewis and Lamb 2007).

Aldous et al. (1998) identify three distinct theoretical accounts of the influences or determinants of fathers' involvement in household tasks and childcare which variously stem from:

- economics – time allocation theory
- sociology – gender-ideology theory
- psychology – family system theory.

Time allocation theory is an extension of human capital theory, where the 'household' decides the most efficient division of time between paid and non-paid activities (Becker 1981; Deutsch et al. 1993). Gender differences in involvement in household rather than market activities are a product of rational decisions aimed at maximising utility based on differences in current or potential income and expertise. If the father has a greater income and the mother is able to perform household tasks more efficiently, then the mother is likely to be allocated a greater proportion of household activities, which include childcare. However, with the increase in female participation in the labour force, there are at least grounds for expecting a shift in this division of household labour between genders.

Time allocation theory stands in contrast with gender-ideology theory. This holds that gender norms provide the basis on which people assign household tasks, specifically the beliefs that individuals have about the appropriateness or otherwise of the tasks in question for each gender (Coltrane 1996). Change in the distribution of household and childcare duties is likely only when there is a prior change in beliefs about gender norms.

Family system theory predicts that the quality of family interactions between father and mother will influence the degree or quality of fathers' interaction with their children (Belsky and Volling 1987; Cowen and Cowen 1987). This is based on the claim that family subsystems – for example, between partners or between individual parents and their children – are interrelated, and that fathers in particular seem less able to separate feelings generated from interactions with their partner and those that relate to their children. Hence discord between partners results in the father's distancing from their children.

In addition to increased female participation in the labour force and a corresponding increase in dual-earner households – which now stand at two-thirds of all households with dependent children – a Department of Trade and Industry report indicated that those working the longest hours (more than 48 hours per week) in the UK are men aged 30 to 49 with children, who are employed in the private sector (Kodz 2003). These changes would suggest that parental (specifically paternal) involvement with children might have declined; however, the reverse seems to be the case.

Gauthier et al. (2004) examined data on 16 industrialised countries and found that the time devoted to childcare for married fathers in full-time employment with children under 5 had risen from 0.4 hours per day in 1960 to 1.2 hours by 2000; in addition, the time devoted by fathers to housework had increased. The activities displaced to make this additional time available were paid employment and personal pursuits, mainly sleep.

Analysing UK-specific data, Fisher et al. (1999) also found increases since the 1960s in fathers' involvement with their children. Further research has found that the greatest increases have occurred among fathers with very young children (O'Brien and Shemilt 2003). However, these observed increases may indicate convergence but do not amount to father/mother parity in terms of time spent on childcare (O'Brien 2005).

Using historical data and UK Time Use Survey data from 2000, Gray (2006) identified both an increase in the time that married men spent engaged in paid work between 1974 and 2000 and in time devoted to childcare – the time they claimed to be *"actively engaging with their children"* – by some 200 per cent (Figure 3.1).

Adjustments in perceptions of gender norms have been cited as explanations for the increase in the time that parents spend with their children, but there are more practical reasons why such an increase may have taken place. The proportion of primary school children being taken to school by car increased from 27 per cent in 1989–91 to 41 per cent by 2006, although the figure had reached 38 per cent by 1995–96 (Department of Transport 2009; Gray 2006). Moreover, concern about threats to children outside the home has increased, resulting in children spending longer at home.

Figure 3.1: Minutes per average day spent on various activities, married men, 1974–2000*

Source: Gray (2006)

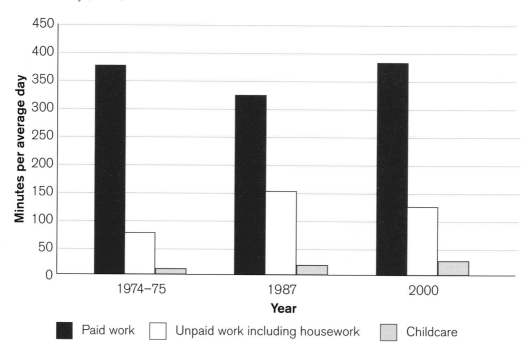

* Data for 2000 include cohabiting couples: prior years assumed also to include cohabiting couple data.

However, the apparent increase in paternal involvement has been contested by some researchers. Analysis of longitudinal datasets, rather than the Time Use Survey data reported above, has indicated that in some cases paternal involvement has decreased. Ferri and Smith (1996) found that men in their thirties in the early 21st century spent less time on childcare than was the case for those in their thirties in 1991. Gray (2006) offers a possible reason for this discrepancy in terms of different modes of data collection: time use surveys record what is actually done with time, while survey questions tap into assumptions about the broader aspects of childcare – not only what is done, but who has the greatest degree of responsibility and decision-making.

3.2 Why is paternal involvement important?

Clearly, paternal involvement in household and childcare activities is relevant to the issue of equitable division of household activities. Using British Household Panel Study data, Kodz (2003) found little evidence of any equal division of household labour. In dual-earner households, where mothers worked 48 or more hours per week, only 20 per cent identified their partner as having the main responsibility for any of the following: washing, cleaning, cooking or grocery shopping. The same research also indicated that for men working long hours, childcare was mainly their partner's responsibility in 68 per cent of cases, compared to 26 per cent for women working long hours.

However, with respect to the influence of paternal involvement on children, it is the content or quality of involvement rather than duration that is critical. The most important aspects are:

- responsive and sensitive interaction
- limit-setting for behaviour
- listening to and talking about children's concerns
- care for wellbeing
- encouraging age-appropriate, independent action (O'Brien 2005).

However, Grossman et al. (2002) hold that the quality of father–infant attachment may be due more to the father's motivation towards fathering and family than it is to sensitivity in interaction with his child, during the child's first year at least.

The impact of paternal involvement on *early* child development, which typically is measured in terms of children's adjustment or their educational outcomes, appears low when compared to maternal involvement. Steele et al. (1999) found that sociability in primary school-age children was predicted by the quality of mother–child attachment, not father–child attachment. However, by secondary school age, paternal involvement appears to be more significant, with quality of play measures predicting teenagers' concepts of self-worth.

In addition, there is evidence that parental involvement in children's education differs by ethnicity. The current authors analysed data from the Longitudinal Study of Young

People in England on reported or perceived involvement in children's education, at age 14, for those fathers who identified themselves as being the more involved of the child's parents in their education ($N = 2632$). After weighting the sample to reflect the prevalence in the population of each ethnic group, the analysis indicated significantly greater difference in the perceived level of involvement between the white group and the black Caribbean, African and mixed groups, who recorded the greatest involvement. The results appear in Figure 3.2.

Figure 3.2: Mean perceived paternal involvement in children's education by father's ethnicity, 2004

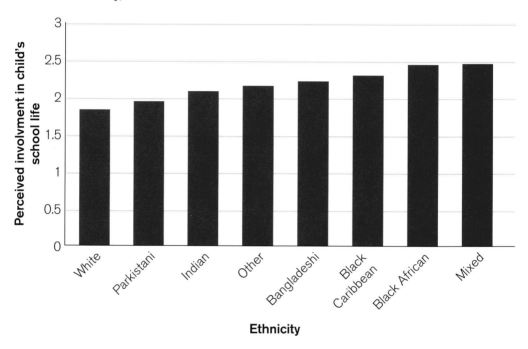

Despite the differences across ethnicity identified in Figure 3.2, it is possible that any differential impact on children's later attainment could vanish when appropriate controls, such as socio-economic level, are included in the analysis.

Analysis using National Child Development Study data found that for boys, by age 16, the child's IQ and father's involvement were all negatively related to being in trouble with the police, but parental criminality was positively related. For girls, non-intact family structure was related to being in trouble with the police; for both genders, family size in childhood and low academic attainment in adolescence were both positively related to being in trouble with the police (Flouri and Buchanan 2002).

Additionally, fathers were more likely to be highly involved when children were not assessed as behaviourally or temperamentally difficult, and more involved in their children's education when their children were doing well academically. However, they tended to be more involved in managing and undertaking outings with sons rather than daughters (Flouri and Buchanan 2003b).

Flouri and Buchanan (2003a) suggest that fathers may find it easier to be involved with children who are not difficult, while children may do better educationally when their fathers are more involved. However, whether such a two-way causal influence actually exists has not been demonstrated. Three UK studies (Feinstein and Symons 1999; Flouri and Buchanan 2004; Hobcraft 1998a, 1998b) all indicate that greater levels of fathers' interest and involvement in their children's education and learning result in better educational outcomes for children, although all three studies used the same National Child Development Study database.

Flouri and Buchanan (2004) constructed an index that combined fathers' behaviour (frequency of outings with, reading to, and management of the child) and a teacher estimate of the father's interest in their child's education at age 7, in order to predict their children's highest school attainment by age 20. After controlling for a large array of background variables, Flouri and Buchanan (2004) identified an effect of father involvement independent of, if weaker than, maternal involvement.

Feinstein and Symons (1999) and Hobcraft (1998a, 1998b) both used the same teacher estimate of fathers' interest in their children's education to predict later outcomes. Feinstein and Symons (1999) measured children's academic attainment at 11 and 16 to 21 years and found that paternal interest predicted academic performance: children with greater levels of paternal involvement did better at later stages of their school career, even when taking into account their level of achievement at earlier time points.

Hobcraft (1998a, 1998b) was concerned not just with educational attainment but with the issue of social exclusion. Low rates of paternal interest were not only found to predict the likelihood of obtaining no educational qualifications in adult life, but low-interest children were four times as likely to leave school with no qualifications as high-interest children. Further, low paternal interest was linked strongly to eight out of 19 outcomes of social exclusion indicators:

● having a degree-level qualification

● high income

● low income

- being in social housing

- receipt of benefits (men particularly)

including those that relate specifically to women:

- non-marital children

- 'psychological malaise'

- teenage motherhood.

Goldman (2005) indentifies three possible mechanisms by which the impact of paternal involvement is actually transmitted or delivered: acquisition of social capital; role modelling; father–child conversations and direct interaction.

Acquisition of social capital here refers to the parents developing contacts, relationships and networks outside the family which have an educational relevance (Coleman 1988). Specifically, this might involve contact with schools and children's teachers and could have a positive impact in terms of:

- overall school environment and quality of teaching (Nord et al. 1998)

- teachers' behaviour towards their specific child (Flouri et al. 2002)

- encouraging early intervention on the part of the teacher, if the child shows problems associated with achievement or behaviour (Nord et al. 1998).

Parent–child conversations centring around education and parental involvement in out-of-school learning have been credited with helping children to think constructively about educationally oriented issues, and more generally rendering parents as teachers (Nord et al. 1998). Fathers differ from mothers in that they tend to be treated as a source of factual information and, as they spend less time with their children and have less knowledge about them, they are more likely to *"speak in ways that challenge children's linguistic and pragmatic abilities"* (Lamb and Tamis-Lemonda 2004, p.9). Furthermore, compared to mothers' interactions with their children, fathers tend to be more playful and more goal-oriented with teenagers.

Role-modelling explanations theorise that children copy parental behaviour and acquire similar attitudes, which places children at risk of acquiring not only positive traits, but also negative ones. However, in positive terms, greater parental interest in education is liable to be replicated in the child. Whether there are particular effects of gender in role modelling is a vexed issue: several small-scale studies have found that fathers interact differently towards daughters and sons, but these findings have not been replicated in large-scale reviews or meta-analyses.

However, positive educationally oriented role modelling such as shared parent–child learning activities and conversations about learning and education does appear to have an impact on educational outcomes (Jodl et al. 2001). Additionally, parental interest in schools demonstrates to children the values placed on education without direct interaction. Indeed, simply selecting a better school, in terms of effectiveness or quality, can enhance children's attainment. In addition, fathers can influence children's education indirectly by supporting maternal involvement in their children's education (Goldman 2005).

Using a sample of 2,722 adolescents, Flouri and Buchanan (2002, 2003a) examined young people's attitudes to school and degree of parental involvement. Parental involvement was measured in terms of interest in their children's schoolwork and the time spent talking with them or listening to their worries. Additionally, the adolescents rated themselves on measures of happiness, self-efficacy and depression and identified instances of conflict at home. The results indicate that father involvement was identified, independent of mother involvement, as contributing importantly to emotional wellbeing and to positive attitudes to education for both boys and girls.

Influences on paternal involvement

Flouri and Buchanan (2003b) identified several different kinds of influences on paternal involvement in children's education, although only dual-parent families with dependent children featured in the research. The most straightforward were those which can be identified as time constraints – the father's level of involvement is likely to be greater if the child is firstborn and has fewer siblings. Additionally, involvement is likely to be greater for fathers who are unemployed, disabled or retired, and in cases where the mother works full time. More complex influences involved interactions between the mother and the father, which can be accounted for in terms of family systems theory. The level of the father's involvement tends to reflect how good relations are between the father and mother. Furthermore, the father's involvement tends to be calibrated with the mother's level of involvement, and tends to be greater, the earlier they are involved with their child's education, although this may reflect individual differences in paternal commitment.

A further source of influence is social advantage: fathers are likely to be more involved if they have higher educational qualifications or occupy a higher socio-economic level. Fathers engaged in manual labour are less likely to be involved in their child's education.

There is evidence of adverse effects of father–child contact. High levels of anti-social behaviour in fathers are associated with higher levels of behaviour and conduct problems in their children, but importantly, this is dependent on the extent of contact between the father and child. The children of resident fathers with high levels of anti-social behaviour had significantly worse conduct problems than the children of non-resident fathers (Jaffee et al. 2003).

There is also evidence that basic contact itself between father and child may be detrimental. Research utilising Avon Longitudinal Study of Parents and Children Survey data found evidence of a gender-specific (boys) detrimental impact of paternal involvement. Taking into account family and individual characteristics, the results indicated that during the early years, boys who spent 15 or more hours a week in the care of their father recorded poorer scores on academic tests at the start of school (Washbrook 2007).

Findings such as these may reflect a difference between the degree of cognitively orientated interaction that fathers and mothers are likely to engage in with their children. Fathers may be substituting such activity for simple monitoring of their child or catering for the child's immediate needs (Washbrook 2007).

3.3 How do diverse family forms affect fatherhood?

A great deal of the research concerning fathers' involvement is based on fathers who are in two-parent families. In the following sections, 'non-standard' families are considered, as well as the likely impact of non-resident fatherhood on children's development.

Using a sample drawn from the British Household Panel Study database of approximately 2,200 men born from 1920 to 1979, Lee (2009) traced the trajectory or pathway of their family lifecourses. Numerous distinct pathways were identified, which were composed of differing combinations of particular stages in the lifecourse. A simple and standard paternal pathway takes the form of the father living with his children throughout the life of the family. However, a non-standard pathway would incorporate additional or alternative life stages, such as non-residence through separation, stepfathering through repartnering and possibly fathering further children. These findings indicate the multiplicity and dynamic nature of family forms, as a total of 81 distinct pathways was identified.

Additionally, Lee (2009) identified changes over time in the prevalence of traditional and non-traditional pathways: 86 per cent of the 1920 cohort who became parents lived with their children throughout the life of the family, and 20 different pathways were identified. In the case of the 1950 cohort, the number who lived with their children throughout the life of the family had reduced to 69 per cent, and 38 pathways were identified. The numbers engaged in the traditional family form in the

1960 and 1970 cohorts stood at 61 and 54 per cent, with 37 and 24 individual pathways identified respectively, although these figures are likely to be subject to some revision as individuals in the 1960 and 1970 cohorts eventually become fathers or experience separation. The evidence indicates that individuals are quite likely to experience different status throughout their life. The following sections examine some of the most important of these and their likely impact on children's development.

Teenage or young fathers and lone fathers

There is a great deal less research on teenage or young fathers[1] than on teenage pregnancies and motherhood. The children of teenage mothers are not invariably fathered by teenagers or young men, but young fathers have a lot in common with teenage mothers.

Teenage or young fathers

Dearden et al. (1995) used National Child Development Study data to assess the antecedents of teen fatherhood, the sample being composed of individuals born during March 1958. The characteristics of teen fathers included an economically impoverished background, a record of truanting and some degree of delinquency; also evident was a tendency to leave school at the minimum age and for their parents to show little interest in education.

Also using data from the National Child Development Study and examining young parenthood, Kiernan (1997) found that like young mothers, young fathers were more likely to be from a lower status socio-economic background and have lower educational attainment than their peers. The consequence is not just that such parents have less to invest in their children initially, but that they are likely to remain economically disadvantaged throughout their life. Evidence for this was identified by the Joseph Rowntree Foundation (Kiernan 1995), using the same dataset. The results indicated that, compared to parents who had had a child at an older age, at 33 years teenage fathers were found to be less likely to own their own home and twice as likely to be unemployed, and hence more likely to be receiving Income Support.

Teenage fathers were also more likely to suffer emotional problems: 19 per cent of those who were assessed as having serious emotional problems at ages seven and 16 became teenage fathers, as opposed to 6 per cent who were assessed as having few problems (Kiernan 1995). Furthermore, as with teenage mothers, teenage fathers show evidence of intergenerational transmission of young parenthood: 22 per

---

1   Teenage fathers are clearly young fathers, but there is no standard definition of 'young fatherhood' – that is, the point at which someone ceases to be a young father.

cent of teenage fathers themselves had teenage mothers, compared with only 13 per cent who had children at a later age (Kiernan 1997).

Bunting (2004) identifies a series of studies, often qualitative and small-scale, which address issues related to teenage or young fatherhood. Relationships during and shortly after pregnancy between the father and the teenage mother, where they exist at all, are almost entirely non-marital (at least initially), and so tend to take the form of cohabitation, 'living apart together' (LATs) or lone parenthood. Subsequent to birth, relationships tend to be shortlived. Allen and Bourke Dowling (1998, cited by Bunting and McAuley 2004) found that approximately 50 per cent of the teenage mothers they interviewed were no longer in a relationship with the father of their child one year later, although the study was essentially qualitative and the sample only included 84 teenage mothers. The study also found that about 55 per cent of fathers had daily contact with their child one year on, and 20 per cent had no contact.

Speake et al. (1996) addressed issues such as barriers to young fathers' contact with their children. A frequently cited barrier was the mother's objection to this contact. In addition, low income was cited as an important reason: this not only limited their ability to provide for their child, but prevented them from establishing a home for their child and the child's mother or their subsequent partner. Moreover, housing policy and housing itself was a barrier to contact: those still living with their own parents found it difficult to establish their own home, and available accommodation for single people often proved to be inconveniently located, incurring additional transport costs and a loss or attenuation of their support network. This point extends to non-resident fathers in general (Simpson and McCarthy 1995).

The support that teenage fathers received was often from paternal grandparents, whether it be in financial, practical or moral terms. They seldom, if ever, cited professional or official support networks: in cases where there was no familial support for young fathers, they were likely to receive no support at all (Speake et al. 1996).

Bunting (2003, cited by Bunting 2004) conducted similar research in Northern Ireland and found that although teenage fathers cited employment problems in relation to difficulties in providing support to their children's mothers, teenage mothers were less inclined to cite financial support as the most important form of support; they were more likely to cite help with parenting tasks.

Lone fathers

Lone fathers are uncommon, and research concerning them rarer still. Lone fathers account for only about 10 per cent of lone parents and 2 per cent of all families with dependent children (McConnell and Wilson 2007). However, unlike other diverse family forms, there is little evidence to suggest that this family form is increasing in prevalence.

Using the 1958 British Birth Cohort, Payne and Range (1998) found that, compared to other men who had become fathers, by age 33, lone fathers had lived with more partners, entered their first relationship earlier, become fathers at a younger age and had more children than lone mothers.

In several respects, the route to lone parenthood taken by fathers contrasts with that of mothers. Lone fathers and mothers show similar levels of prior cohabitation – 24 per cent in the case of fathers and 28 per cent in the case of mothers – but far fewer lone fathers were 'never together' (with the child's mother), compared to lone mothers (6 per cent of lone fathers compared to 26 per cent of lone mothers). However, lone fathers are more likely to have been married or widowed than lone mothers; about 56 per cent compared to 41 per cent in the former case, and 15 per cent compared to 2 per cent in the latter. Additionally, lone fathers are more likely to possess at least one academic qualification than lone mothers, and tend to be older (March and Perry 2003).

Despite these differences, the issues faced by lone fathers are similar to those faced by lone mothers, principally financial disadvantage, often the result of or exacerbated by the separation itself.

Lone fathers' attitudes to their own circumstances and lone fatherhood in general featured in a small-scale study conducted by Gingerbread (2001), a helpline and support network for lone parents. Using a sample of 115 respondents and data from 360 telephone calls to its helpline, the results indicated that 80 per cent of the sample said that in becoming lone parents they were worse off financially, mainly due to the loss of their partner's income or reduced working hours. Very few of the sample (2 per cent) had been the main carer before becoming a lone parent, and since becoming lone parents, they had received almost all of their support from friends, neighbours or family members, principally grandparents, although 22 per cent said that they received no support at all. Approximately 60 per cent of the sample felt that society had a negative view of lone fathers.

Non-resident fathers

Non-resident fathers as a group have received little research attention, possibly because of difficulties associated with gathering reliable data. Blackwell and Dawe (2003) and Lader (2008a), for example, found that the reported frequency of contact between child and non-resident parent depended on whether it was the resident or non-resident parent providing the information. Of resident parents who responded to the 2007 survey, 30 per cent said that their child never sees their non-resident parent. However, only 17 per cent of the non-resident parents said their child never saw them. There is a similar pattern of discrepancy concerning indirect contact (phone, letter, email), although in this case resident parents are in less of a position to provide an accurate assessment of such contact (Lader 2008a).

Despite these difficulties, Lee (2009) found evidence that, while rare, the proportion of fathers who are non-resident at the time of their first child's birth has shown an increase. Analysing data from the British Household Panel Study, only 1.5 per cent of fathers born in the 1920s were non-residential; for those born in the 1960s the figure stood at 5 per cent, although this might decrease if not all the sample have become fathers yet. In examining non-resident fathers' characteristics, Kiernan (2006) found that they had higher levels of social deprivation and lower levels of educational attainment compared to resident fathers. Furthermore, non-residential fathers as a group will include a greater proportion of teenage fathers.

However, there was evidence that non-residential fathers were not entirely disengaged from their children: 63 per cent were registered on the birth certificate; three-quarters saw their children at least once a week, and 24 per cent had become resident with the mother by the time the child was nine months old.

3.4 What happens to relationships between fathers and children when parents separate?

Parental separation and/or divorce marks profound changes in family structure, yet there is evidence that it is neither the event of separation, nor the replacement of one family form with another, that fully explains the apparent negative impact of separation on child outcomes. The situation that existed prior to the disruption needs to be taken into account, along with the prevailing economic conditions that parallel changes in family form and the nature of the relationship between the parents after the break-up.

It is well documented that children who have experienced the separation or divorce of their parents tend to have poorer educational outcomes. However, this may not be as a direct result of the separation or divorce itself. US and Canadian research indicates that children from families that break up do less well educationally prior to disruption than children from families that remain intact, and that it is the level of educational attainment prior to family break up that best explains the child's post-break-up educational attainment or progress (Sun and Li 2001).

Ram and Hou (2003) identified that limited material resources mediate the relationship between family form and children's educational attainment, and that parenting styles and the psychological wellbeing of the parents mediated family form and children's eventual emotional and behavioural outcomes.

Conducting a meta-analysis (i.e. a review and re-analysis of data from previous relevant research), Amato and Gilbreth (1999) found evidence that non-resident fathers' payment of child support, allowing an increased standard of living, is related to enhanced educational outcomes and fewer behavioural problems. Additionally, parental cooperation was found to be associated with children's cognitive and social skills. Earlier research by Heatherington et al. (1982) also indicated the importance of supportive co-parenting between the non-resident father and mother in terms of the father's contact, involvement and positive relationship with their child. More recently, Dunn (2004) found contact between separated parents and supportive co-parenting influenced both the frequency of contact between the father and child and the quality of their relationship. Each of these will be examined in turn.

There is evidence that the frequency of contact between non-residential fathers and their children changes over time. Using ONS data on a sample of 265 resident parents (of whom nine-tenths were mothers), and 179 non-resident parents (of whom nine-tenths were fathers), Lader (2008a) provides information on previous and current contact arrangements between non-resident parents and their children. The percentage of those non-resident parents reporting direct, i.e. face-to-face, contact of at least once a week saw a statistically significant fall from 59 per cent in 2002 to 50 per cent in 2007 (Figure 3.3). However, there was no comparable statistically significant drop in the figures reported by resident parents concerning child–non-resident parent contact, although it is worth repeating that estimates by resident parents concerning such contact tend to be lower than non-resident parents' estimates for frequent contact, and higher for infrequent or no contact.

Figure 3.3: Contact arrangements of non-resident parents, 2002 and 2007*
Source: Lader (2008a)

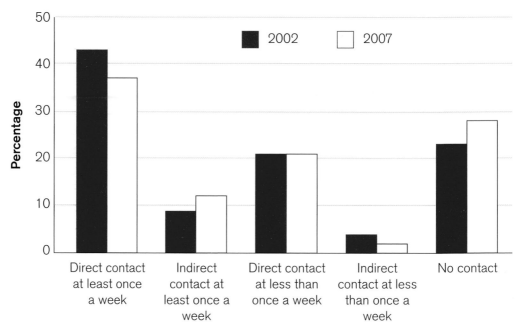

* Sample population weighted.

Levels of contact are closely related not only to background characteristics such as socio-economic status, but also to lifecourse decisions such as remarriage, the nature of any new household that the non-resident parent becomes involved in, and the time since parental separation.

In terms of socio-economic status, 30 per cent of children whose parent occupied the lowest socio-economic occupation group experienced no contact at all with their non-resident parent, compared to 16 per cent in the middle group and 12 per cent in the highest group (Blackwell and Dawe 2003). It is possible that non-residential fathers with greater financial resources are better able to afford the cost associated with higher levels of involvement, such as travelling and funding activities, and indeed to maintain any child support payments that facilitate contact.

The research concerning the effect of non-resident fathers remarrying on contact with their children is conflicting. With its additional demands on parents' time, remarriage has been linked to a decrease in contact (Maclean and Eekelaar 1997). However, other research has found that men who remarry are more likely to maintain contact, which has been explained as a consequence of the tendency of remarried fathers towards greater financial stability.

The arrival of further biological children in later relationships tends to displace to some degree the level of non-resident fathers' involvement with biological children from previous relationships in a way that acquiring step-children does not (Manning and Smock 1999). There is a steep decline in the percentage of children who see their non-resident parent frequently since the separation. Of children whose parents had separated less than a year ago, 70 per cent saw their non-resident parent at least once a week; between one year and less than two years, the figure had dropped to 64 per cent; from two to less than three years, the figure stood at 56 per cent; and only one-third of children whose parents separated three or more years ago saw their non-resident parent at least once a week (Blackwell and Dawe 2003).

In conducting a meta-analysis, Amato and Gilbreth (1999) found that frequency of contact between children and non-resident parents was significantly, although not strongly, associated with children's academic attainment and fewer internalising problems. Additionally these were found only for more recent cohorts of non-resident fathers, possibly because they were more committed to a parental role. Dunn (2004) found unequivocal evidence that both frequency and regularity of direct and indirect contact were related to fewer child adjustment problems and a more positive child–non-resident parent relationship.

However, positive associations with frequency of contact need to be qualified. The relationship between the father and mother is also important: in low-conflict relationships, frequent or regular visits are associated with better child adjustment, but in high-conflict relationships, frequent or regular contact is associated with poorer adjustment. Amato and Gilbreth (1999) conclude that it may be the quality of non-residential father–child contact that is important: that is, what is actually done with the time that they spend together, rather than simply the amount.

Important elements of a high quality parent–child relationship have been identified as:

- warmth and affectionate closeness
- support
- involvement
- monitoring
- an authoritative presence (Dunn 2004).

These have been identified as important elements in non-resident parent–child relationships as well, and associated with positive outcomes in terms of academic attainment and lower externalising and internalising problems (Amato and Gilbreth 1999). However, non-resident fathers report that the nature of their role as a carer can be affected by infrequent contact: authoritative parenting can be difficult to sustain under these circumstances and is effectively replaced by something approaching friendship (Dunn 2004).

Therefore, non-resident fathers face parenting challenges in terms of both the frequency and quality of contact with their children. Research summarised by Dunn (2004) has indicated that, whatever the benefits for children, for fathers, post-separation contact and involvement with their children is associated with enhanced feelings of competence, self-esteem and happiness with family life; they are also less likely to experience adjustment problems after separation.

3.5 How do fathers perceive fatherhood?

Dex (2003b) identified three features of fatherhood that fathers perceived as important: meeting the family's financial needs; meeting the family's emotional needs, but to a lesser extent; and spending time with the family.

A variety of research has identified the primacy afforded to breadwinning across socio-economic and ethnic groups and found it to be linked to fathers often being the higher earners in the family (Burghes et al. 1997). At least one study identified the breadwinning role as being seen as often underpinning emotional support afforded to the family (Reynolds et al. 2003). There was also recognition among fathers that spending time with the family often conflicted with work-related demands. Some individuals expressed regret at concentrating on their career at the expense of the family; others felt that they had sacrificed their career advancement in order to spend more time with their family (Reynolds et al. 2003).

Dex (2003b) also claims that fundamental to their views about their own roles was that fatherhood itself had induced changes in their self-perception. Essentially, this is a change from adolescent irresponsibility to adult responsibility.

It is not uncommon for fathers who rarely or never see their children to cite prevention by an ex-partner as the reason for this, rather than any voluntary disengagement from their children (Simpson and McCarthy 1995; Simpson et al. 2003). This perception of non-resident fathers' plight, whatever its accuracy, indicates the importance of the relationship with the father's former partner. However, this importance extends beyond access to children to the very manner in which the concept of fatherhood itself is constructed.

Ives et al. (2008) conducted research involving a number of focus groups composed of UK men with differing fathering backgrounds. They found that the concept of 'involvement' (or childcare more generally) is central to views of fatherhood, although there are jarring discrepancies in definition depending on lifecourse history. The results indicated a widespread recognition of a distinction between fathers as (just) progenitors of children and fathers as carers of children: while both stood as valid definitions of fatherhood, only the latter was associated with any moral status, and consequently the only means of generating fathers' rights.

However, while non-resident fathers did not dissent from this view, they did tend to regard the former definition as constitutive of being the 'real father'. Whether prevented by accident or design from any sustained contact with their children, or even any contact at all, non-resident fathers identified the biological relation between father and child as an ineradicable link and a means of facilitating or justifying a role as carer. Further, the biological relation was regarded as grounding any role as carer on the most solid of foundations. The perception or construction of fatherhood, whatever the background, places investment in the child as primary, although the perceived right to make this investment can shift according to the father's status.

3.6 How father-friendly is the UK?

Previously in this chapter, the importance of work commitments in relation to fathering has been examined. One area in which it is possible to quantify changes in 'father-friendliness' and changes in fathers' behaviour is legislation and uptake concerning paternal leave from paid employment.

Paternal leave, which is officially sanctioned leave of absence from employment around the time of a child's birth, was first enacted in Sweden in 1974; in the UK, statutory paternity leave was enacted in 2003. To qualify, parents either need to have worked for the same employer for 26 weeks, or need to be a contracted employee; in addition, the mother must have provided notification of her pregnancy and qualify for statutory maternity leave. Further, both parents need to be named on the child's birth certificate, or be named on any adoption certificate, or have legal parental responsibility for children under five (or 18, if they are disabled) (Directgov 2009).

Paternal leave has gained in significance as evidence of the importance of father involvement in children's early years has accumulated. Paternal leave stands as a means of promoting, if not realising, greater father involvement with his child (O'Brien et al. 2007).

Using Millennium Cohort Study data, Tanaka and Waldfogel (2007) found that fathers taking paternal leave and working shorter hours was associated with greater involvement with their children later (8 to 12 months old), where involvement was measured in terms of changing nappies, feeding and getting up at night. Conversely, longer working hours were associated with lower levels of later involvement.

All European Union (EU) countries now have maternal leave entitlements; however, this is not the case for paternal leave. Table 3.1 shows the differing amounts of leave offered to fathers by European country.

Table 3.1: Amount of statutory paternal leave in Europe, 2008

None	Up to 2 weeks	2–6 weeks	2–3 months
Austria	Belgium	Estonia	Iceland
Czech Republic	Denmark	Finland	Italy
Germany	France	Portugal	Norway
Ireland	Greece	Slovenia	Sweden
Poland	Hungary	Spain	
	Netherlands		
	UK		

Nepomnyaschy and Waldfogel's (2007) US-based research found greater levels of later father involvement with their child, but only for those fathers who took two or more weeks' leave around the time of their child's birth. As the USA offers no statutory right to paid paternal leave, those taking two or more weeks tend to be US-born, well educated and in middle- or high-prestige jobs. However, it ought to be pointed out that in the sample used, 98 per cent of fathers did take at least some time off work, although about two-thirds of these fathers only took a maximum of a week's leave. Fathers who are more financially disadvantaged are less likely to experience high involvement with their children during their early years.

The availability and duration of any leave period is likely to influence the involvement of fathers with their children, but so too is the pay associated with the period of leave. Some countries such as Sweden pay a rate of 80 per cent of income and have an estimated 80 per cent take-up. The UK has a flat rate of £123.06 (€140 approximately) per week, or 90 per cent of earnings if lower than this. The proportion of those who took paternity leave exclusively in 2005 was only 50 per cent; a further 30 per cent incorporated additional leave entitlement, while the remainder took no paternal leave at all (Smeaton and Marsh 2006). Across Europe the pattern of paternal leave take-up is not uniform: fathers are more likely to take leave or take it for a lengthier period if their partners have higher education and/or earnings, or if they work in the public sector or female-dominated occupations (Moss 2008). Where parental leave is offered – that is, leave that either parent is entitled to take, and usually after the initial period of maternal or paternal leave – it is seldom taken by fathers, even when it is paid at a relatively high rate. The UK offers a total of 13 unpaid weeks of parental leave. A 2005 survey estimated only 8 per cent of fathers had taken such parental leave in the first 17 months of their child's life, and of these, only one-quarter had taken a week or more (Moss 2008). These findings are consistent with the time allocation theory or human capital theory introduced earlier: fathers are unlikely to take additional time off work if there is a choice to be made as to which partner takes time off, and fathers earn the most.

Parent–child relationships: dependence and independence

Stephen A. Hunt

Key statistics

These statistics are cited from independent research, ranging from small, qualitative studies to large-scale, representative surveys.

- 72 per cent of parents perceive themselves to be less strict than their own parents.

- There is a clear intergenerational trend towards smacking – the older the respondent, the more likely they are to have used smacking as a means of managing children's behaviour.

- One in seven parents have used physical punishment, despite claiming to disapprove of it.

- 84 per cent of parents felt that commercial companies targeted products at their children 'too much'.

- One-third of households in Great Britain had internet access in 2000, rising to 65 per cent of households in 2008.

- 50 per cent of 5- to 10-year-olds and 95 per cent of 11- to 16-year-olds had their own mobile phone in 2009.

- The under-16 conception rate stood at 9 per 1,000 in 1998 and 8.3 per 1,000 in 2007 (provisional figures).

- The maternity rate for girls under 16 in 2001–02 was 12 times higher in the most deprived areas compared to the least deprived. ▶

- Pregnant girls in less deprived neighbourhoods are more likely to have an abortion: the under-16s abortion rate per conception was 77 for the least deprived areas and 50 per cent for the most deprived in 2001–02.

- 71 per cent of adults reported playing in the street or area near their home every day when they were children, compared to only 21 per cent of children in 2007.

- There has been a 20 per cent decline in the time spent eating at home, and correspondingly more time spent eating out between 1975 and 2000.

- The consumption of convenience food has increased by 300 per cent since 1977.

- The proportion of men and women classified as obese rose from 17 to 24 per cent and 20 to 24 per cent respectively between 1997 and 2007. The corresponding rise for children was 10 to 16 per cent.

- The consumption of five or more portions of fruit or vegetables declines with income, particularly in the case of men.

- There has been a downward trend in young people's smoking from 13 per cent to 6 per cent between 1996 and 2007.

- 14 per cent of 16- to 18-year-olds were Not in Education, Employment or Training (NEET) in 1985, compared to 10 per cent in 2008.

- The proximity of grandparents to their grandchildren varies with age and education.

Introduction

This chapter looks at various features of the parent–child relationship and how these may have been subject to change over recent decades. It begins by examining how trends in parenting have changed over the last 25 years and the possible implications. Legal changes that relate to parenting, particularly with respect to physical punishment, are examined, along with parents' attitudes to these changes. The chapter also looks at marketing, advertising, the advent of new technology and their effects on parenting. In addition, parents' concerns about the speed at which their children enter into young adulthood, the risks perceived by both parents and children and the influence that these might have on parenting are examined. It looks at the trajectories that children take towards independence, and concentrates on those young people who are at risk of social exclusion, specifically Not in Education, Employment or Training (NEET). Finally, the role of grandparents in family life is considered.

These issues are examined by addressing each of the following questions:

4.1   Are there trends in parenting?

4.2   Has the way in which parents control and discipline their children changed?

4.3   Has there been a growth in consumerism and materialism?

4.4   How has technology affected parenting?

4.5   Are children growing up 'too fast'?

4.6   How do parents and children perceive risk?

4.7   What are the trends in lifestyle-related health?

4.8   What are the pathways to independence?

4.9   Has the role of grandparents in family life altered?

4.1 Are there trends in parenting?

Currently there are (and perhaps always have been) concerns about teenagers' or young people's behaviour – or more accurately, their 'problem behaviour'. Collishaw et al. (2004) reported that there has been an increase in teenage problem behaviour such as lying, disobedience and stealing over the last 25 years, and this is regardless of family structure. Although the levels were lower in two-parent families, levels of problem behaviours in these families, lone-parent families and step-families have all increased.

Research conducted by the Nuffield Foundation was designed to determine whether parenting or changes in parenting were wholly or partly responsible for the deterioration in adolescents' behaviour. The author of the report summarises the findings in the following terms:

> " We found no evidence for declining standards of parenting overall and this leads us to believe this factor does not generally explain the rise in problem behaviour. " (Nuffield Foundation 2009a)

However, definite trends in parenting practice were discerned (Nuffield Foundation 2009b). The numbers of parents and teenagers spending quality time together rose in the case of mothers, from 62 to 70 per cent over the 25-year period, and in the case of fathers, from 47 to 66 per cent over the same period. The research also identified trends in the amount of time that parents spent caring for their children, indicating a rise from about 20 minutes a day in the 1970s to about 70 minutes in the 1990s.

Parental expectations about their children's good behaviour rose between 1986 and 2006. Seven out of eight measures, including expectations about doing their homework and being polite, showed an increase.

Monitoring of children by parents also showed changes: 79 per cent of parents in 1986 asked where their children were going; by 2006, this had risen to 85 per cent. Moreover, the numbers of parents asking what their children were doing had risen over the same period, from 47 to 66 per cent. In addition, the report found a narrowing of differences in parenting based on income and family structure: in 1994, the children of lone parents were more likely to be out late without their parent knowing where they were; however, by 2005 this was no longer the case. The report's positive take on contemporary parenting was balanced with an acknowledgement that the challenges parents face have changed, and that parenting may be becoming more stressful. This seems to be particularly true for lone parents and low-income families: the proportion of families from the low-income group that reported distress increased by 50 per cent between 1986 and 2006. The challenges include:

- the fact that young people are now reliant on their parents for longer

- the concerns that parents feel about new technology, such as mobile phones and the internet

- perceived risks which might have surfaced in terms of increased monitoring.

The authors conclude, from the increase in young people with problem behaviour, that it may be due to peer pressure or 'wider cultural influences'. Many of these issues, such as adolescents and peer pressure, and parents' and adolescents' risk perceptions, are returned to throughout this chapter.

There is evidence that parenting younger children in Britain has changed: it appears to be less authoritarian than it may have been previously. Anderson et al. (2002) examined parents' views on their relationship with their children, among other things. A variety of research methods were used, including a survey of 692 parents (469 mothers and 196 fathers). The results indicated that 72 per cent of parents perceived themselves to be less strict than their own parents. Parents' perceptions of their relationship with their own children were marked by change: their children were seen to have become more assertive, less obedient and less respectful towards their parents than they were, and the parents and children seem to have entered a more equal relationship.

4.2 Has the way in which parents control and discipline their children changed?

The research in the previous section indicated societal shifts in parenting. Of course, family practices can be affected directly by changes to the law, and this section looks at how changes to the law have altered parents' use of and attitudes to physical punishment. The legal position of parents with respect to the physical punishment of their children was stated in a judicial remark by Chief Justice Cockburn in 1860:

> " *By the law of England, a parent ... may for the purpose of correcting what is evil in the child, inflict moderate and reasonable corporal punishment, always, however, with this condition, that it is moderate and reasonable.* " (quoted in Whitehead 2007)

This position remained unchanged until the 21st century, when legislation brought the country into line with the European Convention on Human Rights 1950. In England and Wales the current legal position on the physical punishment of children is derived from reforms enacted in Section 58 of the Children's Act 2004, which outlaw the physical punishment of children leaving any *"lasting physical marks"*. Legally, this means that if the physical punishment (i.e. assault and injury) occasions actual bodily harm, the parents are liable to prosecution; if the punishment constitutes only common assault, then the parents are able to use the defence of 'reasonable chastisement'. The defence of 'reasonable chastisement' under similar conditions also exists in Scotland, but Section 51 of the Criminal Justice (Scotland) Act 2003 prohibits adults from delivering blows to the head, shaking and using an instrument to 'punish' children. The position in Northern Ireland was effectively rendered the same as that in England and Wales with the implementation of Article 2 of The Law Reform (Miscellaneous Provisions Northern Ireland) Order 2006.

However, several European states have outlawed any corporal punishment directed at children: Austria, Bulgaria, Croatia, Cyprus, Denmark, Finland, Germany, Greece, Hungary, Iceland, Latvia, Norway, Romania, Sweden and Ukraine.

The current legal status of the physical chastisement of children in England is the subject of some debate. The NSPCC declares it 'ambiguous', although it should be noted that the NSPCC is opposed to corporal punishment of children in all its forms

(NSPCC 2009).[1] However, a recent review of the current status of Section 58 of the Children's Act stated: *"The current legal position is clear and appropriate, but can be difficult to understand. It is neither correct nor incorrect to say, 'smacking is legal'"* (Department for Children, Schools and Families 2007, p.15, para. 42). The review did not advise any revision of the existing law.

The review also contains the results of a survey (Sherbert Research 2007) concerning parents' attitudes to the 'physical punishment' of children, which essentially amounts to smacking – other forms of physical chastisement have largely vanished. The sample was composed of 1,822 parents in England and Wales both with and without dependent children (1,204 and 618 respectively). The results indicate that smacking[2] was or had been used by only 24 per cent of parents in order to manage or improve their child's behaviour, but there is a clear intergenerational trend: the older the respondent, the more likely they are to have used smacking as a means of managing children's behaviour. Only 7 per cent of young parents (15- to 24-year-olds) said that they use or have used smacking, compared to 44 per cent of those aged 65 or older, with a steady rise in percentage with age in between. This relationship was reversed in terms of alternative 'time out' techniques, which include the 'naughty step', which have been used by 38 per cent of young parents, but only by 5 per cent of older parents (Figure 4.1); across all parents, 26 per cent employed some form of 'time out' technique.

---

1   The NSPCC is not the only organisation opposed to corporal punishment of children: some 400 organisations support the Children are Unbeatable! Alliance. This opposes the legal justification of common assault against children on the grounds of 'reasonable chastisement', and seeks to place children on the same footing as adults with respect to the law.

2   Other methods that parents used to manage their child's behaviour which were more commonly cited than smacking were: praising good behaviour; reasoning with them; preventing them from doing something they like; rewarding good behaviour; sending them to their room; shouting at them; setting a good example; 'grounding' them; creating a diversion; counting to three; and making them take time out (IpsosMORI 2007).

Figure 4.1: Percentage of parents by age using particular techniques of child management, 2007

Source: IpsosMORI (2007)

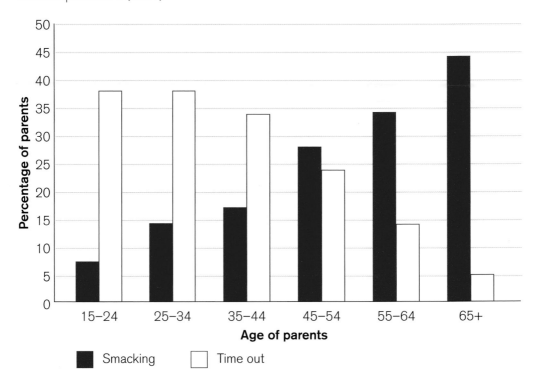

It should be noted that when asked directly in the same survey whether they had ever smacked at least one of their children, 57 per cent of respondents indicated that they had, and 29 per cent indicated that they had smacked at least one of their children at some point during the last 12 months. As might be expected, there are clear differences in the proportion of parents administering physical punishment and the age of their children. These are indicated in Figure 4.2 with data from the same survey.

Figure 4.2: Percentage of parents physically punishing children during the last 12 months by child's age, 2007

Source: IpsosMORI (2007)

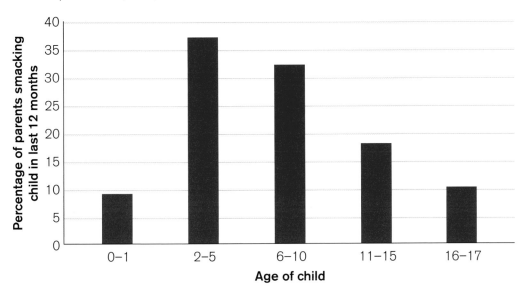

The most commonly mentioned reason for smacking a child was to stop them doing something dangerous to themselves. The proportion of parents citing this reason and various others is presented in Figure 4.3.

Figure 4.3: Parents' reasons for physically punishing children, 2007
Source: IpsosMORI (2007)

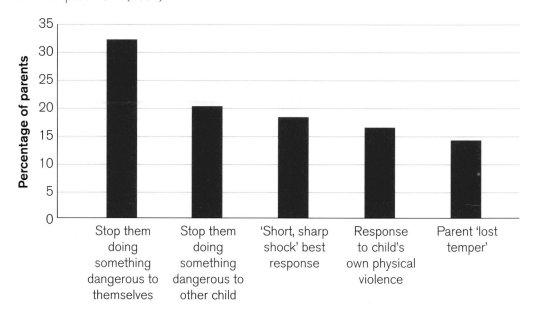

Reason for physical punishment

Using a sample of 1,250 parents of 0- to 12-year-olds throughout Britain, Ghate et al. (2003) found evidence of intergenerational transmission of the use of physical punishment: parents who had experienced harsh discipline themselves were more likely to apply such discipline to their children. Furthermore, research conducted by Sherbert Research (2007), which is considered in more detail below, found that among children who had not been smacked, smacking was not regarded as an acceptable form of punishment, while those who had been smacked were more likely to consider it acceptable. Ghate et al. (2003) suggest that such transmission might be challenged by changing social attitudes and negative appraisal by individuals of their own experiences of physical punishment; however, whether this is the case was not demonstrated.

Parents' attitudes to physical punishment

A survey conducted in 1998 for the ONS, using an adult rather than parental sample, found that 88 per cent agreed with the statement *"It is sometimes necessary to smack a naughty child"* (IpsosMORI 2007). An IpsosMORI survey conducted in 2007 indicated that the figure stood at 52 per cent (IpsosMORI 2007). Although this is taken as evidence of a shift in attitude towards smacking, the 2007 survey indicated that a majority of parents think that the law should allow parents to smack their children. As Figure 4.4 shows, it is only among the youngest age group of parents that the percentage agreeing that *"The law should allow parents to smack their children"* falls below 50 per cent, and agreement with the statement increases with age. In total 59 per cent of the sample agreed with the statement and only 22 per cent disagreed. The same figure of 59 per cent of respondents were opposed to a change in the law forbidding the smacking of children in an earlier survey conducted by Populus, reported in *The Times* (Booth 2004). Again, the 18 to 24 age group showed greatest opposition to the current situation, with 59 per cent stating that smacking should become a criminal offence.

In an IpsosMORI (2004) poll commissioned by the Children Are Unbeatable! Alliance ($N = 2004$), when asked whether children should be given as much protection from being hit as adults, 71 per cent agreed that they should, and only 10 per cent were opposed to such a change. The younger age group, parents and women expressed the strongest opposition (76 per cent, 74 per cent and 73 per cent respectively). When asked whether *"It is wrong for someone to hit a child in their family"*, 56 per cent agreed and 31 per cent disagreed.

Boyson and Thorpe (2002) identified a series of pre-legislation concerns current in countries which now have outlawed the physical chastisement of children. These included:

- an increased opportunity for the state to intervene in domestic affairs

- the threat of possible criminal proceedings against parents for minor transgressions

- a concern that children will become out of control.

Boyson and Thorpe (2002, p.2) claim that these concerns were unfounded and that *"no negative effects have been documented following legal reform"*, although it must be stressed that there were issues concerning the authors' access to accurate data.

Figure 4.4: Percentage of parents agreeing or disagreeing that *"The law should allow parents to smack their children"*, 2007
Source: IpsosMORI (2007)

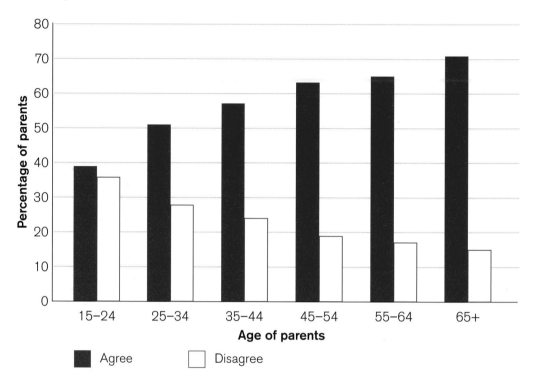

Alongside the views of parents, a study for the Department for Children, Schools and Families (2007) used interviews with children on their attitudes and experiences of corporal punishment. About two-thirds of the children reported that they had been smacked at some point. This finding highlights an apparent inconsistency between the reported administration of smacking by parents and the reported experience of smacking by children, which has been replicated in other research. For example, Ghate et al. (2003) found that although 40 per cent of parents stated that physical punishment was never acceptable, and half said that it was only acceptable sometimes, 88 per cent admitted that they had used physical punishment at some stage. The corollary is that one in seven parents had used physical punishment, despite claiming to disapprove of it.

Children's attitudes to physical punishment

Qualitative research concerning the attitudes of children aged four to 16 ($N = 64$) towards punishment indicated that smacking is the most feared punishment: it is feared due to the distress or humiliation associated with its administration rather than the pain that it causes (Sherbert Research 2007). The children in this study tended to regard discipline and punishment as necessary, but the role of smacking was questioned. It was associated with parents' lack of control, setting a poor example and damaging communication between parent and child. In addition, smacking was regarded as antiquated or obsolete, and placed in a historical context among other forms of physical punishment, possibly administered to their parents, such as the cane, which have vanished.

Alternative punishments were identified, such as denial of access to TV or toys, which involved greater inconvenience and time for the child to consider the behaviour leading to the punishment. However, understanding what the punishment received was for remained the most important aspect of making it effective. Children who experienced punishment without explanation or clear justification reported that they were less likely to consider their behaviour, and more likely to feel anger at their parents and isolation from them after they had been punished (Sherbert Research 2007).

4.3 Has there been a growth in consumerism and materialism?

This section examines the factors that might dispose individuals, particularly children, towards consumerist behaviour or materialistic values, and the factors which might actively promote such behaviour or values. Initially this is considered in terms of the influence that changes in family form may have in promoting materialistic values in children, specifically parental separation.

Consumerism, materialism and family structure

Research conducted in the USA set out to test the influence of family structure and family disruption (divorce or separation) on the consumer attitudes and behaviour of young adults (Rindfleisch et al. 1997; Roberts et al. 2003). Consumer attitudes were measured in terms of 'materialism', which is defined as a *"set of centrally held beliefs about the importance of possessions in one's life"* (Richins and Dawson 1992, p. 308). These beliefs are apparent in terms of the degree to which material possessions are a primary source of an individual's satisfaction or dissatisfaction with their own life. Generally, high levels of materialism are treated as a negative trait, associated with low self-esteem and dissatisfaction with life. Materialism in practice is measured in terms of three sub-dimensions, specifically:

- the centrality of material possessions in life

- happiness – the extent to which material possessions are necessary for wellbeing and satisfaction in life

- success – the level of success associated with ownership of material possessions.

Rindfleisch et al.'s (1997) study looked at materialism among 261 young adults aged 20 to 32 years, approximately half of whom had experienced the divorce or separation of their parents. The results indicated that those who had experienced their parents' divorce or separation scored higher on the materialistic measure, in terms of both the overall score and scores on the subscales of centrality and happiness. These results were partly replicated by Roberts et al. (2003) who, using a younger sample of 11- to 15-year-olds (N = 669), found only the happiness subscale exhibiting a difference – those whose families had been disrupted by divorce were more likely to associate happiness with possessions. The reason suggested for this difference was that those who have experienced parental separation or divorce are more likely to value material possessions as a surrogate.

Rindfleisch et al.'s (1997) post-hoc analysis indicated that family resources mediated the relationship between family form and the 'happiness' dimension of materialism. Further analysis by Roberts et al. (2003) indicated that the link between family form and materialism – measured in terms of 'happiness' – was mediated by 'family stressors' (but not resources): that is, the greater the recorded stress, the greater the likelihood of associating happiness with material wealth for those from families which had experienced marital breakdown or separation. This indicates not only the association between separation or divorce and consumer attitudes, but the likely exacerbating impact of a high-stress divorce on children. As Roberts et al. state: *"Low-stress divorces lead to less negative outcomes for children"* (2003, p.304).

Roberts et al. (2003) also found that lack of family resources predicted a higher association of happiness with material wealth, irrespective of whether the parents were ever divorced. The implications are that any increase in rates of separation for parents with dependent children is likely to impact on the materialistic values current in a society, as will levels of deprivation.

Consumerism, materialism and media literacy

While the issues above might dispose individuals to consumerism or materialism, advertising is seen as actively promoting these values. Dittmar (2004) argues that consumer brands are linked to 'identity construction', and even more strongly so for adolescents than for adults. Furthermore, there is evidence that children from deprived areas seem to place greater importance on material possessions than children from more affluent areas, as shown in Figure 4.5 (Nairn et al. 2007).

Figure 4.5: Attitudes to material wealth of young people aged 9–13 years by affluence of area, 2006

Source: Nairn et al. (2007)

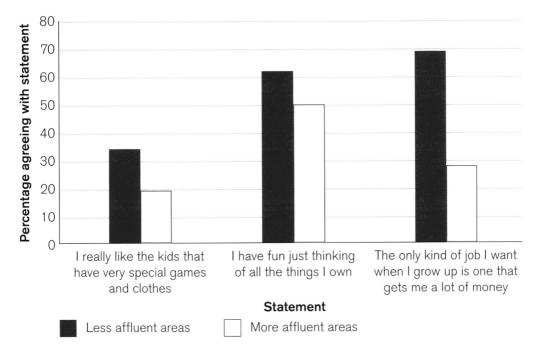

The data in Figure 4.5 indicate, for example, that 34 per cent of children from deprived areas, but only 19 per cent of children from affluent areas, agreed with the statement *"I really like the kids that have very special games and clothes".* The authors suggest that the differences may be due to differences in exposure to TV. In more deprived areas, 43 per cent of the 9- to 13-year-olds that they studied watched TV every weekday in bed before going to sleep, compared to 10 per cent in the more affluent areas, and in both areas the amount of TV watched was correlated with materialism.

As well as the amount of TV watched, concerns also exist about TV advertising directed at or appealing to children. The target for advertisers is both children's spending power and their likely influence over family spending decisions. For example, US research has indicated that 65 per cent of car purchases are influenced by children (Williams 2007).

Some European countries have subjected such advertising to restrictive legislation. In 1995, Norway introduced a complete ban on television advertising to children, and Sweden followed in 1996. Over the same period, Belgium and Greece introduced partial restrictions on TV advertising directed at children. Belgium prevented adverts from immediately preceding or following children's programmes, and in Greece, toy adverts were forbidden between 7am and 10pm.

The annual spend on children-themed food and drink advertising across all media in the UK for 2007 was £61 million (Department of Health 2008). Recently, the UK has placed a series of restrictions on advertising food high in fat, salt or sugar: in 2007, advertisements featuring such products were banned *"in or around"* programmes aimed at children aged four to nine.[3] The age range was extended in 2008 to cover all children under 16 years, and by 2009 all channels were expected to comply. Children also watch a great deal of non-children's TV, which is exempt from these restrictions.

A children-themed advert is defined as containing one or more of the following:

- a connection to a children's TV programme, film, book or computer game

- licensed characters

- a free toy, gift or collectable

- a novelty product or packaging design that *"appeals to children"* (Department of Health 2008).

Where concerns exist about advertising aimed at children, they derive in part from the presumption that children do not have the capacity to deal with adverts yet, and therefore are exploited more easily. That is, they lack media or, more precisely, advertising literacy, where advertising literacy is defined as possessing the skills of analysing, evaluating and creating persuasive messages across a variety of contexts and media.

With respect to children, advertising literacy centres around two distinct abilities: to discriminate between adverts and TV programmes; and to identify persuasive intent, i.e. to be aware that any such communication only features positive information. The latter is seen as the more demanding skill, and hence is likely to develop at a later age. Once acquired, these abilities provide children with a 'cognitive defence' against commercials (Krunkel et al. 2004); however, young children, particularly those aged six or below, are unlikely to have such a comprehensive cognitive defence.

Accounts of the acquisition of media or advertising literacy are extrapolated from more general theories of children's psychological or cognitive development. Piaget's

---

3   The definition of a programme aimed at children is that the proportion of children watching exceeds their prevalence in the population by 20 per cent (see Office of Communications 2006). This definition would have included only 2 of the 10 most popular TV programmes with children under 10 years, based on viewing figures collected over two weeks in September 2007 (*Which?* 2007).

account of child development may not have great currency within contemporary research in developmental psychology, due to a failure to cohere with a growing body of experimental evidence, but nonetheless it is frequently cited in communications research (Gunter et al. 2005).

Piaget's theory involves the child progressing through a number of stages. The latter three stages, seen as relevant to the development of media literacy, are:

- the pre-operational stage (two to seven years) – characterised by an absence of logical thought that renders children unable to distinguish adverts from programmes

- the concrete operational stage (7 to 12 years) – where children can think logically but in concrete rather than abstract terms, enabling them to identify persuasive intent

- the formal operational stage (12 years and over) – where children are able to reason abstractly, and hence to evaluate critically advertising and its associated intentions.

A more contemporary psychological account which has implications for child development is 'theory of mind'. This also identifies children's early years as a period during which they have not yet developed the cognitive architecture or functions required to render them media literate, making them potentially more susceptible to advertising (Moses and Baldwin 2005).

Recent accounts of cognitive development have identified two processes that may be required for understanding advertisements: metacognition and multiple perspectives. Metacognition allows children to identify and reflect on the 'mental' states of TV characters while viewing; additionally, it allows children to relate their existing knowledge to new information and draw conclusions beyond what is immediately presented, based on the relationships identified. In addition, by the age of eight, children are thought to be able to take multiple perspectives in terms of advertising. These allow children to form an opinion about an advertisement through realistic weighting of the evidence, judging it for its appeal and aesthetic qualities. Additionally, by the same age, children already show evidence of incredulity and a critical faculty; while identifying the role of adverts as primarily informative, they are aware that adverts exist to sell products (D'Alessio et al. 2009). The corollary of this is that younger children in general are thought to be more susceptible to advertising.

However, Livingstone and Helsper (2006) found no evidence that younger children are influenced disproportionately by advertising, although this should be the case if young children lack media literacy. Instead they suggest that different processes of persuasion that vary with media or advertising literacy are effective at different ages. Younger children are more likely to be persuaded by peripherals such as celebrity association, lively presentation and the appealing appearance of the product or service, while older children and teenagers are more likely to be affected by presentation of arguments associated with the product or service. Therefore, while age is important with respect to the possible effect of advertising, children or young people's psychological maturation or development is the main barrier to consumption and this is addressed by advertisers.

Reviewing research concerning the unintended effect of advertising, Buijzen and Valkenburg (2003) conclude, on the weight of evidence, that there is a modest but discernible relation between increased exposure to advertising and increased materialism, at least for those in early childhood and adolescence.

Parents' attitudes to children-themed advertising

A 2003 poll found that 84 per cent of parents felt that companies targeted their children 'too much'. The related concerns reported included additional encouragement of children to spend, children developing a throwaway attitude, and a growth in children's dissatisfaction (National Family and Parenting Institute 2003).

In addition, concern has been expressed about new markets and advertising, particularly product tie-ins that seem to be aimed particularly at young children, as well as new technologies such as computer games and mobile phones which are marketed at children (Gunter et al. 2005). Parents expressed concern not just about the marketing of new technologies but marketing *via* new technologies, such as the internet and particularly text messages, as such marketing is difficult for parents to monitor (National Family and Parenting Institute 2003). The impact of new technologies on family life is examined in the following section.

4.4 How has technology affected parenting?

This section examines how parents have approached the issues and challenges raised by technology, from those associated with the long-established medium of TV to more recent forms: the internet and mobile phones.

Hanley (2002) identified three broad areas of concern that parents might have about new technology usage and children's TV viewing:

- they may find it difficult to know how to monitor their children's TV viewing and internet activities without being either neglectful or intrusive

- they may not have consistent, effective or fully thought-through plans on how to monitor their children's media usage

- they may feel unsure about what constitutes a danger to children.

Television

CHILDWISE estimated that in 2008 nine in 10 children aged five to 16 years had access to a multichannel TV at home, four in 10 had a multichannel TV in their own room, and children watched about 2.7 hours of TV per day (CHILDWISE 2009). Parental attitudes towards TV indicated that the watershed (9pm) was seen as a valued feature of TV regulation, and that there was a feeling in general that TV was regulated effectively. However, concerns were voiced about programming prior to the watershed, particularly about soaps and police or crime dramas. Additionally, concern was also expressed about adverts.

The techniques that parents employed in monitoring and controlling children's TV viewing included:

- the prohibition of certain programmes and endorsement of others

- changing channels or switching off the TV

- sending children out of the room when something unsuitable was being broadcasted

- discussing the content of concern

- limiting the time that children were allowed to watch TV

- random checks on children's viewing.

Almost all the parents felt their children's TV viewing was under control, although the ages of greatest concern were 10 to 14 years.

Internet

Using General Household Survey data, the ONS reported that one-third of households in Great Britain had internet access in 2000 (the first time this question was asked); by 2001 the figure had risen to 39 per cent, and by 2005 to 55 per cent. The figures for the UK, available since 2006, indicate that in 2006, 14.26 million households (57 per cent) had access to the internet; by 2008 this had risen to 16.46 million or 65 per cent of all households, and 86 per cent of these had broadband access (ONS 2008h). Currently there are plans to levy a charge of some £6 a year on all households with a landline in order to fund a programme furnishing all households in the UK with broadband internet access (Woods 2009).

This general growth in household internet access is mirrored in the access that children now have to the internet. The CHILDWISE (2009) trends report indicated that currently, almost all 5- to 15-year-olds have access to a computer at home, and nearly half own their own personal computer or laptop, with two-fifths of 7- to 16-year-olds having access to the internet in their own room.

Access to the internet gives individuals the opportunity to engage with a series of rapidly evolving or developing interactive services, such as multiplayer games; content streaming services such as Spotify for music and YouTube for audiovisual material, message boards, weblogs (blogs) and a range of social networking sites such as MySpace (which has an age restriction of 14 years and above), Facebook, Bebo and the more recent mobile phone-driven Twitter (all three with an age restriction of 13 years and above).

Universal internet access has brought with it a range of positive and negative perceived and actual impacts on users, including children. Table 4.1 summarises the principal benefits and risks associated with children's use of the internet.

Table 4.1: Opportunities and risks associated with children's internet usage, 2008

Source: Hasebrink et al. (2008)

Opportunities	Risks
• Access to global information	• Illegal content
• Educational resources	• Paedophiles, 'grooming', strangers
• Social networking for old or new friends	• Extreme or sexual violence
• Entertainment, games and fun	• Other harmful or offensive content
• User-generated content creation	• Racist or hate material and activities
• Civic or political participation	• Advertising or commercial persuasion
• Privacy for expression of identity	• Bias or misinformation (advice, health)
• Community involvement or activism	• Exploitation of personal information
• Technological expertise and literacy	• Cyberbullying, stalking, harassment
• Career advancement or employment	• Gambling, financial scams
• Personal, health or sexual advice	• Self-harm (suicide, anorexia, etc.)
• Specialist groups and fan forums	• Invasion or abuse of privacy
• Shared experiences with distant others	• Illegal activities (hacking, downloading)

Compared to TV, more serious worries were expressed by parents in Hasebrink et al.'s (2008) study about children's exposure to the internet, particularly by parents who lacked experience of the internet. The concerns appeared to stem from parental awareness of the size of the internet and of its inherently unregulated nature: even where parents had confidence in children's self-regulation there was a residual concern about their accidental exposure to unsuitable material. The concerns were balanced to some extent by an awareness of the internet's potential, particularly in educational terms. The techniques employed in monitoring and controlling children's internet usage included:

- placing the computer where usage was visible
- controlling when the computer was turned on
- sitting with the child (especially younger or new users)
- children being required to keep their parents informed of all internet use
- random checks on usage
- no or limited random surfing
- time-limits on usage
- use of filtering controls (software blocking or rating services).

However, filtering controls were often criticised for requiring too high a level of technical knowledge for many parents.

Often, the dangers associated with the internet or cyberspace are characterised in terms of the child as a potential victim. However, the internet also offers the opportunity for the child to become a perpetrator, not simply in terms of role reversal (such as the potential victim of cyberbullying becoming a bully) but by presenting new opportunities to engage in what amounts to criminal activity. Sharing files with copyright content is common but illegal, yet parents seldom express concern about their children engaging in this sort of activity.

Mobile phones

The CHILDWISE (2009) trends report indicates that mobile phone ownership for 5- to 16-year-olds stands at about 75 per cent. More specifically, 50 per cent of 5- to 10-year-olds have their own mobile phone, and this figure rises to 95 per cent among 11- to 16-year-olds (CHILDWISE 2009). Recently the French Government announced plans to prevent the advertising of mobile phones to children under 12 and to stop the sale of mobile phones to children under six years. These moves were motivated by concerns about the heightened health risks associated with children's exposure to the microwave radiation (LIMRadiation) emitted by mobile phones (Allen and Macrae 2009). Currently the British Government has not taken equivalent steps.

Health risks notwithstanding, mobile phones offer parents a means of remaining in contact with their children on a permanent basis. Using qualitative research with a sample of 26 two-parent families with at least one child aged between 12 and 16, Lewis, Sarre and Burton (2007) found that although monitoring children via phone was universal, some parents expressed misgivings about the presence of mobile phones in their children's lives. They felt that they were no longer able to monitor who was phoning their children; they did not know the phone numbers of their children's friends, which meant that they could not check or contact the parents of their children's friends; and while they could contact their children, they could not always be certain where they actually were. A further area of parental concern was that, like the internet, which can be accessed from a mobile phone, mobile phones also provide a medium for advertising – in this case, via text messaging, which largely escapes parental scrutiny.

Some of the children in the research conducted by Lewis, Sarre and Burton (2007) admitted that 'other children' exploited the potential of the mobile phone in order to deceive their parents, such as telling them that they were in one place deemed to be acceptable when in fact they were elsewhere. However, this may change in the near future. Technology now exists to allow a mobile device (phone or even a watch) to be tracked on the internet. In theory, parents will be able to locate the precise whereabouts of their child's phone or watch, if not the child themselves, at any time (Daily Mail Reporter 2009). Currently, this innovation is being marketed in terms of increasing children's safety and reducing parental concerns. However, it has not been met with universal approval. Some parents have expressed concerns that tracking children may be interfering or undermining parent–child trust. Further concerns have been expressed that if a parent can use a tracker to locate the whereabouts of their child, then so can someone else (Goldacre 2006).

4.5 Are children growing up 'too fast'?

Evidence indicates that young people's transitions into many areas of adulthood, such as joining the labour force and living independently from the parental home, are subject to greater delay than they have been previously. The issue of whether children are growing up 'too fast' appears to be composed largely, if not entirely, of concerns about the age at which young people initiate sexual activity.

Particular concerns have been raised about the premature 'sexualisation' of children, especially where it is orchestrated principally to further corporate interests and is realised via the media. These concerns have been articulated in at least two recent US books: *So sexy so soon* (Levin and Kilbourne 2009) and *The Lolita effect* (Durham 2008). Yet a report by the American Psychological Association Task Force on the Sexualization of Girls makes clear that, to date, there is very little research on the effects of the media on young girls (Zurbriggen et al. 2007).

There is no evidence that children are growing up any faster in physical terms: the average age of puberty has not declined significantly over recent decades, at least in the UK. The average age of menarche (onset of menstruation) in the UK currently stands at 12 to 13 years. Between the late 19th century and the mid-20th century, the average age fell by a year or more in many European countries, including the UK. This decline has been termed a 'secular trend', which ceased around the 1960s and now may even be reversing, at least in western Europe. The onset of menarche is related to a variety of factors, principally genetic, psychological, socio-economic and nutritional, and the latter two at least have improved considerably since the 19th century (Patton and Viner 2007; Whincup et al. 2001).

The picture in the USA is somewhat different: recent research has suggested that the average age of menarche has declined further (Whincup et al. 2001). Herman-Giddens (2007) argues that until the 1960s, the factors influencing the trend in decreasing age of menarche were largely positive in health terms, such as improvements in nutrition and decline in the incidence of infectious diseases. However, further decline in the average age of menarche is likely to be due to less positive factors such as obesity, reduction in physical activity and chemical pollution. Herman-Giddens (2007) also cites other possible factors such as exogenous hormones, and even the hypersexualisation of culture.

Murrin and Martin (2004) reported that children were becoming sexually active at a younger age: boys tended to have their first sexual experience at the age of 13, and girls at the age of 14, with the most frequent age at which sexual intercourse first takes place being 16. Around 1950, the average age was 20, although the decade with the steepest decline in the average age at which individuals lost their virginity was the 1950s. Predictors of earlier sexual activity include coming from a disrupted home, gaining no qualifications, learning about sex from peers rather than school and reaching puberty earlier than average (Murrin and Martin 2004).

However, there is an abiding problem with research concerning human sexual activity, and that is the reliability of the evidence. For example, response rates for surveys can be compromised if the area researched is sensitive, as is the case with respect to sexual behaviour (Fife-Schaw 1995). The most obvious and perhaps most reliable indicator of sexual behaviour is pregnancy and, in this case, teenage pregnancy, which is discussed below.

Teenage conception, pregnancy and motherhood

Teenage conception, pregnancy and motherhood often raises moral, social and economic concerns. Central to these is the longstanding association between teenage motherhood and social disadvantage: the association between poor educational attainment and teenage motherhood, for example, has been observed Europe-wide (Berthoud and Robson 2001).

The rate of teenage pregnancy, both in the UK and in continental Europe, has varied considerably over previous decades. This section will examine these rates and the possible factors influencing them.

The first family planning centre designed for young unmarried people was established by Helen Brook in 1964. Later in the same decade two important pieces of legislation were passed: the Abortion Act 1967, which legalised abortion and placed it on demand; and the National Health Service (Family Planning) Act 1967, which allowed local authorities to give contraceptive advice to people who were unmarried. However, the uptake of services provided by organisations such as the Family Planning Association by individuals below the age of 16 was very low, at least until the early 1970s (Leathard 1980, cited in Paton 2002).

Two significant developments in family planning occurred in 1974: contraception was made free to all via the National Health Service, and the then Department of Health and Social Security issued clarification concerning the legality of providing contraception to under-16s without parental consent. These milestones in family planning in the 1960s and early 1970s certainly preceded a discernible reduction in under-16 pregnancy rates between 1971 and 1981 (Figure 4.6).

Figure 4.6: Conception rates for teenagers under 16 years, England and Wales, 1971–2007*

Source: ONS (2002b); Shrosbree (2009)

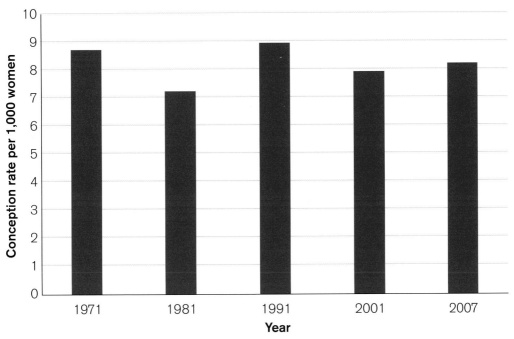

* Figures for 2007 are provisional.

Clarification concerning the legality of providing contraception to under-16s without parental consent was reissued in 1980. However, in 1984 the Appeal Court, returning a judgment in the case of *Gillick* v. *West Norfolk and Wisbech Area Health Authority* ([1986] AC 112), prohibited the administration of contraception to under-16s without parental consent; this was reversed subsequently by a Law Lords ruling in 1985 which re-established the right to contraception without parental consent. It has been argued that, allied to a reduction in funding for community health services and concerns over confidentiality led to a decline in under-16s' attendance at family planning clinics and a subsequent increase in teenage conception rates during the 1980s (Brook 2009). However, this account has been contested: Paton (2002) found neither evidence that the *Gillick* ruling had an impact on under-16 conception rates, nor that greater access to family planning reduced under-16 conception rates; indeed, there was some evidence that greater access is associated with greater rates of teenage pregnancy, possibly by raising the likelihood of underage teenagers engaging in sexual activity to begin with (Paton 2002) or, as Paton (2008) remarks elsewhere, by increasing the likelihood of teenagers engaging in risky sexual behaviour.

Since the 1980s there have been two government initiatives designed to reduce teenage conception rates. The first was part of the 1992 Health of the Nation initiative, which aimed at a 50 per cent reduction in under-16 pregnancies by 2000. The period from 1990 to 1995 saw a 16 per cent reduction in under-16 pregnancies, which coincided with an expansion of young people's services: the number of health authorities providing specialist services for young people rose from 52 per cent to 85 over this period (Brook 2009). After a brief rise in conception rates in the mid- to late 1990s, which coincided with a shortlived scare about the safety of the contraceptive pill, the downward trend resumed: the 1998 conception rate for under-16s stood at 9 per 1,000.

The second government initiative, the Teenage Pregnancy Strategy, was initiated in 1999, prompted by concern about the higher rate of teenage pregnancies or births in the UK compared to other European Union (EU) countries. Teenage birth rates across EU Member States for 1970 and 1998 appear in Figure 4.7.

Figure 4.7: Teenage birth rates for EU Member States, 1970 and 1998
Source: Unicef (2001)

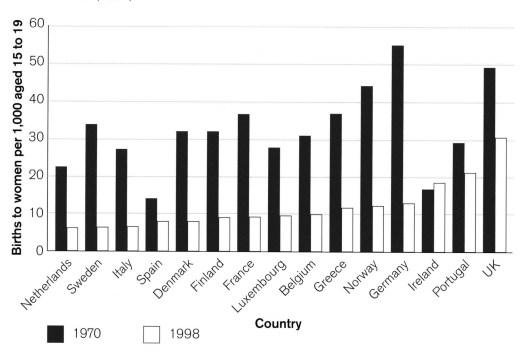

Figure 4.7 indicates a clear reduction in teenage births from 1970 to 1998 for all EU countries except Ireland, which had a relatively low rate of teenage births in 1970 and a fractional increase by 1998.

The stated objective of the Teenage Pregnancy Strategy was to reduce under-18 pregnancies by half from the 1998 baseline over the course of the ensuing decade and to establish a downward trend in under-16 conceptions. There is evidence of a reduction in the teenage conception rate during this period, but this was neither uniform across all social groups, nor is the continued rate of reduction such that the stated target is likely to be met by 2010. The under-16 conception rate stood at 9 per 1,000 in 1998; by 2006 it had reduced to 7.8. The pattern was similar for 15- to 18-year-olds, where the conception rate dropped from 46.6 per 1,000 to 40.6 over the same period.

However, recently the rates for all teenagers have shown an increase. The increase in the conception rate for teenage girls under 16 was particularly steep: provisional figures show a rise from 7.8 conceptions per 1,000 in 2006 to 8.3 in 2007 – a 6.4 per cent increase. In absolute terms there was a 4.7 per cent increase in the number of conceptions for this age group between 2006 and 2007, with three-quarters of these conceptions belonging to 15 year-olds. Conception rates for 15- to 18-year-olds also showed an increase to 41.7 from 40.6 (Shrosbree 2009).

The Teenage Pregnancy Strategy reputedly marked a turning point in the approach to the issue of unintended teenage pregnancy in the UK, being based on evidence rather than moral judgement. The strategy had five main themes:

- joined-up action

- a national media campaign

- support for the parents of teenagers

- prevention – including improving sex and relationship education and access to contraception

- support for teenage parents (Department for Children, Schools and Families 2008b).

The strategy further involved identifying the risk factors associated with teenage pregnancy. The most important included:

- that the teenager's own parent had been a teenage parent

- poor educational attainment, particularly if it showed a deterioration over time (Kiernan 1997)

- intended truancy

- NEET at 16 (Bynner and Parsons 1999).

Perhaps the single most important risk factor is socio-economic status: there is a tenfold increase in the likelihood of becoming a teenage mother for girls from the lowest socio-economic level (unskilled labour), compared to those from the highest (professional) level (Botting et al. 1998). Further research has identified the importance of area deprivation (McLeod 2001; Sloggett and Joshi 1998) and expectations about becoming a parent by 20 (Allen et al. 2007). Bradshaw et al. (2005) found an apparent association between higher levels of teenage pregnancy and areas with higher concentrations of ethnic minorities, but this was eliminated when socio-economic deprivation was taken into account.

Using data from 2001–02, Uren et al. (2007) found an association not only between area deprivation and conception rates, but also between area deprivation and conception outcome – maternity or abortion. Teenage conception rates by outcome from 1971 to 2007 are presented in Table 4.2.

Table 4.2: Teenage conception rates by age at conception outcome, rates per 1,000 conceptions, England and Wales, 1971–2007

Source: ONS (2002b); Shrosbree (2009)

	Type of pregnancy									
	Leading to maternity					Leading to abortion				
Age	1971	1981	1991	2001	2007	1971	1981	1991	2001	2007
Under 14*	0.5	0.4	0.5	0.5	0.5	0.5	0.7	0.7	0.7	0.7
14	2.8	1.7	2.6	2.2	2.0	2.4	2.9	3.5	3.5	3.8
15	13.5	7.1	9.8	8.0	7.0	6.9	8.7	9.3	9.4	10.5
All <16*	5.5	3.1	4.3	3.5	3.2	3.2	4.1	4.6	4.5	5.1
16	41.0	21.5	25.0	21.9	19.4	13.0	16.2	17.1	18.5	20.0
17	68.5	36.7	41.5	37.2	34.0	15.2	20.1	22.7	26.6	28.0
18	95.0	54.6	57.0	52.2	50.8	16.7	21.6	26.6	31.4	33.1
19	114.5	73.0	66.2	61.1	62.0	16.4	21.0	28.6	33.4	34.9

* Rates for girls aged under 14, under 16 and under 20 are based on the population of girls aged 13, 13 to 15 and 15 to 19, respectively.

Uren et al.'s (2007) research indicated that maternity and abortion rates increase with deprivation; that for girls under 16 the rate of abortion was three times greater for those in the most deprived areas compared to the least: 6.6 compared to 2.1 per 1,000 girls aged 13 to 15, and in the case of maternity the rate was 12 times higher: 21 per 1,000 compared to 1.7. The same trend was observed for older teenagers: the abortion rate for 15- to 17-year-olds was more than twice that for those in the most deprived areas compared to those in the least deprived (27.9 as opposed to 11.5 per 1,000 women aged 15 to 17). The maternity rate was nine times higher (43.1 as opposed to 4.8).

However, there is also evidence that pregnant teenagers in less deprived areas are more likely to have an abortion: i.e. the greater the deprivation, the lower the abortion rate *per conception* for both under-18s and under-16s. In the case of under-18s, the abortion rate in the least deprived areas is 71 per cent of conceptions, and in the most deprived, 31 per cent; for the under-16s the equivalent figures are 77 per cent and 50 per cent respectively. These figures suggest that there is a socio-economic distinction, perhaps realised in terms of a subtle gradation, between those teenagers who tend to opt for abortion and those who tend to opt for motherhood. Recent evidence of the importance of teenagers' socio-economic status in conception rates and the eventual outcome of pregnancy has been indentified by Lee et al. (2004). This is returned to later in this section, when the relation between unplanned or unwanted teenage pregnancy and eventual motherhood is considered.

A further influence on the likelihood of abortion is age. As Figure 4.8 indicates, the likelihood of abortion decreases with age: 66 per cent of 14-year-olds have legal abortions, for 16-year-olds the figure falls to 51 per cent.

Figure 4.8: Percentage of teenage pregnancies leading to legal abortions by age, England and Wales, 2007

Source: Shrosbree (2009)

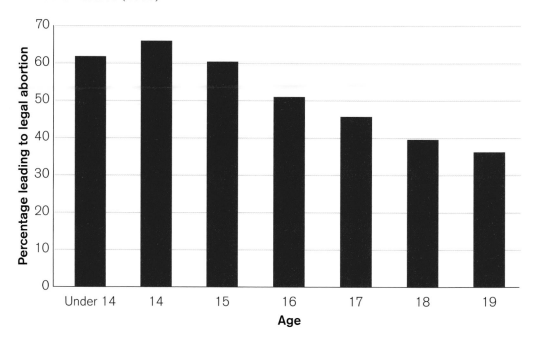

There is a question as to whether the 1998 rate of teenage conception or births in the UK is constitutive of a problem at all. Lawlor and Shaw (2004) argue that the teenage birth rates found in the UK are high only when compared to other western European countries; considered globally in the context of 46 industrialised nations, England and Wales have only moderate rates of teenage births (Singh and Darroch 2000). Lawlor and Shaw (2004) further point out that while the number of sexually active teenagers has increased and historically the age of menarche has decreased, thus increasing the at-risk population, nonetheless the rate of teenage births has gone downwards over the past 30 years.

While the rate of teenage pregnancies has fluctuated, an increasing proportion of teenage births now occur outside marriage. In 1971 the rate was 26 per cent, in 1981 the figure was 47 per cent, in 1996 the figure stood at 88 per cent, and by 2006, 93 per cent of live births to women aged under 20 in England and Wales occurred outside marriage (Kiernan 1997; ONS 2007).

However, the pattern of teenage pregnancy and motherhood is not uniform over ethnic groups. Using data from the Labour Force Survey 1987–99, Berthoud and Robson (2001) found that Bangladeshi young women had the highest rates of teenage pregnancy (75 per 1,000), followed by Caribbean and Pakistani teenagers, with rates of 44 and 41 per 1,000 respectively. White British teenagers had a rate of 29 per 1,000 and Indian teenagers the lowest, with 17 per 1,000. However, South Asians (Indian, Pakistani, Bangladeshi) had the highest rate of marriage among young mothers: approximately 85 per cent, compared to 47 per cent for white and 15 for Caribbean.

There are also differences by country in terms of the association between teenage motherhood and socio-economic disadvantage. Berthoud and Robson (2001) found considerable variation: the disadvantage experienced by teenage mothers was most acute in the Netherlands, and least acute in Austria, where it almost vanished entirely. In the case of the UK, it was far closer to the situation in the Netherlands than Austria. Berthoud and Robson (2001) also consider the issue of the association between disadvantage and teenage motherhood, specifically in terms of whether it exists simply because it is disadvantaged teenagers who are most likely to become mothers, or whether teenage motherhood itself exacerbates any disadvantage that the teenager is experiencing already. An analysis using National Child Development Study data conducted by Hobcraft and Kiernan (1999) found that while poverty tends to track individuals throughout their life, and the more disadvantaged teenagers tend to become young mothers, there was an explanatory role for teenage motherhood independent of background: that is, the age at which the first child is born accounts for more of the risk of poorer outcomes than the mother's socio-economic background.

Unplanned or unwanted teenage pregnancies and motherhood

The Social Exclusion Unit (restructured and renamed the Social Exclusion Task Force in 2006) identified that one of the principal problems associated with teenage motherhood is that it can worsen the level of disadvantage that the mother already experiences. The occurrence of unplanned pregnancy has been given the following broad account by the Social Exclusion Unit (1999): mixed messages about sex from the adult world and an accompanying lack of knowledge about contraception dispose teenagers to both sexual activity and pregnancy; and once pregnant, to opt for motherhood as the most viable lifestyle or economic option, given their otherwise low expectations of education and employment opportunities (Social Exclusion Unit 1999).

In reviewing largely qualitative research, Duncan (2007) offers an alternative account of teenage motherhood, if not pregnancy rates, which explicitly incorporates a sociocultural element. Predicated on the claim that working-class teenagers experience a different sociocultural environment from middle-class teenagers, working-class teenagers grow up in an environment where early motherhood is both common and uncensored (Phoenix 1991), and where self-esteem, identity and social inclusion are centred around motherhood, with participation in the labour market being secondary to this (Duncan and Edwards 1999). Unplanned teenage pregnancy is less likely to be regarded as unwanted, being aligned more closely with family expectations concerning early motherhood and occurring within a network of family support. The environment inhabited by middle-class teenagers is different: identity is derived, chronologically at least, from higher education and labour market position, and while motherhood eventually may be no less central to middle-class mothers' identity, it is realised after educational and career achievements. In a small-scale qualitative study, Arai (2009) found that the most isolated and least well-supported teenage mothers were middle-class or older, but still teenage, married women who were geographically distant from their families.

Furthermore, case study research suggests that rather than preventing participation in education, training and/or employment, early motherhood can prove to be a spur to participation for some – participation that would have been less likely without motherhood (Graham and Dermott 2005; Phoenix 1991). There is also evidence that relatives, particularly the teenager's mother, might be supportive of their daughter's impending motherhood, and so act as an impediment to termination (Duncan 2007).

Attitudes to and consequences of teenage motherhood

Results from the British Social Attitudes Survey reported by Clarke and Thomson (2001–02) indicated that attitudes towards teenage pregnancy in the population are largely negative: it was identified as a 'problem' by 92 per cent of respondents, and 56 per cent agreed that 'a lack of morals' was one of the main causes of teenage pregnancy. Additional 'causes' were identified by 66 per cent of the respondents as stemming from TV and advertising putting too much pressure on teenagers to have sex before they were ready. In addition, there was a widespread assumption that teenagers were neither ready nor able to bring up children.

Countering the construction of teenage pregnancy as a problem, Arai (2009) found that teenage mothers often characterise their own motherhood in a positive manner, particularly in (eventual) terms of family support. Arai (2009) does concede , however, that the mothers might be utilising a 'consoling plot' when recounting their own experiences and attitudes – that is, unduly emphasising (although not fabricating) positive elements.

Whether involuntary teenage pregnancy is a social problem or symptomatic of a wider social malaise is open to debate. However, what is clear is that there are specific social and health disadvantages associated with teenage motherhood. The children born to teenage mothers tend to have lower than average birthweight, and tend to be brought up in a lone-parent family. Teenage mothers are more likely to leave school at the minimum age and to have lower educational outcomes than their peers; they are also likely to experience unemployment and low incomes when employed. Moreover, there is an elevated rate of infant mortality associated with teenage pregnancy, running at 60 per cent higher than for older women (Botting et al. 1998). There is even evidence of longer-term disadvantages associated with teenage pregnancy. Using the National Survey of Health and Development concerning individuals born in 1946, longitudinal research found teenage parenthood in general to be associated with poorer coronary heart disease risk factors by the age of 52. That these extend to both the mother and father indicates that they are not the product of the biological impact of an early pregnancy, but the result of lifestyle factors. These lifestyle factors seem rooted in a lifelong occupancy of low socio-economic status, lower educational attainment and poorer health behaviours, such as smoking and lack of exercise, at least insofar as they were observed in the sample (Hardy et al. 2009).

4.6 How do parents and children perceive risk?

This section concerns parents' and adolescents' risk perceptions generally and examines the impact that these may have on parenting approaches to younger children and adolescents. The following section applies these to the issue of health-related lifestyle choices and, in particular, examines the implications that they may have for adolescents' risk-taking behaviour.

Parents and risk

The Nuffield Foundation (2009b) reports that through examination of published research, parents now exercise more control over younger children than they have done previously, especially in terms of restricting the range of out-of-home activities available to their children.

There is evidence of a shift in parental attitudes with respect to the perceived safety of children, which may go some way to explaining this change. Playday conducted a UK-wide survey in 2007, involving 1,030 children and 1,031 adults. The results indicated that 71 per cent of adults reported playing in the street or area near their home every day when they were children, compared to only 21 per cent of children today. The principal reason for this change was the attitude that parents took to the risk posed by increased volume of traffic (Lacey 2007).

Citing Hillman et al. (1990), Joshi and MacLean (1995) found that the proportion of independent journeys to school by seven- to eight-year-olds had dropped from 80 per cent in 1971 to 9 per cent in 1990. However, it is not just practical considerations which have informed these changes but also parental risk perceptions. Joshi and MacLean (1995) examined the reasons for parental accompaniment of children to or from school. "Stranger danger" was the reason most frequently given, with three-fifths of parents of children aged seven to nine years old citing it. This was followed by *"child not able to cross roads"* cited by half of parents, and *"school being too far away"* cited by approximately one-third of parents.

Research concerning people's risk perceptions of technological hazards has indicated that it is not the likelihood of a particular negative event occurring by which it is judged to be high risk, but other considerations. These include whether exposure to the hazard is perceived as voluntary, controllable, known, equitable or dreaded, and the numbers likely to be affected by the hazard – the more affected, the greater the risk (Slovic 2000; Slovic et al. 1982). Latterly, attention has been paid to the influence of emotion, particularly in terms of emotional associations with risk judgements and risk-taking behaviour. Where there is a conflict between emotion and calculation, the emotional response usually dictates the judgement or decision (Slovic et al. 2002). Risks are also subject to 'social amplification': some risks assume greater importance because they receive greater attention, particularly through the media, rather than because of their likely eventuality (Kasperson et al. 1988).

The implications for parental risk perceptions are that they are likely to be related only tenuously to the likelihood of particular events occurring, and are likely to be influenced by the attention that a risk has received, the feelings associated with a risk and the possible severity of its consequences. Murrin and Martin (2004) found that parents were most worried about quite rare events affecting their children, such as abduction, but were less concerned about far more likely events, such as accidents in the home. The 10 concerns most frequently cited by parents appear in Table 4.3.

Table 4.3: Concerns expressed by parents about their children and statistical likelihood of the event, 2002–03*

Source: Murrin and Martin (2004)

Risk	Per cent of parents expressing this concern	Likelihood
Hit by a car or lorry	45	Medium
Abducted or murdered	42	Medium
Damaging health by eating too much sugar and too many sweet things	38	High
Too much time watching television or playing computer games	36	High
Growing up too fast	33	High
Becoming the victim of crime	32	High
Eating too much junk food	31	High
Having friends who are a bad influence	28	High
Getting a serious illness	28	Medium
Becoming the victim of physical violence	27	High

* Medium is a likelihood of less than 1/100; higher is any likelihood that is greater than this.

Lewis, Sarre and Burton (2007) reported a strong sense from parents that their children were now growing up in communities that were more dangerous than those in which they themselves had grown up, and that the risks children faced lay outside the home. The parents' approach to managing their children's exposure to such hazards was dependent on their children's age and recognition of their growing independence. The approach to parenting with respect to older children involved negotiating a delicate balance between protecting children and alienating them. The approach adopted towards the older children approaching 16 and above involved setting ground rules for behaviour in the home and keeping in touch by phone when they were away. There was recognition that attempts to control children's behaviour outside the home, however well intentioned, might simply serve to alienate them. The management of younger children's (12 to 15 years) exposure to risks principally involved regulating or managing their time away from home, so as to reduce as far as possible their opportunities to 'loiter' and encourage their 'purposeful use of time'. However, there were widespread expressions of bafflement concerning how to control the kind of friends that their children made.

In addition to the use of rules, Lewis, Sarre and Burton (2007) highlight the pivotal role that trust plays with respect to parents managing their children's exposure to possible risks:

> " ... *most families relied on a complicated set of negotiations with their children, in which the degree to which they trusted their children and their children's judgement played a major part in how far the parents were prepared to let go* ... " (p.86)

Lewis, Sarre and Burton (2007) identify the way in which parents can experience a growing sense of powerlessness as their children increase their independence, with parents having little choice but to rely on trust and negotiation rather than a dictatorial approach. However, the trust that parents have in their children may be somewhat misplaced: there were frequent examples of children misleading their parents and deliberately withholding information. The motivation was not just to avoid punishment, but also to prevent their parent from worrying needlessly.

Adolescence and risk

Over the last century, while the health of children and older people has improved the mortality rate for adolescents (15 to 19 years) from injury and suicide has increased from 11 per cent of total deaths between 1901 and 1910 to 57 per cent in 2003. This increase is linked to health inequalities – inequalities which are more pronounced in adolescence due to the greater ethnic diversity of younger generations. There is also evidence to suggest that risk behaviours such as binge drinking, delinquency and illicit drug use could be contributing to the development of health and social inequalities that eventually have an impact on mortality rates (Viner and Cole 2005).

Adolescents are more likely than adults to engage in risky behaviour. Furthermore, evidence suggests that while adolescent risk-taking behaviour is generally experimental, risk-taking behaviours tend to be clustered in individuals, so individuals who binge-drink are also more likely to smoke (Benthin et al. 1993). The source of adolescent risk-taking is less clear: it may stem from a sense of invulnerability (unrealistic optimism) or a general failure to appreciate certain activities as risky (Cohen et al. 1995).

There is a further issue strongly associated with adolescent risk-taking: that of peer pressure. Evidence from criminology indicates that adolescents tend to commit crimes in groups of two or more, but adults tend to act alone (Gardner and Steinberg 2005). Hensley (1977) examined the phenomenon of 'risky shift' – that in specified conditions, group decisions tend to be more risky than individual decisions – and found a greater shift towards risk from adolescents than those of college age. However, the sample was small and the risky scenarios were abstract hypothetical choice dilemmas rather than ones relating to real-life situations.

However, using a sample of more than 300 individuals and both hypothetical and real-world scenarios, Gardner and Steinberg (2005) found that there was a decline in risk-taking and risky decision-making between adolescence and adulthood. Furthermore, they found that risky shift operated as a function of age: while all groups' decisions became more risky than individuals', the group decisions of middle and late adolescents were more risky than those of adults. A slight disposition towards risk-taking behaviour among adolescents, then, is likely to be exacerbated or compounded by peer influence, an influence to which adolescents have heightened levels of susceptibility to in any case. This susceptibility may be due to limitations in adolescents' psychosocial functioning in areas such as self-reliance, which then has an impact on their capacity to act independently.

The concern that parents express about the influence of their children's friends is then well grounded; however, it is likely to be the children of parents who are indifferent to their child's activities outside the home who are at greatest risk from any negative peer influence (Murrin and Martin 2004).

4.7 What are the trends in lifestyle-related health?

The trends in and health consequences of lifestyle choices concerning diet or exercise, smoking, alcohol consumption and drug use, particularly in terms of their impact on children and adolescents, are examined in this section.

> *Many of the current most common causes of morbidity and premature mortality are linked to a range of individual behaviours such as diet, physical activity levels, smoking and drinking. Current government health strategies place a strong emphasis on reducing ill health through promoting healthy lifestyles.* (ONS 2009b, p.96)

Before examining what people actually do, it is worth considering some of the psychological underpinnings of people's risky lifestyle choices. Previously the nature of people's risk perceptions was considered and this has a bearing on lifestyle choices, helping to explain why lifestyle shifts are slow to occur. The negative health consequences of poor dietary choices and smoking are not immediate but long-term and cumulative, while the benefits (such as they are) are immediate. Furthermore, exposure to the risks associated with particular food choices, smoking and drinking is largely voluntary, and continued exposure is under the individuals' apparent control. These factors serve to minimise the risks psychologically, if they are considered at all. People also have a tendency to be unduly optimistic about the chances of experiencing both positive and negative events, termed 'optimistic bias', which may also contribute to particular lifestyle choices (Weinstein 1980).

Changes in diet and eating

Obesity made its first appearance in the international classification of diseases only as recently as 1948.[4] Obesity has now reached epidemic levels internationally, in both the developed and developing world, and affects all age groups (Kipping et al. 2008). The simple explanation for the increased incidence of obesity is that individuals' energy consumption has increased. Interestingly, while corresponding decreases in levels of physical activity may have contributed to the rise of obesity and positive associations have been identified between obesity and inactivity, the degree to which inactivity is responsible for obesity has not been established (British Medical Association Board of Science 2005).

Obesity is one of the most obvious results of poor dietary choices. Ultimately the consequence for the UK population of such poor choices, such as consuming too much saturated fat, salt and sugar and too little fruit, vegetables and oily fish, is an estimated 70,000 preventable or premature deaths a year[5] (Strategy Unit 2008a).

Western society has become conducive to weight gain, given the greater prevalence and consumption of energy-rich foods and drinks and increase in sedentary occupations, car usage and TV viewing as a pastime (leisure activity). Even though the

---

4   A commonly used metric to assess whether an adult individual is overweight is the Body Mass Index (BMI). The BMI is weight (kg)/height (m)^2. An adult is defined as overweight if their BMI is above 25kg/m^2 and obese if their IBM is above 30kg/m^2 (British Medical Association Board of Science 2005). The situation for children is more complex, as the figures are adjusted for every six months of the child's life, i.e. the BMI definition of overweight and obese in children is age-dependent (see Cole et al. 2000).

5   Dietary recommendations intended to eliminate these premature deaths involve reducing daily salt intake from an average 9g to 6g, saturated fat intake by 2.3 per cent, added sugar intake by 1.75 per cent, and increasing fruit and vegetable intake to five a day (Strategy Unit 2008a).

precise relations between the factors thought to cause weight gain remain obscure, the evidence of widespread weight gain is clear. The period 1997–2007 saw the proportion of men in the UK aged 16 and over classified as obese rise from 17 per cent to 24 per cent. For women the figure rose from 20 per cent to 24 per cent. Additionally, 41 per cent of men and 32 per cent of women were classified as overweight. The total figures for those classified as overweight or obese by 2007 stood at 65 per cent of men and 56 per cent of women.

A similar pattern is evident among children. Between 1995 and 2007 there was a 6 per cent rise in children classified as overweight or obese. By 2007, 30 per cent of all children aged between 2 and 15 years and 16 per cent of all children were classified as obese. This is over a period when average birthweights have changed little. Projections indicate that one-fifth of boys and one-third of girls will be obese by 2020 (British Medical Association Board of Science 2005).

There has been a marked change in the British diet and eating habits since the 1970s. For example, between 1975 and 2000 there was a 20 per cent decline in the time spent eating at home, and correspondingly more time spent eating out. Approximately one in six meals are now eaten outside the home (Strategy Unit 2008b). By 2005 the UK was spending £27.6 billion on eating out, a figure which had risen by 29 per cent since 1995 (Strategy Unit 2008a).

However, perhaps the most striking change is the introduction of and growth in the consumption of convenience foods, such as ready meals, which has increased by 300 per cent since 1977 (Strategy Unit 2008a). Convenience foods such as pizza have become widely available only since the 1970s, but are now firmly established in the national diet. Between 1993 and 2005 the fast food industry increased its sales by 73 per cent. Trends in the consumption of various convenience foods between 1974 and 2007 are indicated in Figure 4.9, which shows a sharp rise since 1974, but a current levelling off or even slight decline.

Figure 4.9: UK household purchased quantities of convenience food, average per person per week, 1974–2007*

Source: Department for Environment, Food and Rural Affairs (2008)

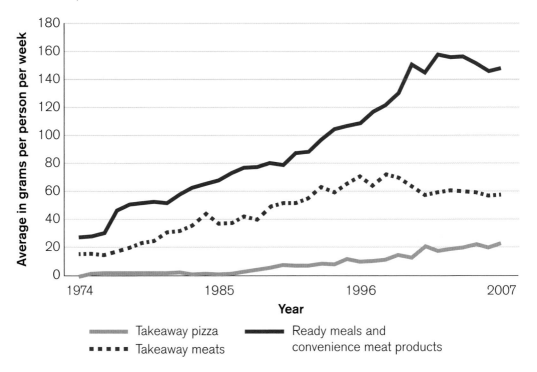

* Adjusted National Food Survey Figures 1974–2000, Expenditure and Food Survey figures 2001–02 onwards.

The growth in eating out and the consumption of convenience foods has led to concerns about the decline of the 'family meal' and people's health. Concerns about this decline may be well placed, if overstated. The Nuffield Foundation (2009b) cites evidence that there has been a slight overall decline in family meals since the 1970s; additionally, the numbers of teenagers eating family meals with their parents once a week or more dropped from 83 per cent in 1986 to 72 per cent in 2006.

The health implications associated with the rise in the consumption of convenience foods and eating out are considerable. Typically, convenience foods are high in fat, sugar and salt, and food eaten out tends to have a greater sugar content and slightly greater fat content. Essentially, such foods are energy-rich. For example, it is estimated that it takes one to two hours of 'extremely vigorous' activity to burn off calories equivalent to a single large-size children's meal ($>=$ 785 kcal) from a fast food restaurant.

When examining food choices, Viner and Cole (2006) found that increases in the BMI for those between 16 and 30 years were linked to consumption of takeaway meals at a rate of at least twice a week, and two or more soft or fizzy drinks a day. The issue of soft or fizzy drinks has particular relevance for children. These drinks are the greatest single source of non-milk extrinsic or 'added' sugar in the average child's diet, and children from a low-income background get even more of their sugar from soft drinks than those from higher income families – with boys from low-income families in particular having the highest added sugar intake (Strategy Unit 2008a).

The issue of high or increased calorific intake may extend beyond processed or convenience foods and soft drinks. The sugar content of fruit has increased in recent decades: apples have approximately 50 per cent more sugar content than they did 30 years ago, so consequently most fruit juice contains approximately the same amount of sugar as soft drinks, about 10g per 100g (Leak 2004). Chickens now contain twice the calories as they did approximately 100 years ago, due to an increase in their fat content and concomitant decrease in protein content. This has been attributed to changes in intensive farming methods (Wang et al. 2004). Further claims have been made about the decline in the mineral content of vegetables, but these are more controversial (Purvis 2005).

Parental influence and children's diets

The diet of the average child in the UK mirrors that of a typical adult's, but generally contains an even greater proportion of sugars and saturated fats (Strategy Unit 2008a). There is evidence that the early years are critical in terms of later health outcomes. Using the 1970 British Cohort Study, Viner and Cole (2005) found that watching more than two hours of TV at the weekend as a child predicted (not to be confused with caused) later adult obesity. Each extra hour watched at weekends at age five increased the likelihood of adult obesity by about 7 per cent.

Research further indicates that childhood obesity is determined before the age of five, but not at birth. By the age of five years a child's weight has little relation to their birthweight, but predicts their likely weight by age nine (Viner and Cole 2005).

Personal preferences, peers, school and the media all exercise an influence on children's dietary habits, but the strongest influence during early childhood comes from parents. Parents act as providers, enforcers and role models (Clark et al. 2007). Parents with dietary or nutritional knowledge are more likely to influence their children's diet positively: levels of such knowledge in mothers were found to be associated with greater levels of children's consumption of both fruit and fibre and lower consumption of fat (Gibson et al. 1998; Variyam et al. 1999). Correspondingly, Lake et al. (1997) found evidence of the intergenerational transmission of obesity: using the 1958

National Child Development Study, children with two overweight parents were themselves more likely to be overweight and at greater risk of obesity in adulthood. Being overweight as a child also disposes the individual to being overweight as an adult by about 50 per cent, as does being the child of overweight parents.

Using a sample of 226 families, Perez-Pastor et al. (2009) found an increased chance of obesity in children if their parents were obese, by gender. Daughters had a greater chance of being obese if their mothers were themselves obese, but not if their fathers were. Conversely, boys were more likely to be obese if their fathers were, but not if their mothers were. The implication of these findings is that the transmission of obesity is less likely to be genetic as behavioural: the authors attribute the difference to 'behavioural sympathy' – daughters copying mothers' lifestyle, and boys copying fathers'.

Clark et al. (2007) examined the literature concerning not what children were eating, but the complementary issue of how parents fed their children, particularly in relation to children's weight gain. Parental food behaviours included:

- control over availability and portion size

- pressure to eat

- using food to reward, to pacify or as a treat.

An early study identified by Clark et al. (2007) had indicated the effect and importance of parental monitoring on the food choices of children aged four to seven. The results indicated not only the positive influence of parental monitoring, but also children's inherent food preferences, their own knowledge about the nutritional or health properties of food, and what they thought their mothers' attitudes to these were likely to be. Children allowed to make free food choices selected a large proportion that were high in sugar, but when simply told that their mothers would monitor their selection, the children's choices were significantly lower in added sugar. When their mothers actually monitored the children's choices, they were lower in total calories, saturated fat and salt than previously (Klesges et al. 1991). These findings suggest that children might well be aware of the kinds of food that parents approve and disapprove of, and what they are expected to eat, yet still seek to evade these constraints when the opportunity presents itself.

However, parental restrictions of child food consumption, particularly snacks, can be counterproductive. Clark et al. (2007) report only one cross-sectional study that failed to find a relationship between parental restriction of a favourite food and child weight. Fisher and Birch (1999) found that restricted foods were subject to greater attention from children than when they were not restricted. Several reasons for this relationship have been suggested: restricted foods become more desirable and subject to greater consumption in the absence of parental control; furthermore, self-control may become attenuated and children possibly develop tendencies to 'eat without hunger'. This should not be interpreted as restriction causing weight gain, but rather as being associated with it. Children may be overweight already, or perceived as being overweight, prior to any imposition of restrictions.

Socio-economic differences in diet and their implications for children's health

Research has indicated a link between parental dietary or nutritional knowledge, which has a positive association with children's diets, and socio-economic variables, such as education (Wardle et al. 2000). When combined with the tendency towards intergenerational transmission of obesity, this suggests that the children most at risk from obesity and other health issues associated with poor dietary habit will be those from families with low socio-economic capital.

Knowledge of a healthy diet is a starting point in making dietary changes, and this differs by socio-economic group. The Food Standards Agency Consumer Survey found that although 78 per cent of respondents had heard of the recommended 'five-a-day' portions of fruit or vegetables, only 58 per cent claimed to have achieved this. Of the respondents in the Food Standards Agency (2008) study, 89 per cent from the upper third socio-economic level correctly identified the five-a-day recommendation, but only 67 per cent from the lowest third did so. These differences in dietary awareness were reflected in behaviour. Figure 4.10 shows that the claimed consumption of five or more portions of fruit or vegetables a day declines with income, particularly in the case of men.

Figure 4.10: Consumption of five or more portions of fruit and vegetables per day by income group and gender, 2007*
Source: ONS (2009u)

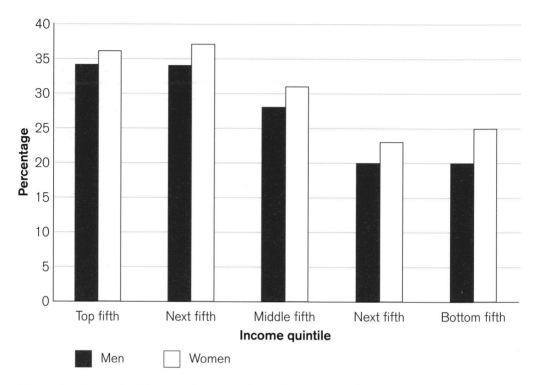

* Equivalised household income (income adjusted by the size of the household) has been used to rank the households into five groups of equal size. The bottom fifth (quintile) group is the 20 per cent of households with the lowest incomes.

The distribution of those who are overweight or obese is not uniform throughout the population. Children from families with manual backgrounds were found to be more likely to be overweight as adults than children from non-manual backgrounds (Power and Moynihan 1988). When examining a sample of 2,127 individuals aged four to 18, Jebb et al. (2003) found those with Asian heritage almost four times as likely to be obese as white individuals.

Obesity has risen and is expected to continue to rise for many groups within the population. Zaninotto et al. (2006) studied adult population estimates of obesity from 2003 and projections to 2010: they found that obesity levels in both manual and non-manual groups for men are expected to increase by about 6 per cent, with greater levels of obesity for the manual group. However, women are predicted to remain at more or less the same level between 2003 and 2010, but with greater levels of obesity for the non-manual group, which stood at 19 per cent in 2003, compared to 28 per cent in the manual group.

Centre for Longitudinal Studies briefings (Centre for Longitudinal Studies 2006) provide a summary of research using longitudinal data concerning obesity, diet and exercise which highlight the likely precursors of being overweight or obese. These are frequently related to socio-economic differences. Using the 1970 British Cohort Study, Viner and Cole (2006) examined changes in individuals' BMI from adolescence through to early adulthood. They found that it was young people from the high socio-economic groups who were more likely to have reduced their BMI. Using the 1958 National Child Development Study data and covering the period 1990–99, Parsons et al. (2005a) found that any lifestyle changes in terms of physical activity or diet were slow to take place. Those that were evident included greater consumption of fruit and vegetables largely by those from higher socio-economic levels, or with a lower BMI. However, reduction in the consumption of fried food was evident among those from lower socio-economic levels.

Using the 1958 National Child Development Study, Parsons et al. (2005) found for both genders that those who took more physical activity at ages 11, 33 and 42 years had a lower BMI, and by age 42 the most active men and women had an appreciably lower BMI than the least active. Viner and Cole (2006) found that four-plus hours of sedentary behaviour a day at 16 years of age was associated with increased BMI by the age of 30.

Consequences of being overweight or obese

The physiological consequences typically associated with being overweight are gathered under the title 'metabolic syndrome'. These include: high levels of blood pressure, blood sugar and cholesterol and abdominal obesity. The health outcomes associated with metabolic syndrome include type-2 diabetes (non-insulin dependent diabetes controlled by diet or tablets) and cardiovascular disease.

Type-2 diabetes has shown a 10.9 per cent increase over the last 30 years in the male adult population, with the steepest growth occurring in the most recent years. The period 1979–2000 saw an increase within the range 4.3–6.9 per cent; between 2000 and 2005, the increase was 11.2 per cent. Thomas et al. (2009) also argue that if all the respondents in their study had maintained a BMI below $22.5 kg/m^2$, then 68 per cent of all the diabetes cases that they observed could have been prevented.

Type-2 diabetes was largely restricted to adults and extremely rare in children: now its prevalence in children in the UK is growing, and obesity is one of the most important risk factors associated with its development (Haines et al. 2007). The appearance of diabetes in the young increases the risk of complications of the ailment later in life, including cardiovascular disease, kidney failure, visual impairment and limb amputation.

A heightened risk of cardiovascular disease is related to being overweight. Cardiovascular disease denotes a group of conditions, including stroke and heart disease, which are caused by a narrowing of blood vessels due to build-up of fat and cholesterol. In 2006, cardiovascular disease was the second most commonly reported longstanding illness in Great Britain. The physical consequences of being overweight or obese are paralleled by a number of negative psychological and social effects. These include low self-esteem, depression and body dissatisfaction, and appear to have a greater impact on girls than boys. Moreover, girls' life chances appear to be affected by being obese: they are less likely to be accepted to university, married or economically well off (British Medical Association Board of Science 2005).

Children's attitudes to those overweight or obese

There is evidence that the negative attitudes of others towards those who are overweight, which may well contribute to the psychological consequences of being overweight, are present already at quite a young age. Children's attitudes to overweight or obese individuals are not charitable and appear to have worsened over the decades. In a 1961 study, 10- to 11-year-olds were given pictures of children suffering various disabilities and obesity, and were asked who they would like to be friends with – invariably, the obese child was ranked last. This was repeated in 2001: the results indicated that the children's social reaction had worsened (British Medical Association Board of Science 2005). A US study reportedly found children as young as four regarding those who were overweight as *"stupid and ugly"* (Devlin 2008).

Smoking

The fatalities associated with smoking account for one-fifth of UK deaths annually. Approximately half of the individuals who start smoking during adolescence and continue lifelong will die of a smoking-related disease, and of these, half will die after the age of 70 and half before, experiencing an average reduction of 21 years of life (Doll et al. 1994).

The prevalence of smoking among the adult population in Great Britain has shown a considerable decrease in recent decades. In 1974, 45 per cent of those aged 16 or above smoked; by 2007, the figure stood at 21 per cent (Figure 4.11).

Figure 4.11: Percentage of adults smoking in Great Britain, 1974–2007*
Source: ONS (2009u)

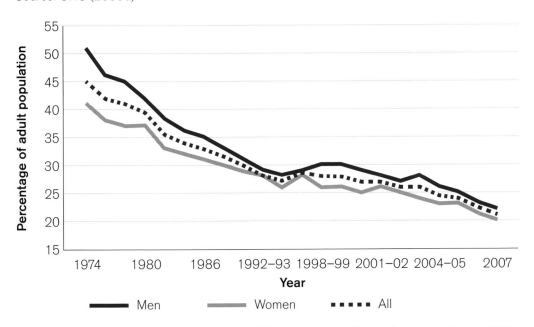

* Adults are those aged 16 and over. From 1988 data are for financial years. Between 1974 and 2000–01 the surveys were run every two years. From 2000–01 data are weighted to compensate for non-response and to match known population distributions.

Research indicates that smoking has been more prevalent in lower socio-economic groups. This continues to be so despite reductions across the population as a whole, as indicated by time trend analysis of General Household Survey data (Davy 2007). According to data from the ONS Omnibus Survey, individuals whose occupations were classified as 'routine or manual' were almost twice as likely to smoke as those whose occupations were classified as 'managerial or professional' (30 per cent, as opposed to 16 per cent), and one-third were more likely to smoke than those in intermediate occupations (19 per cent). Figures from the General Household Survey, the original source of these questions, present a similar pattern (Lader 2008b).

The reduction in the proportion of adult smokers has had an impact on the proportion of children exposed to secondhand or environmental smoke (passive smoking). The inhalation of environmental smoke has been linked to a permanent increase in the risk of asthma and wheezing in younger children, impaired lung function and time off school, in the case of older children.

From the 1980s to 2000 the numbers of children exposed to passive smoking have almost halved. In addition to the general reduction in smoking, the decrease is also attributed to restrictions on smoking in public places. However, children with parents who smoke did not see a reduction in their exposure (Jarvis et al. 2000). Children and young people who remain exposed to environmental smoke are likely to be concentrated in lower socio-economic groups. As well as passive smoking, for most parents their own adolescent children's smoking, alcohol consumption or drug use is of concern. The following sections examine the prevalence of these activities among young people.

Adolescents and smoking

The Drug Use, Smoking and Drinking among Young People in England 2007 survey found that only 6 per cent of young people claimed to be regular smokers (smoking at least one cigarette per week, although the average was six cigarettes per day) – the lowest figure it had ever recorded. This drop exceeds the stated government target of a reduction to 9 per cent by 2010 (Lynch 2008a). The pattern in young people's smoking is indicated in Figure 4.12 and essentially indicates a slow downward trend since 1996, with a precipitous fall between 2006 and 2007 to a low of 6 per cent. The data also indicate a greater prevalence of smoking among teenage girls than boys, the reverse of adult smoking patterns as indicated in Figure 4.11. Furthermore, the difference in prevalence between socio-economic groups in adults does not hold in the case of recent teenagers or young people, those born between 1971 and 1985 (Davy 2007).

Figure 4.12: Percentage of young people aged 11–15 in England smoking
Source: Lynch (2008a)

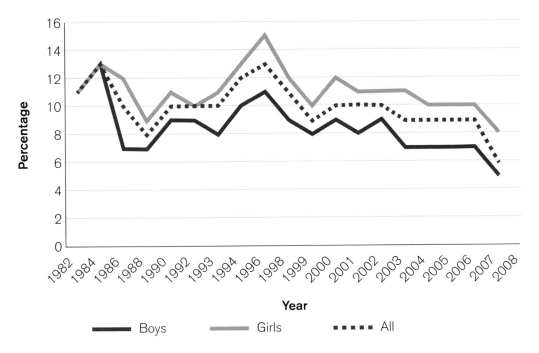

In a US research study, Slovic (2000) identified a number of misconceptions that adolescents held about smoking, which may explain its general prevalence. Young smokers and non-smokers were found to be aware of the likely harm from long-term smoking. However, young smokers were less aware of the short-term impact of smoking, particularly the likelihood and consequences of addiction. A belief in the short-term harmlessness of smoking and an underestimation of the difficulties of quitting mean that many young smokers expect to quit before they become exposed to health risks. The likelihood is that these expectations will not be realised. Slovic (2000) reports findings from the Teenage Attitudes and Practices Survey that, while 32 per cent of those who smoked one pack a day expected to give up in five years' time, six years later only 13 per cent had done so (Allen et al. 1993). Allied to this is that young smokers tend to feel personally less at risk from the health impacts of smoking (Benthin et al. 1993). It may be that corrections to these misconceptions result in the patterns of smoking apparent among the adult population. The rates of quitting are not uniform: Davy (2007) found that cessation rates – at least for those born after 1955 – tend to be higher among non-manual smokers than manual; there is every indication that this trend is likely to continue. Although fewer individuals now smoke, of those who do, it is those who are classified as manual that tend to remain smokers. The consequence is that an increasing proportion of the children who are exposed to environmental smoke will be from lower socio-economic levels, as are the adults who will experience the most serious long-term health impacts of smoking.

Those from higher socio-economic levels tend to respond more to health-related warnings about tobacco consumption. These have far less impact on those from lower socio-economic levels, who tend to be more responsive to cost (Townsend et al. 1994). Addressing the link between the prevalence of smoking and socio-economic status may depend more on manipulating the price of tobacco, or promoting the money to be saved from quitting, rather than providing additional information or reinforcing information about the health effects of smoking.

Alcohol

Adolescents and alcohol

Concerns about excessive drinking and any drug use tend to be concerns about the behaviour of adolescents or young adults, and as discussed previously, drinking, smoking and other risk-taking behaviours tend to be clustered together. Thus Lynch (2008b) found that those who reported that they had recently drunk alcohol also were more likely to report being regular smokers. Regular smoking was more likely among those who indicated that they had taken drugs; also, those who truanted from school or had been excluded from school were more likely to be regular smokers.

Tellingly, the Drug Use, Drinking and Smoking among Young People in England 2007 survey was known as the 'Smoking among Secondary Schoolchildren' survey until 1998. Lynch (2008b) found that one in five 11- to 15-year-olds had drunk alcohol in the past week, this figure having declined from 26 per cent since 2001. However, the level of consumption increased with age. Only 3 per cent of 11-year-olds had drunk alcohol in the past week, but 41 per cent of 15-year-olds claimed they had, with no difference apparent between boys and girls. Figure 4.13 shows the rate of alcohol consumption by gender.

Figure 4.13: Mean alcohol consumption (units) in the last week by gender, 1990–2000

Source: Lynch (2008b)

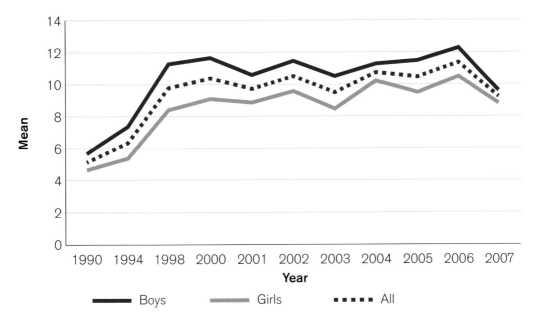

The rate of alcohol consumption between 1990 and 2007, presented in Figure 4.13, does not show any consistent trend. However, there are clear patterns relating to those who have consumed alcohol in the past week: these have been identified as those who were older, white and who had truanted or been excluded from school. Socio-economic distinctions were not evident. In addition, drinking alcohol in the previous week was related to a propensity to take drugs.

Drugs

Adolescents and drugs

The issue of drug-taking is frequently couched in terms of its impact on adolescents or young people. One-quarter of 11- to 15-year-olds reported ever having taken drugs in 2007, compared to 29 per cent in 2001.[6] Over the same period, a fall was evident in the number of young people reporting that they had taken drugs over the past year,

---

6   Although data was gathered on young people's drug use from 1998, the method of collection was altered in 2001, and the data prior to this is not comparable with that gathered from 2001 onwards (Clemens et al. 2008).

from 20 per cent to 17 per cent (Clemens et al. 2008). As with the consumption of alcohol, the incidence of drug use increased with age from 6 per cent of 11-year-olds to 31 per cent of 15-year-olds, although there was little difference by gender. Only 5 per cent of young people reported usually taking drugs at least once a month.

Class A drugs – cocaine, Ecstasy, crack, heroin, LSD, 'magic mushrooms', amphetamines prepared for injection (Home Office 2009) – reportedly had been taken by only 4 per cent of young people: a figure which had remained approximately stable since 2001. The most frequently taken drug was cannabis, but the most frequently reported first drug experience, at 51 per cent, was sniffing a volatile substance such as glue.

Thus the data available does not point to any recent growth in drug consumption by adolescents. As with previously considered risk-taking behaviours, the young people more likely to have taken drugs share many of the characteristics of those who were the most likely to have drunk alcohol and who are regular smokers. Additional factors include being older, male and having truanted or been excluded from school.

4.8 What are the pathways to independence?

Benthin et al. (1993) remark that for at least some young people, engaging in risk-taking behaviour may provide the only perceived path to realising certain goals, such as achieving independence from their parents.

Children's transitions to young adulthood and independence appear to have changed qualitatively over recent decades. There no longer appears to be a *normative ordering along a single pathway (comprising a school-to-work transition followed some years later by a household-and-family-formation transition)"* (Jones 2002, p.2). This kind of pathway perhaps was uniquely prevalent in the 1950s and early 1960s. A more recent form of transition involves 'back-tracking', where young people oscillate between the family and the outside world. At the same time as seeking greater autonomy and psychological independence, many young people stay at home longer so that their financial and physical dependency is prolonged. Perhaps more important than characterising a series of 'non-standard' transitions is Jones's (2002) identification of a 'youth divide' in terms of young people's life chances, which is perceptible in the kind of transition that young people make to adulthood and independence, specifically 'slow-track' and 'fast-track'.

The 'slow-track' pattern occurs mainly within middle-class families but also increasingly in affluent working-class families; it may be influenced as much by factors such as lack of affordable housing, ineligibility for benefits, wariness of commitment to relationships and unstable relationships, as by lifestyle choices. 'Fast-track' patterns involve young people leaving home, entering or attempting to enter the labour market and becoming parents precipitously. Due to the erosion of much welfare support, grants and adequate minimum wages for people at the outset of work careers, they are exposed to considerable risk, perhaps leading eventually to social exclusion.

Jones (2002) suggests that the emphasis placed by recent governments on encouraging families to support themselves may have increased young people's tendency to rely on within-family transference of material resources. In other words, strengthening processes of intergenerational transmission of resources may have led to a widening of the gap between rich and poor.

Risk of social exclusion can involve, or perhaps culminate in, young people becoming NEETs. NEETs stand as a group for whom transition into the labour force and economic independence has effectively stalled. Figures for England in 2008 indicate that 10.3 per cent of 16- to 18-year-olds are NEETs; in 2007 the figure stood at 9.7 per cent, and in 1997 the figure stood at 8.9 per cent. Figure 4.14 shows the trend over the period for which records are available (1985–2008) and although 2008 is higher than 2007, the trend has been one of fluctuation around the 8 to 10 per cent level.

Figure 4.14: Percentage of 16- to 18-year-olds in England classified as NEET, 1985–2008

Source: Department for Children, Schools and Families (2009)

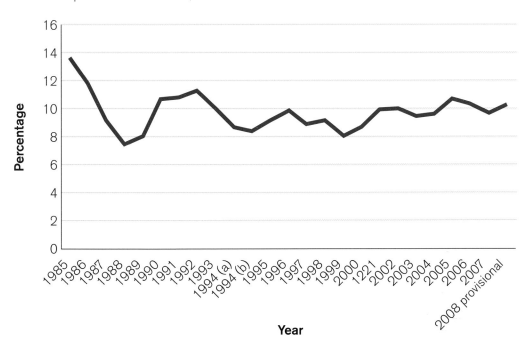

Often, NEET status is explained in terms of early experiences likely to heighten the individual's risk of social exclusion, such as truancy and school exclusion. However, a recent explanatory approach has been to consider how multiple problems and processes of social exclusion combine and what their effect is over time (Webster et al. 2005). Webster et al. (2005) identified a series of likely factors associated with, or predictive of, social exclusion and youth offending and stressed the importance of the intergenerational transmission of disadvantage. These include neighbourhood, employment opportunities, family form and social capital.

Post-war de-industrialisation, the subsequent decline in employment opportunities and abandonment of public housing by the better off (by 1995 half of all local authority households had no breadwinner) have led to a geographical concentration of economic or social disadvantage, and higher levels of NEETs are found in such areas.

The nature of the labour market open to young adults at risk of exclusion, particularly those with few or no qualifications, also limits their opportunities for later inclusion and participation. Areas with a high concentration of NEETs tend to be characterised by the prevalence of low-wage employment. The interventions intended to enhance individuals' transition into the labour market are likely to have little effect, given that the local labour market will be characterised by unstable and low-wage employment opportunities, as Webster et al. state:

> *Young men and women who hold consistently conventional orientations to work continue to circulate around the bottom of the labour market, moving in and out of poor work and unemployment.* (2005, p.4)

Frequently, those at risk of exclusion have been brought up in lone-parent families. Although poor life chances might be associated with having been brought up by a lone parent, this might reflect the influence of poverty rather than anything inherent in lone parenthood and concomitant parenting styles. Financial privation renders it more difficult for parents to be effective.

4.9 Has the role of grandparents in family life altered?

Grandparents' integration with the rest of their family and particularly grandchildren can be gauged to some extent at least by frequency of contact. The data from ONS shown in Figure 4.15 indicates that in 2001, more than 60 per cent of grandparents saw their grandchildren at least once a week, 10 per cent saw them less than once every three months, and 2 per cent did not see them at all.

Figure 4.15: Frequency of grandparents' contact with their grandchildren, Great Britain, 2001*
Source: ONS (2003b)

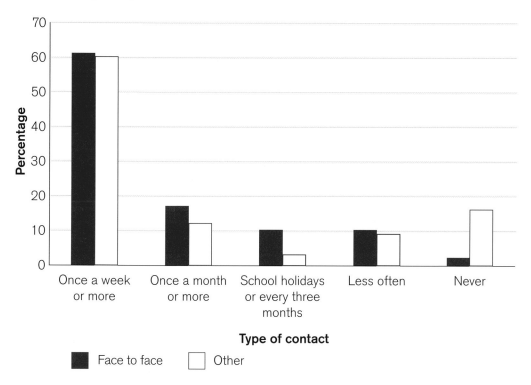

* 'Other' included letter, telephone, fax, email.

The number of three-generation households had declined from about 25 per cent in the 1960s to fewer than 10 per cent in 1998 (Dench and Ogg 2002). Analysis of Millennium Cohort Study data has indicated that only 4 per cent of families had a resident grandparent (Hawkes and Joshi 2007b). However, there were differences by ethnic group. Bangladeshi and Pakistani households tend to be larger than white ones, partly because such households are more likely to contain grandparents, parents and children, and there are also differences by ethnicity in perceived ideal family size, particularly in terms of the number of children (ONS 2003b).

Murphy et al. (1999) estimated that approximately 60 per cent of adults aged between 30 and 50 years, with a living mother, lived within half an hour of them. Clarke (2004) found that proximity varied with age and education. Approximately 75 per cent of those under 70 years lived within half an hour of at least one grandchild; additionally, those with lower educational attainment tended to live closer to their grandchildren (Gray 2005). In a nationally representative survey of 870 grandparents, Clarke (2004) found that grandparents with lower levels of education and those who had manual jobs were more likely to live nearer their grandchildren and had frequent contact with them.

Gray (2005) cites two studies that indicate that the threshold distance – i.e. the distance beyond which the grandparent's involvement in childcare declines – is between 15 and 20 minutes' journey (Arthur et al. 2003; Meltzer 1994).

Despite the constraints that the geographic dispersion of family members creates, Hawkes and Joshi (2007b) found that one in four families received some kind of childcare support from grandparents and that almost all families received some kind of financial support from them. The financial support was more frequent for couple families at 90 per cent than for lone parents at 80 per cent. This difference may be because lone parents are less likely to maintain close relationships with both sets of grandparents. However, the greatest proportion of grandparent childcare is where grandparents provide informal (unpaid) care in the (temporary) absence of parents – usually to enable mothers to take up paid employment. Usually, such childcare is provided by the maternal grandmother (Koslowski 2009).

Gray (2005) identifies the importance of grandparent childcare in allowing mothers the freedom to join or rejoin the workforce if they cannot afford formal childcare or have working hours that preclude the use of formal childcare. Koslowski (2009) cites various estimates of the unpaid value of grandparent childcare: these ranged from £3,886 million a year, through £50 billion to £220 billion.

The importance of (mainly paternal) grandparents for teenage or young fathers was considered in Chapter 3. More generally, grandparents provide the greatest degree of childcare support during their grandchildren's very early years. Of those parents who received grandparent childcare support (from the maternal grandparent only) for their nine-month-old child, only 54 per cent were still receiving it when their child was three years old (Hawkes and Joshi 2007a). The role of grandparents, however, may be subject to pressures derived from the shrinking family: as a childcare resource they remain one of a decreasing number of options in the absence of, or reduction in, the number of other family members such as uncles and aunts. The demand for grandparents to provide informal childcare support is likely to increase, yet, as Gray (2005) points out, rising employment rates amongst the over 50s is likely to act as an impediment to grandparental childcare. Koslowski (2009) comments that the willingness of grandparents to provide childcare support is unlikely to be open-ended, and may not be sustainable.

Recession and family relationships

5

Claire James

Introduction

This final chapter looks at international evidence of the effects of previous recessions on family life, specifically the Great Depression and economic recessions experienced in the 1980s and 1990s. In addition, it examines the current situation of UK families and the likely impact of specific instances of economic hardship, particularly in terms of those most at risk.

5.1 Families in the Great Depression

The earliest in-depth research into the effects of economic hardship on family relationships used studies of a cohort of children born in Berkeley, CA, in 1928–29 who were followed from early childhood, and an older group in Oakland, CA, who were born in 1920–21 and studied from early adolescence onwards.

A high proportion of both middle-class and working-class families in these studies suffered significant income loss in the Great Depression of the 1930s. As fathers' breadwinning ability reduced, mothers and older children took on more responsibility for generating family income. The reaction of the father to this situation and their psychological temperament before it developed seemed to be the key factors linking income loss to family wellbeing. Fathers who tended to be unstable before the Depression frequently became more irritable and explosive in temperament following a heavy loss of income. In these families, marital tension increased. These fathers were also more punitive and arbitrary in disciplining their children (Elder Jr et al. 1986). Mothers' parenting was not affected in the same way, although it has been suggested that the type of measures used may not have been sensitive to mothers' responses to stress (Conger et al. 1992).

Inconsistent or arbitrary parenting increased the risk of child problem behaviour, which could exacerbate the situation further. Even otherwise calm fathers could be arbitrary and punitive towards 'difficult' children, those young children who had showed problem behaviour before the Depression. It was found that where mothers were undemonstrative rather than affectionate – all these risks were heightened (Elder Jr et al. 1986).

The differences found between the two groups were attributed largely to the different ages of the children at this time of stress. The gender of the child was found to make a significant difference. For boys from the Berkeley study, those whose families experienced deprivation at a young age were less likely to be judged as goal-oriented and socially competent as adolescents. This impact was not found for the girls in this study (Elder Jr et al. 1986). For the boys in the Oakland study, who were in their teenage years during the Depression, the impact of family deprivation on their development was quite different. Boys from deprived families took on roles of responsibility such as paid jobs contributing to the family finances, and emerged from the experience generally more resilient and resourceful than others (Elder Jr et al. 1986). For the older girls, the impact of deprivation in adolescence was more negative. Both teenage boys and girls could be targets of rejecting behaviour by fathers, but this was somewhat more so for girls. In addition, girls were more affected by fathers' rejecting behaviour than boys. Daughters of rejecting fathers were less likely to aspire towards high goals and held a lower opinion of themselves. In particular, when the girls in the study were separated into those judged physically 'attractive' and those judged 'unattractive', it was found that the latter were more likely to be rejected by fathers. Physically attractive daughters were not likely to be maltreated by their fathers, no matter how severe the economic pressure. This effect of physical appearance was not found for the adolescent boys (Elder Jr et al. 1985).

5.2 Families in the USA during the 1980s agricultural recession

A combination of factors led to an agricultural crisis in the USA in the 1980s. Many small farmers were unable to pay their debts and lost their farms, with a dramatic effect on rural communities which had been prosperous in the 1970s. The Iowa Youth and Families Project recruited families who had children in the seventh grade (12- or 13-year-olds) during autumn 1989, following them to the present day. A comparison of wellbeing and relationships between families with different levels of economic stress led to the development of a family stress model. This model suggested that in families under economic pressure, this led to depressed mood in both parents. Depressed mood then had a direct impact on marital conflict and quality of parenting. In turn, the quality of the marital relationship affected parenting. Parenting was linked to children's adjustment (Conger and Elder Jr 1994).

Unlike the findings from the Great Depression studies, the emotions and behaviour of both mothers and fathers were affected almost equally by financial difficulties, and disruptions in each parent's interaction with their child had adverse consequences for adolescent development (Conger et al. 1992, 1993). However, findings on the relationships between different factors were not always consistent. For example, in a study of adolescent boys, both marital conflict and mothers' and fathers' depressed mood were found to be related directly to parenting (Conger et al. 1992), whereas in the equivalent study of girls, parents' depressed mood did not affect their parenting directly; rather it affected it indirectly by increasing marital conflict (Conger et al. 1993).

Additional pathways were indicated by the research. Simons et al. (1994) found that economic pressure had a direct effect on young people's adjustment as well as an indirect effect through parenting. However, in general, the evidence supported the proposed model of family functioning.

5.3 Families in Finland in the 1990s recession

During the severe economic crisis of the early 1990s in Finland, unemployment rose from 3.5 per cent in 1990 to 18.4 per cent in 1994 (Kinnunen and Feldt 2004). Although the unemployment rate was higher in lower socio-economic groups, the recession affected families from all social classes. Business enterprises went bankrupt and their entire personnel were laid off. Many families had taken out loans during the preceding boom and experienced difficulties in paying them off. Moreover, the general cost of living went up, affecting all families (Solantaus et al. 2004).

Researchers were unsure as to whether the family stress model developed in the USA would apply to Finnish society, because the Finnish welfare state should buffer families from the worst financial deprivation. Yet despite a more generous welfare state, particularly in terms of unemployment benefits, and a strong norm of dual-earner families, economic stress was found to have a significant impact on family relationships and parenting (Leinonen et al. 2002; Solantaus et al. 2004), highlighting the importance of stress rather than absolute deprivation in family relationships.

The general implications of a recession for families can be serious. Studies on couples and whole families show that economic pressure is linked to psychological distress (depressed mood or irritability) for both men and women, and that this has a negative effect on couple interaction (Conger et al. 1992, 1993, 1999; Leinonen et al. 2002; Solantaus et al. 2004). Furthermore, Papp (2009) found that conflicts about money tend to be more pervasive, problematic and recurrent than conflicts over other issues. Gudmunson et al.'s (2007) research indicated that more frequent disagreements led to more frequent fights and a decrease in quality time together. All three of these factors contributed to men and women perceiving their marriage as less secure for the future.

5.4 UK families and recession

The International Monetary Fund issued a report in March 2009 stating that the global economy would contract by 0.5 to 1 per cent during 2009, the first time that the global economy has failed to grow since the Second World War. Additionally, those countries with the most advanced economies were expected to experience the severest recessions, although an upturn, conditional on the appropriate implementation of a collection of measures, was predicted to take place by 2010 (International Monetary Fund 2009). The stalling of the world economy is a product or consequence of the 2008 financial crisis and the sudden evaporation of credit from global financial systems.

The following sections examine the impact that various features of a recession are likely to have on UK families, beginning with the most critical of all – unemployment.

Unemployment

The British Chambers of Commerce predicted, in January 2009, that over the next two years, UK unemployment would rise to a peak of 3.1 million, affecting some 10 per cent of the workforce (British Chambers of Commerce 2009). As an example, Experian is cited in the *Guardian* as predicting that around 1,400 retail businesses will fail during 2009 (Inman 2009).

The TUC and Fawcett Society have drawn attention to the greater impact that this recession is expected to have on female employment, compared to the recession of the 1990s, where retail distribution and hotels and catering held up relatively well compared to manufacturing and construction. They point out that women are making a greater financial contribution to family incomes than ever before, and approximately one-quarter of all families are headed by lone parents (90 per cent of whom are women). Women may also face particular barriers to finding new jobs because of family responsibilities (Fawcett Society 2009; TUC 2009). However, women have been partly protected so far from the recession because 38 per cent work in the public sector – for example, in public administration, education and health – which has not suffered job losses to the same extent as the private sector as yet. The ONS (2009u) has reported that, to date, men have been more affected than women in the current recession which started in 2008, as the increase in the unemployment rate for men was higher than that for women in the first quarter of 2009, compared to the first quarter of 2008.

Unemployment has been linked to negative consequences for individuals' mental health (Warr et al. 1988). These are not due entirely to associated financial loss. Jahoda (1982, cited in Gershuny 1994) identified five key psychological benefits of employment:

- time structure

- social contact

- collective effort or purpose

- social identity or status

- regular activity.

Jahoda argued that the lack of these was a significant cause of poorer mental health among the unemployed. In addition, job security can be an important factor in health and wellbeing. Burchell (1994) found that men who are in insecure employment at the disadvantaged end of the labour market had about the same level of psychological disadvantage as unemployed men.

A US study on recently unemployed jobseekers (male and female) and their partners found that women who lost their jobs were as depressed as the men. The main gender difference was that for male jobseekers, their partners were on average about as depressed as they were, whereas for female jobseekers, their partners were affected much less. This difference did not seem to be due to the smaller financial impact of female job loss, since income loss was a poor predictor of depression (Howe et al. 2004). For the female partners of male jobseekers, the correlation between their own and their partner's depressive symptoms appeared to be due partly to stressful life events experienced in common. Also, it was mediated partly by their partner's anger-irritation and depressive symptoms, and by the disruption of their relationship. However, in these couples the effects were not all one-way, since, although male jobseekers were not affected by their partner's depressive symptoms, they were affected by their partner's anger-irritation (Howe et al. 2004).

In Finland, Kinnunen and Feldt (2004) found that the longer the total spell of unemployment a man had experienced during the last five years, the poorer his wife's marital adjustment. It was suggested that this could be indicative of men's accumulated problems of social functioning, such as heavy drinking during long periods of unemployment.

In an Australian qualitative study, Lobo and Watkins (1995) describe how couples use different strategies to cope with late-career unemployment. Usually, spouses were supportive at first, seeing redundancy as a short-term phase, but this could become more difficult in the longer term. Many marriages were put under serious strain by the experience. Research indicated that the husband's unemployment had more of a negative impact on the marital relationship in couples with more traditional gender role expectations (Larson 1984).

The impact of unemployment is not confined to the couple relationship. Research with Canadian undergraduates has demonstrated that parental job insecurity or job loss may affect their children by shaping how they perceive paid employment and the labour market. Fathers' experiences of unemployment seemed to be particularly relevant, perhaps because they were more likely to be the main breadwinner in the family. The undergraduates' perceptions of their fathers' job insecurity influenced how positive their own beliefs about work were, and their motivation and feelings of alienation from the world of work. This effect was stronger, the more strongly the young people identified with their fathers (Barling et al. 1998). In addition, these perceptions were related to their belief in the world as being unjust. This belief was linked to negative mood, and negative mood was strongly correlated with grade performance (Barling and Mendelson 1999). Furthermore, perceptions of a parent's job insecurity were linked to students' cognitive difficulties (for example, ability to concentrate), which in turn affected their grades. This effect was greater, the more strongly that the students identified with the parent. For mothers the effect was found only in students whose identification with their mother was high (Barling et al. 1999).

In a national US study, single mothers' employment instability (compared to those steadily employed in jobs paying a living wage) was associated with an increased risk of school drop-out and decline in adolescents' self-esteem and mastery. This effect did not seem to be mediated by differences in income (Kalil and Ziol-Guest 2004).

Analysis of the post-war divorce rate in the USA shows a small but significant correlation between the divorce rate and the unemployment rate in the previous year (South 1985). In the Netherlands, Fischer and Liefbroer (2006) found that lower consumer confidence is linked to higher rates of divorce and relationship break-up. Household-level research supports these findings. Lampard (1994) found that individuals who experience unemployment during one calendar year have a 70 per cent increased chance of divorce in the following year.

Blekesaune (2008) used data from the British Household Panel Survey between 1991 and 2005, and found that unemployment increased the risk of partnership dissolution, and that the difference between the effects of male and female unemployment was not statistically significant. In the analysis, the financial impact of unemployment seemed to be key. Around half of the impact of male unemployment on marital stability could be accounted for by their female partner's perception of their financial situation. The factors linking female unemployment and marital instability were not identified. This research suggests that UK divorce rates are likely to rise as unemployment rises.

Mortgages and repossession

The Council of Mortgage Lenders predicted that by the end of 2009, 500,000 households would be more than three months in arrears. It also predicted that repossessions would rise from 45,000 in 2008 to 75,000 in total in 2009, with the caveat that a significant number of these would be cases of properties being abandoned or property fraud, and a sizeable share would be buy-to-let mortgages (Council of Mortgage Lenders 2008).

Nettleton and Burrows (1999) interviewed adults and children whose homes were repossessed during the 1990s and who had subsequently moved into social housing, and explored the causes and consequences of repossession. In these families, repossession was never an isolated problem but was associated with other family stresses such as job loss or relationship break-up. Often, these problems had been the cause of families being unable to keep up mortgage repayments.

Two factors increase a family's risk of repossession: having only one adult in the household, and having children (in particular, larger families with three or more children) (Bowie-Cairns and Pryce 2005). In 1992, 36 per cent of lone parents faced repayment difficulties compared to 18 per cent of couples with children under 16. In addition, lower socio-economic status increases the probability of repayment difficulty and arrears.

Families in the current recession whose homes are repossessed may find it much harder to access social housing. Families in many areas already face a wait of several years for social housing, with almost 1.8 million households on waiting lists (Local Government Association 2009).

The majority of couples that Nettleton and Burrows (1999) interviewed during the 1990s recession reported suffering from depression. The stress of repossession put severe strain on relationships, with individuals blaming themselves and each other. Some couples separated, temporarily or permanently. Some men said that they had left because they could not cope with the sense of failure. Parents and relations were an important source of support for some, but others found that the stigma of 'failure' meant that they felt unable to ask for help.

It was difficult for families to move on and build a new life, as they could be pursued for outstanding debt for up to 12 years. Where couples had separated, women were particularly vulnerable, since having children resident with them made them easier for companies to locate and pursue settlement of debt. Sometimes these debts had been incurred by their ex-partners and put in their joint names without the women's knowledge. In addition, being a lone parent made it more difficult to take on paid work.

Both parents and children felt shame at moving from owner status to that of tenant. It was difficult to prevent children from knowing what was going on, and difficult for the children themselves to be a part of a process that neither they nor their parents could control. Afterwards, most stayed at the same schools, although for many this meant long journeys. Those who changed schools and those whose family was moved repeatedly by the council found it the most difficult. Some children worried about their parents' wellbeing, some had short-term behaviour problems and others were insecure and lacking in self-confidence following the move.

Debt

Currently, excluding mortgages, the average household debt in the UK (including households with no debts) is more than £9,500 (Credit Action 2009). In terms of families with dependent children, a 2007 review showed that 7 per cent of lone parents and 5 per cent of couples with children were spending more than one-quarter of their gross income on unsecured credit repayments. Further, 27 per cent of lone parents and 8 per cent of couples with children were at least two months behind on one payment, either mortgage, household bill or other debt, and 29 per cent of lone parents and 20 per cent of couples with children identified either their mortgage, other credit and bills or their total repayments as being a heavy burden (Department for Business Enterprise and Regulatory Reform 2007).

Using British Household Panel Study data for 1995 and 2005 to examine the consequences of debt, Brown et al. (2005) found that, after controlling for other factors, individuals with outstanding consumer debt (credit cards, instalment loans on purchases and overdue bills) and those who have higher amounts of such debt were significantly less likely to report complete psychological wellbeing. This was not found for mortgage debt. Debt appeared to increase couple conflict in two ways: as a subject for dispute in itself, and by increasing each person's stress level.

Consumer debt has been found to contribute to changes towards more frequent marital conflict five years later, in addition to the impact of economic pressure (Dew 2007). Large increases in consumer debt predicted a decrease in marital satisfaction, while mortgage debt did not. The main impact of mortgage debt was to increase work hours and decrease couples' time together. Consumer debt also decreased couples' time together, but an increase in work hours was not detected (Dew 2008). However, being in arrears or having difficulty meeting mortgage payments has been shown to have a mental health impact of similar magnitude to that of a job loss or relationship break-up (Taylor et al. 2007).

Managing debt can be more difficult for those who are financially marginalised – those who have no access to standard bank loans, for example, since home credit companies or doorstep lenders charge much higher rates of interest. Any reluctance of banks to lend will mean that more people are likely to find themselves financially marginalised.

It is likely that those with relationship difficulties to start with will be more profoundly affected by economic stress (Conger et al. 1999). Lacking the buffering effect of a supportive relationship, individual stress, unhappiness and negative couple interaction are likely to interact and reinforce each other.

Furthermore, families' pre-recession economic state is likely to influence significantly the impact of additional economic stress. Dearing et al. (2001) found that changes in family income had a much greater impact on the wellbeing of children from poorer families. During the first three years of children's lives, changes in income-to-needs had little impact on children from non-poor families. However, for those whose families were below the poverty threshold at any period during the study, these changes had a significant effect on school readiness, receptive language (understanding requests) and expressive language.

Thus the effect of any of the negative consequences of recession is likely to be disproportionately greater for those families that enter the recession already disadvantaged.

Appendix: data sources

Annual Population Survey

The Annual Population Survey combines results from the Labour Force Survey, the Scottish, Welsh and English Local Labour Force Surveys, and for a limited time, the Annual Population Survey Boost Sample. The survey aims to provide enhanced annual data for England, covering a target sample of more than 300,000 individuals.

Further information: http://www.esds.ac.uk/government/aps/

Annual Survey of Hours and Earnings

The Annual Survey of Hours and Earnings provides information on the levels, distribution and make-up of earnings and hours for employees in Great Britain. It is based on a sample of employee jobs taken from HM Revenue & Customs and from employers. In 2007, the survey was based on approximately 142,000 returns.

Further information: http://www.statistics.gov.uk/statBase/product.asp?vlnk=13101

Avon Longitudinal Study of Parents and Children

This is is long-term health research project with respondents drawn from a particular region of the UK: Avon. It recruited 14,000 mothers during pregnancy from 1991 to 1992, and the health and development of their children has been followed since then.

Further information: http://www.bristol.ac.uk/alspac/

British Cohort Study

The British Cohort Study, initially titled the British Births Survey, collected data about the births and families of babies born in the UK in one particular week in 1970. It was designed initially to examine the social and biological characteristics of the mother in relation to neonatal morbidity, and to compare the results with those of the National Child Development Study. The Northern Ireland sample was dropped subsequently from the seven successive sweeps, which have monitored the respondents' health, education, social and economic status.

Further information: http://www.esds.ac.uk/longitudinal/access/bcs70/l33229.asp

British Household Panel Survey

This survey is conducted by the Institute for Economic and Social Research and was initiated in 1991 with 5,500 respondents from Great Britain. It tracks the same individuals over successive years; in 2001 a further 2,000 respondents were added from Northern Ireland.

Further information: http://www.iser.essex.ac.uk/survey/bhps

British Social Attitudes

This survey, initiated in 1983, is administered by the National Centre for Social Research annually, face-to-face with a current sample of 3,600. It covers a range of social, economic, political and moral issues. Some core issues or questions feature every year, others less frequently.

Further information: http://www.britsocat.com/Body.aspx?control=HomePage

Drug Use, Smoking and Drinking among Young People

This survey is commissioned and the results published by the National Health Service Information Centre. Currently it is conducted by the National Centre for Social Research and the National Foundation for Educational Research. It has been running since 1982, and originally was called 'Smoking among Secondary Schoolchildren'. The survey ran biannually until 1998, and has been an annual undertaking since then. In 2007 the sample size was 7,831 young people (secondary school students) aged 11 to 15, drawn from England.

Further information: http://www.data-archive.ac.uk/findingData/snDescription. asp?sn=6005

Effective Provision of Pre-school Education

This project is the largest European longitudinal study of a national sample of 3,000 young children, specifically of their development between the ages of three and seven. The project looked at background characteristics, the child's home environment and pre-school settings, and later developmental and intellectual outcomes. The project has been extended and will continue to follow the young people until their post-16 choices of education, training and employment.

Further information: http://eppe.ioe.ac.uk/index.htm

Family Resources Survey

This survey collects information on the incomes and circumstances of private households in the UK (or Great Britain before 2002–03). It is sponsored by the Department for Work and Pensions. (Note that no questions concerning ethnicity are asked in Northern Ireland.)

Further information: http://www.dwp.gov.uk/asd/frs/

Labour Force Survey

This survey is a quarterly sample survey of 60,000 households in Great Britain. Its purpose is to provide information on the UK labour market for the development of labour market policies. The questionnaire design, sample selection and interviewing are carried out by the Social and Vital Statistics Division of the Office for National Statistics, on behalf of the Statistical Outputs Group.

Further information: http://www.statistics.gov.uk/statbase/Source.asp?vlnk=358&More=Y

Longitudinal Study of Young People in England

This survey was initiated in 2004 with an initial sample of 15,770 young people in England aged between 13 and 14. The survey contains sample boosts for deprivation factors and ethnicity to ensure an adequate representation of the relevant sub-populations. It is concerned with the transition between secondary school and further education, training or the workplace. The survey gathers data on the young person's family background, personal characteristics, attitudes, experiences and behaviour, income, family environment, schools and educational attainment.

Further information: http://www.esds.ac.uk/longitudinal/access/lsype/L5545.asp

Millennium Cohort Study

This study began in 2001 by following the families of nearly 19,000 children aged nine months in the UK, with over-representation from areas of high child poverty and high minority-ethnic populations. The sample population for the study was drawn from all live births in the UK over 12 months from 1 September 2000 in England and Wales and 1 December 2000 in Scotland and Northern Ireland. There have been three follow-up surveys to date at ages three, five and seven. The study focuses on the social and economic backgrounds of the children, and child development in terms of education, health, employment and parenting of the next generation.

Further information: http://www.cls.ioe.ac.uk/studies.asp?section=000100020001

National Child Development Study

This is a longitudinal study of 17,414 children born in the first week of March 1958. Initially designed to examine the social and obstetric factors associated with stillbirth and death in early infancy, the study contains medical, demographic, social, psychological, educational and economic aspects of the respondents' lives. Follow-ups have been made on seven occasions, the most recent being in 2004.

Further information: http://www.cls.ioe.ac.uk/studies.asp?section=000100020003

National Survey of Health and Development

This survey, the oldest of the British birth cohort studies, has data from birth to age 60 on the health and social circumstances of 5,362 individuals born in England, Scotland or Wales in March 1946. It was designed to identify lifecourse influences on normal and healthy ageing.

Further information: http://www.nshd.mrc.ac.uk/

New Earnings Survey

This survey began in 1972 and was replaced by the Annual Survey of Hours and Earnings in 2004. It was a repeated cross-sectional sample giving information on earnings and employment for one week in April each year in Great Britain.

Further information: http://www.data-archive.ac.uk/findingData/snDescription.asp?sn=2245

ONS Omnibus Survey ('Opinions')

This survey was initiated in 1990, and was designed to provide information quickly in relation to policy issues. It has been run 12 times a year for most of its existence, although there was a period when it was run eight times a year. It features approximately 1,800 individuals aged 15+, one from each household approached. From January 2008, Opinions became a part of the Integrated Household Survey.

Further information: http://www.esds.ac.uk/government/omnibus/

Women and Employment Survey

This survey, taken in 1980, is a cross-sectional representative sample of 5,588 women aged 16 to 59 in Great Britain, and 800 husbands, in order to establish the place of employment or unemployment in women's lives.

Further information: http://www.esds.ac.uk/findingData/snDescription.asp?sn=1746

References

Aldous, J., Mulligan, G.M. and Bjarnason, T. (1998) Fathering over time: what makes the difference? *Journal of Marriage and the Family,* **60(4)**, 809–820.

Ali, R., Binmore, R., Dunstan, S., Greer, J., Matthews, D., Murray, L. and Robinson, S. (2009) *General Household Survey 2007: overview report.* London: Office for National Statistics.

Allen, E., Bonell, C., Strange, V., Copas, A., Stephenson, J., Johnson, A.M. and Oakley, A. (2007) Does the UK government's teenage pregnancy strategy deal with the correct risk factors? Findings from a secondary analysis of data from a randomised trial of sex education and their implications for policy. *Journal of Epidemiology and Community Health,* **61(1)**, 20–27.

Allen, K.A., Moss, A., Giovino, G.A., Shopland, D.R. and Pierce, J.P. (1993) Teenage tobacco use: data. Estimates from the Teenage Attitudes and Practices Survey, United States. *Advance Data from Vital and Health Statistics,* **224**, 1–20.

Allen, P. and Macrae, F. (2009) France cracks down on children's mobile phone use, but Britain still ignoring warnings. *Daily Mail,* 11 January. Online at http://www.dailymail.co.uk/health/article-1112123/France-cracks-childrens-mobile-phone-use-Britain-ignoring-warnings.html

Amato, P. and Gilbreth, J.G. (1999) Non-resident fathers and children's well-being. *Journal of Marriage and the Family,* **61(3)**, 557–573.

Anderson, N., Marray, L. and Brownlie, J. (2002) *Disciplining children: research with parents in Scotland.* Edinburgh: Scottish Executive Central Research Unit.

Arai, L. (2009) What a difference a decade makes: rethinking teenage pregnancy as a problem. *Social Policy and Society,* **8(2)**, 171–183.

Arthur, S., Snape, D. and Dench, G. (2003) *The moral economy of grandparenting.* London: National Centre for Social Research.

Barling, J. and Mendelson, M. (1999) Parents' job insecurity affects children's grade performance through the indirect effects of beliefs in an unjust world and negative mood. *Journal of Occupational Health Psychology,* **4(4)**, 347–355.

Barling, J., Dupre, K.E. and Hepburn, C.G. (1998) Effects of parents' job insecurity on children's work beliefs and attitudes. *Journal of Applied Psychology,* **83(1)**, 112–118.

Barling, J., Zacharatos, A. and Hepburn, C.G. (1999) Parents' job insecurity affects children's academic performance through cognitive difficulties. *Journal of Applied Psychology,* **84(3)**, 437–444.

Barlow, A., Burgoyne, C., Clery, E. and Smithson, J. (2008) Cohabitation and the law: myths, money and the media. In A. Park, J. Curtice and K. Thomson (Eds), *British Social Attitudes: the 24th report* (pp.29–51). London: Sage.

Barlow, A., Duncan, S., James, G. and Park, A. (2001) Just a piece of paper? Marriage and cohabitation. In A. Park, J. Curtice and K. Thomson (Eds), *British Social Attitudes: the 18th report. Public policy, social ties* (pp.29–57). London: Sage.

Barnes, M. and Bryson, C. (2004) *Keep time for children: the incidence of weekend working.* London: National Centre for Social Research.

Barrett, H. (2004) *UK Family trends: 1994–2004.* London: Family and Parenting Institute.

Beck, U. (1992) *Risk society: towards a new modernity.* London: Sage.

Becker, G. (1981) *A treatise on the family.* Cambridge, MA: Harvard University Press.

Becker, G.S., Landes, E.M. and Michael, R.T. (1977) An economic analysis of marital instability. *Journal of Political Economy,* **85(6)**, 1141–1187.

Bell, A., Bryson, C., Barnes, M. and O'Shea, R. (2005) *Use of childcare among families from minority ethnic backgrounds.* London: National Centre for Social Research.

Bellamy, K. and Rake, K. (2005) Money, money, money: is it still a rich man's world? Online at http://www.fawcettsociety.org.uk/documents/£££20Audit%20full%20report.pdf

Belsky, J. and Volling B.L. (1987) Mothering, fathering, and material interaction in the family triad during infancy: exploring family systems processes. In P.W. Berman and F.A. Pederson (Eds), *Men's transitions to parenthood: longitudinal studies of early family experience* (pp.37–64). Hillsdale, NJ: Erlbaum.

Bengston, V.L. (2001) Burgess Award Lecture: beyond the nuclear family – the increasing importance of multigenerational bonds. *Journal of Marriage and the Family,* **63(1)**, 1–16.

Benthin, A., Slovic, P. and Severson, H. (1993) A psychometric study of adolescent risk perception. *Journal of Adolescence,* **16(2)**, 153–168.

Berrington, A. (2004) Perpetual postponers? Women's, men's and couple's fertility intentions and subsequent fertility behaviour. *Population Trends,* **117**, 9–19.

Berthoud, R. (2001) Teenage births to ethnic minority women. *Population Trends,* **104**, 12–17.

Berthoud, R. and Robson, K. (2001) The outcomes of teenage motherhood in Europe. *Innocenti Working Paper.* Florence: Unicef Innocenti Research Centre.

Bianchi, S.M., Milkie, M.A., Sayer, L.C. and Robinson, J.P. (2000) Is anyone doing the housework? Trends in the gender division of household labour. *Social Forces,* **229(1)**, 191–228.

Blackwell, A. and Dawe, F. (2003) *Non-resident parental contact.* London: Office for National Statistics.

Blekesaune, M. (2008) Unemployment and partnership dissolution. *ISER Working Paper series.* Colchester: Institute for Social and Economic Research, University of Essex.

Boheim, R. and Ermisch, J. (2001) Partnership dissolution in the UK: the role of economic circumstances. *Oxford Bulletin of Economics and Statistics,* **63(2)**, 197–208.

Booth, J. (2004) Majority want right to smack their children. *The Times,* 12 April. Online at http://www.timesonline.co.uk/tol/news/uk/article821585.ece

Botting, B., Rosato, M. and Wood, R. (1998) Teenage mothers and the health of their children. *Population Trends,* **93**, 19–28.

Bowie-Cairns, H. and Pryce, G. (2005) Trends in mortgage borrowers' repayment difficulties. *Housing Finance,* **11(July)**, 1–12.

Bowlby, J. (1969) *Attachment and loss.* Harmondsworth: Penguin.

Boyle, P.J., Kulu, H., Cooke, T., Gayle, V. and Mulder, C.H. (2006) The effect of moving on union dissolution. *MPIDR Working Paper.* Rostock: Max Planck Institute for Demographic Research.

Boyson, R. and Thorpe, L. (2002) *Equal protection for children: an overview of the experience of countries that accord children full legal protection from physical punishment.* London: NSPCC.

Bradshaw, J., Finch, N. and Miles, J.N.V. (2005) Deprivation and variations in teenage conceptions and abortions in England. *Journal of Family Planning and Reproductive Health Care,* **31(1)**, 15–19.

Brannen, J., Moss, P., Owen, C. and Wale, C. (1997) *Mothers, fathers and employment: parents and the labour market in Britain 1984–1994.* London: Department for Education and Employment.

Bray, H. (2008) 2006-based national population projections for the UK and constituent countries. *Population Trends,* **131**, 8–18.

British Chambers of Commerce (2009) UK GDP set to fall more than in 1990s recession. Press release.

British Medical Association Board of Science (2005) *Preventing childhood obesity.* London: British Medical Association.

British Social Attitudes Information System (2009) *British Social Attitudes Survey.* Online at http://www.britsocat.com/Body.aspx?control=HomePage

Brook (2009) *Teenage conceptions: statistics and trends.* London: Brook.

Brown, S., Taylor, K. and Wheatley Price, S. (2005) Debt and distress: evaluating the psychological cost of credit. *Journal of Economic Psychology,* **26(5),** 642–663.

Buijzen, M. and Valkenburg, P.M. (2003) The effects of television advertising on materialism, parent–child conflict, and unhappiness: a review of research. *Journal of Applied Developmental Psychology,* **24(5)**, 437–456.

Bunting, L. and McAuley, C. (2004) Research review: teenage pregnancy and parenthood: the role of fathers. *Child and Family Social Work,* **9(3)**, 295–303.

Bunting, M. (2004) *Willing slaves: how the overwork culture is ruling our lives.* New York: HarperCollins.

Burchell, B. (1994) The effects of labour market position, job insecurity, and unemployment on unemployment and psychological health. In D. Gallie, C. Marsh and C. Vogler (Eds), *Social change and the experience of unemployment* (pp.188–212). Oxford: Oxford University Press.

Burghes, L., Clarke, L. and Cronin, N. (1997) *Fathers and fatherhood in Britain. Occasional Paper.* London: Family Policy Studies Centre/Joseph Rowntree Foundation.

Bynner, J. and Parsons, S. (1999) *Young people not in employment, education or training and social exclusion. Analysis of the British Cohort Study 1970 for the Social Exclusion Unit.* London: Social Exclusion Unit.

Callender, C., Millward, N., Lissenburgh, S. and Forth, J. (1997) *Maternity rights and benefits in Britain 1996.* Norwich: The Stationery Office.

Centre for Longitudinal Studies (2006) *CLS briefings: obesity, diet and exercise.* London: Centre for Longitudinal Studies.

Chan, T.W. and Halpin, B. (2008) *The instability of divorce risk factors in the UK.* Oxford: University of Oxford.

Chartered Management Institute (2009) *Managers in the UK.* Online at http://www.managers.org.uk/content_1.aspx?id=10:293id=10:290id=10:9

CHILDWISE (2009) *CHILDWISE trends report.* Online at http://www.childwise.co.uk/childwise-published-research-detail.asp?PUBLISH=53

Clark, H.R., Goyder, E., Bissell, P., Blank, L. and Peters, J. (2007) How do parents' child-feeding behaviours influence child weight? Implications for childhood obesity policy. *Journal of Public Health,* **29(2)**, 132–141.

Clarke, L. (2003) *Grandparenthood in Britain.* Paper presented at the 8th Australian Institute of Family Studies Conference, Centre for Population Studies, London School of Hygiene and Tropical Medicine, 12–14 February.

Clarke, L. (2004) *Grandparenthood in Britain.* Online at http://www.aifs.gov.au/institute/afrc8/clarke2.pdf

Clarke, L. and Cairns, H. (2001) Grandparents and the care of children: the research evidence. In B. Broad (Ed.), *Kinship care: the placement choice for children and young people* (pp.11–20). Lyme Regis: Russell House.

Clarke, L. and Thomson, K. (2001–02) Teenage mums. In A. Park, J. Curtice, K. Thomson, L. Jarvis and C. Bromley (Eds), *British social attitudes: public policy, social ties* (pp. 59–79). London: National Centre for Social Research.

Clemens, S., Jotangia, D., Nicholson, S. and Pigott, S. (2008) Drug use. In E. Fuller (Ed.), *Drug use, smoking and drinking among young people in England in 2007,* (pp.17–106). London: NHS Health and Social Care Information Centre.

Cohen, L.D., Macfarlane, S., Yanes, C. and Imai, W.K. (1995) Risk-perception: differences between adolescents and adults. *Health Psychology,* **14(3)**, 217–222.

Cole, T.J., Bellizzi, M.C., Flegal, K.M. and Dietz, W.H. (2000) Establishing a standard definition for child overweight and obesity worldwide: international survey. *British Medical Journal,* **320(7244)**, 1240–1243.

Coleman, J.S. (1988) Social capital in the creation of human capital. *American Journal of Sociology,* **94(supp.)**, S95–S120.

Collishaw, S., Maughan, B., Goodman, R. and Pickles, A. (2004) Time trends in adolescent mental health. *Journal of Child Psychology and Psychiatry,* **45(8)**, 1350–1362.

Coltrane, S. (1996) *Family man: fatherhood, housework, and gender equity.* New York: Oxford University Press.

Conger, R.D. and Elder Jr, G.H. (1994) Families in troubled times: the Iowa Youth and Families project. In R.D. Conger and G.H. Elder Jr, *Families in troubled times: adapting to change in rural America* (pp.3–20). Hawthorne, NY: Aldine de Gruyter.

Conger, R.D., Conger, K.J., Elder Jr, G.H., Lorenz, F.O., Simons, R.L. and Whitbeck, L.B. (1992) A family process model of economic hardship and adjustment of early adolescent boys. *Child Development,* **63(3)**, 526–541.

Conger, R.D., Conger, K.J., Elder Jr, G.H., Lorenz, F.O., Simons, R.L. and Whitbeck, L.B. (1993) Family economic stress and adjustment of early adolescent girls. *Developmental Psychology,* **29(2)**, 206–219.

Conger, R.D., Rueter, M.A. and Elder Jr, G.H. (1999) Couple resilience to economic pressure. *Journal of Personality and Social Psychology,* **76(1),** 54–71.

Council of Mortgage Lenders (2008) *Market commentary, 18 December 2008.* Online at http://www.cml.org.uk/cml/publications/marketcommentary/109

Cowen, C. and Cowen, P.A. (1987) Men's involvement in parenthood: identifying the antecedents and understanding the barriers. In P.W. Berman and F.A. Pederson (Eds), *Men's transformation to parenthood: longitudinal studies of early family experiences* (pp. 145–174). Hillsdale, NJ: Erlbaum.

Credit Action (2009) *Debt facts and figures, 2 March 2009.* Online at http://www.creditaction.org.uk/assets/PDF/statistics/2009/march-2009.pdf

Crompton, R. and Lyonette, C. (2005) The new gender essentialism: domestic and family 'choices' and their relation to attitudes. *British Journal of Sociology,* **56(4)**, 601–620.

Crompton, R. and Lyonette, C. (2009) Who does the housework? The division of labour within the home. In A. Park, J. Curtis, K. Thomson, M. Phillips and E. Clery (Eds), *British Social Attitudes: the 25th report* (pp.33–80). London: Sage.

D'Alessio, M., Laghi, F. and Baiocco, R. (2009) Attitudes toward TV advertising: a measure for children. *Journal of Applied Developmental Psychology,* **30(4)**, 409–418.

Daily Mail Reporter (2009) Worried parents can track children with GPS locator watch. *Daily Mail,* 7 January. Online at http://www.dailymail.co.uk/sciencetech/article-1106883/Worried-parents-track-children-GPS-locator-watch.html

Dale, A., Lindley, H., Dex, S. and Rafferty, A. (2008) Ethnic differences in women's labour market activity. In J. Scott, S. Dex and H. Joshi (Eds), *Women and employment: changing lives and new challenges* (pp.81–106). Cheltenham: Edward Elgar.

Davy, M. (2007) Socio-economic inequalities in smoking: an examination of generational trends in Great Britain. *Health Statistics Quarterly,* **34**, 26–34.

Daycare Trust (2009) *Childcare Costs Survey 2009.* London: Daycare Trust.

Dean, H. (2008) Flexibility or flexploitation? Problems with work–life balance in a low-income neighbourhood. In T. Maltby, K. Kennet and K. Rummery (Eds), *Social policy review 20: analysis and debate in social policy, 2008* (pp.113–132). Bristol: Policy Press.

Dearden, K., Hale, C. and Woolley, T. (1995) The antecedents of teen fatherhood: a retrospective case-control study of Great Britain youth. *American Journal of Public Health,* **85(4)**, 551–554.

Dearing, E., McCartney, K. and Taylor, B. (2001) Change in family income-to-needs matters more for children with less. *Child Development,* **72(6)**, 1779–1793.

Dench, G. and Ogg, J. (2002) *Grandparenting in Britain.* London: Institute of Community Studies.

Department for Business Enterprise and Regulatory Reform (2007) *Tackling over-indebtedness: annual report 2007.* London: Department for Business, Enterprise and Regulatory Reform.

Department for Business Enterprise and Regulatory Reform (2009) *Work and Families Act 2006.* Online at http://www.berr.gov.uk/whatwedo/employment/employment-legislation/workandfamiliesact/index.html

Department for Children, Schools and Families (2007) *Review of Section 58 of the Children's Act 2004.* London: Department for Children, Schools and Families.

Department for Children, Schools and Families (2008a) *The impact of parental involvement on children's education.* London: Department for Children, Schools and Families.

Department for Children, Schools and Families (2008b) *Departmental report 2008.* London: Department for Children, Schools and Families.

Department for Children, Schools and Families (2009) *Participation in education, training and employment by 16–18 year olds in England.* Online at http://www.dcsf.gov.uk/rsgateway/DB/SFR/s000849/SFR12_2009Ratesv2.xls#'A13'!A1

Department for Education and Employment (1998) *Green Paper: meeting the childcare challenge – executive summary.* London: Department for Education and Employment.

Department for Environment, Food and Rural Affairs (2008) *UK household purchased quantities of food and drink.* Online at https://statistics.defra.gov.uk/esg/statnot/efsstatnot.pdf

Department for Work and Pensions (2009a) *Quintile distribution of income for individuals by various family and household characteristics, United Kingdom.* Online at http://research.dwp.gov.uk/asd/hbai/hbai2007/excel_files/chapters/chapter_3_excel_hbai08.xls

Department for Work and Pensions (2009b) *Lone parents.* Online at http://www.dwp.gov.uk/welfarereform/parents.asp

Department for Work and Pensions (2009c) *About us.* Online at http://www.dwp.gov.uk/aboutus/

Department of Health (2008) *Changes in food and drink advertising and promotion to children.* London: Department of Health.

Department of Transport (2009) *Transport trends: 2008 edition. Section 4: variations in personal travel and access to services.* London: Department of Transport.

Desforges, C. and Abouchaar, A. (2003) *The impact of parental involvement, parental support and family education on pupil achievement and adjustment: a literature review.* Research Report. London: Department for Education and Schools.

Deutsch, F.M., Lussier J.B. and Servis, L.J. (1993) Husbands at home: predictors of paternal participation in child care and housework. *Journal of Personality and Social Psychology,* **65(6)**, 1154–1166.

Devlin, K. (2008) Four-year-olds think fat people are 'stupid and ugly'. *Daily Telegraph,* 5 August. Online at http://www.telegraph.co.uk/news/uknews/2504562/Four-year-olds-think-fat-people-are-stupid-and-ugly.html

Dew, J. (2007) Two sides of the same coin? The differing roles of assets and consumer debt in marriage. *Journal of Family and Economic Issues,* **28(1)**, 89–104.

Dew, J. (2008) Debt change and marital satisfaction change in recently married couples. *Family Relations,* **57(1)**, 60–71.

Dex, S. (2003a) *Work and family life in the 21st century.* York: Joseph Rowntree Foundation.

Dex, S. (2003b) *Families and work in the twenty-first century.* York: Joseph Rowntree Foundation.

Dex, S., Ward, K. and Joshi, H. (2006) Changes in women's occupations and occupational mobility over 25 years. Paper for Women and Employment Survey, Centre for Longitudinal Studies.

Dex, S., Ward, K. and Joshi, H. (2008) Changes in women's occupations and occupational mobility over 25 years. In J. Scott, S. Dex and H. Joshi (Eds), *Women and employment: changing lives and new challenges* (pp.54–80). Cheltenham: Edward Elgar.

Directgov (2009) *Parents: parental leave.* Online at http://www.direct.gov.uk/en/Parents/Moneyandworkentitlements/WorkAndFamilies/Parentalleaveandflexibleworking/DG_10029416

Dittmar, H. (2004) Are you what you have? *The Psychologist,* **17(4)**, 206–210.

Doll, R., Peto, R., Wheatley, K., Gray, R. and Sutherland, I. (1994) Mortality in relation to smoking: 40 years' observations on male British doctors. *British Medical Journal,* **309(7455)**, 901–911.

Duncan, S. (2005) Mothering, class and rationality. *Sociological Review,* **53(11)**, 50–76.

Duncan, S. (2007) What's the problem with teenage parents? And what's the problem with policy? *Critical Social Policy,* **27(3)**, 307–334.

Duncan, S. and Edwards, R. (1999) *Lone mothers, paid work and gendered moral rationalities.* London: Macmillan.

Duncan, S. and Phillips, M. (2008) New families? Tradition and change in modern relationships. In A. Park, J. Curtice and K. Thomson (Eds), *British Social Attitudes: the 24th report* (pp.1–28). London: Sage.

Duncan, S. and Smith, D.P. (2006) Individualism versus the geography of 'new' families. *Families Social Capital ESRC Research Group Working Papers.* London: South Bank University.

Dunn, J. (2004) Annotation: children's relationships with their nonresident fathers. *Journal of Child Psychology and Psychiatry,* **45(4)**, 659–671.

Dunn, J. and Deater-Deckard, K. (2001) *Children's views of their changing families.* York: Joseph Rowntree Foundation.

Dunnell, K. (2007) The changing demographic picture of the UK: national statistician's annual article on the population. *Population Trends,* **130**, 9–21.

Durham, M.G. (2008) *The Lolita effect: the media sexualization of young girls and what we can do about it.* Woodstock, NY: Overlook Press.

Dustmann, C. and Preston, I.P. (2007) Racial and economic factors in attitudes to immigration. *B.E. Journal of Economic Analysis Policy,* **7(1)**, Article 62.

Dyhouse, C. (2008) Gaining places: stagnation and growth in the proportion of women in universities. ESRC research project summary, ESRC RES-000-22-0139. Online at http://www.esrc.ac.uk/ESRCInfoCentre/Plain_English_Summaries/LLH/health_wellbeing/index456.aspx

Ehrman, R. (2009) *The power of numbers: why Europe needs to get younger.* London: Policy Exchange.

Elder Jr, G.H., Caspi, A. and van Nguyen, T. (1986) Resourceful and vulnerable children: family influence in hard times. In R.K. Silbereisen, K. Eyferth and G. Rudinger (Eds), *Development as action in context* (pp.167–186). New York: Springer-Verlag.

Elder Jr, G.H., van Nguyen, T. and Caspi, A. (1985) Linking family hardship to children's lives. *Child Development,* **56(2)**, 361–375.

Ellison, G., Barker, A. and Kulasuriya, T. (2009) Work and care: a study of modern parents. Equality and Human Rights Commission, research report 15. Online at http://www.equalityhumanrights.com/en/publicationsandresources/Documents/Equalities/Work_and_care_modern_parents_15_report.pdf

Equal Opportunities Commission (2005a) *Britain's hidden brain drain: final report. The EOC's investigation into flexible and part-time working.* Manchester: Equal Opportunities Commission.

Equal Opportunities Commission (2005b) *Then and now: 30 years of the Sex Discrimination Act.* Manchester: Equal Opportunities Commission.

Equal Opportunities Commission (2005c) *Reasons for working part-time, 2004.* Online at http://83.137.212.42/sitearchive/eoc/Default5a09.html?page=17923

Ermisch, J. (2001) Births outside marriage: the real story. *The Edge,* **8**, 8–9.

Ermisch, J. and M. Francesconi (2001) Family structure and children's achievements. *Journal of Population Economics,* **14(2)**, 249–270.

Ermisch, J., Francesconi, M. and Pevalin, D.J. (2001) *Outcomes for children of poverty. Research report no. 158.* London: Department for Work and Pensions.

European Trade Union Confederation (2006) *The European Union's Lisbon Strategy.* Online at http://www.etuc.org/a/652

Eurostat (2009a) *Live births outside marriage: share of all live births (%).* Online at http://epp.eurostat.ec.europa.eu/tgm/table.do?tab=table&init=1&language=en&pcode=tps00018&plugin=0

Eurostat (2009b) *Employment rate by gender.* Online at http://epp.eurostat.ec.europa.eu/tgm/table.do?tab=tablelanguage=enpcode=tsiem010tableSelection=1footnotes=yeslabeling=labelsplugin=1

Eurostat (2009c) *Gender pay gap in unadjusted form in percentage (national sources: 1994 to 2006).* Online at http://epp.eurostat.ec.europa.eu/portal/page/portal/product_results/search_results?mo=containsallms=gender+pay+gapsaa=p_action=SUBMITl=usco=equalci=,po=equalpi=

Fawcett Society (2009) *Are women bearing the burden of the recession?* London: Fawcett Society.

Feijten, P., Boyle, P., Feng, Z., Gayle, V. and Graham, E. (2009) Stepparenting and mental health. In J. Stillwell, E. Coast and D. Kneale (Eds), *Fertility, living arrangements, care and mobility* (pp.151–170). London: Springer.

Feinstein, L. and Symons, J. (1999) Attainment in secondary school. *Oxford Economic Papers* **51(2)**, 300–321.

Ferri, E. and Smith, E. (1996) *Parenting in the 1990s.* London: Family Policy Studies Centre.

Fife-Schaw, C. (1995) *Surveys and sampling issues.* In G. Breakwell, S. Hammond and C. Fife-Schaw (Eds), *Research methods in psychology* (pp.99–115). London: Sage.

Fischer, T. and Liefbroer, A.C. (2006) For richer, for poorer: the impact of macroeconomic conditions on union dissolution rates in the Netherlands, 1972–1996. *European Sociological Review,* **22(5)**, 519–532.

Fisher, J.O. and Birch, L.L. (1999) Restricting access to palatable foods affects children's behavioral response, food selection and intake. *American Journal of Clinical Nutrition,* **69(6)**, 1264–1272.

Fisher, K., McCulloch, A. and Gershuny, J. (1999) *British fathers and children. Report for Channel 4 Dispatches.* Colchester: Institute of Social and Economic Research, University of Essex.

Flouri, E. and Buchanan, A. (2002) Father involvement in childhood and trouble with the police in adolescence: findings from the 1958 British cohort. *Journal of Interpersonal Violence,* **17(6)**, 689–701.

Flouri, E. and Buchanan, A. (2003a) The role of father involvement and mother involvement in adolescents' psychological well being. *British Journal of Social Work,* **33(3)**, 399–400.

Flouri, E. and Buchanan, A. (2003b) What predicts fathers' involvement with their children? A prospective study of intact families. *British Journal of Developmental Psychology,* **21(1)**, 141–153.

Flouri, E. and Buchanan, A. (2004) Early father's and mother's involvement and child's later educational outcomes. *British Journal of Educational Psychology,* **74(2)**, 141–153.

Flouri, E., Buchanan, A. and Bream, V. (2002) Adolescents' perceptions of their fathers' involvement: significance to school attitudes. *Psychology in the Schools,* **39(5)**, 575–582.

Food Standards Agency (2008*) Consumer attitudes to food standards, wave 8: UK report.* London: Food Standards Agency.

Ford, R. (2008) Is racial prejudice declining in Britain? *British Journal of Sociology,* **59(4)**, 609–636.

Gardner, M. and Steinberg, L. (2005) Peer influence on risk taking: risk preference, and risky decision making in adolescence and adulthood – an experimental study. *Developmental Psychology,* **41(4)**, 625–635.

Gauthier, A.H., Smeeding, T. and Furstenberg Jr, F.F. (2004) Do we invest less time in children? Trends in parental time in selected industrialised countries since the 1960s. *Population and Development Review,* **30(4)**, 647–671.

George, A. and Hansen, K. (2007) *Millennium Cohort Study: childcare. Briefing 11.* London: Institute of Education.

Gershuny, J. (1994) The psychological consequences of unemployment: an assessment of the Jahoda thesis. In D. Gallie, C. Marsh and C. Vogler (Eds), *Social change and the experience of unemployment* (pp.213–230). Oxford: Oxford University Press.

Gershuny, J. (2000) *Changing times: work and leisure in postindustrial society.* Oxford: Oxford University Press.

Ghate, D., Hazel, N., Creighton, S., Finch, S. and Field, J. (2003) *The national study of parents, children and discipline in Britain: summary of key findings.* London: Policy Research Bureau.

Gibson, E.L., Wardle, J. and Watss, C.J. (1998) Fruit and vegetable consumption, nutritional knowledge and beliefs in mothers and children. *Appetite,* **31(2)**, 205–228.

Gimson, S. (2008) *Listening to mother: making Britain mother-friendly. Discussion paper.* Online at http://www.familyandparenting.org/Filestore//Documents/PolicyDiscussionPapers/motherhood-FINAL_web.pdf

Gingerbread (2001) *Becoming visible: focus on lone fathers.* London: Gingerbread.

Goldacre, B. (2006) How I stalked my girlfriend. *Guardian,* 1 February. Online at http://www.guardian.co.uk/technology/2006/feb/01/news.g2

Goldman, R. (2005) *Fathers' involvement in their children's education.* London: National Family and Parenting Institute.

Government Equalities Office (2009) *Flexible working: benefits and barriers – perceptions of working parents.* London: Government Equalities Office.

Graham, H. and Dermott, E. (2005) Qualitative research and the evidence base of policy: insights from studies of teenage mothers in the UK. *Journal of Social Policy,* **35(1)**, 21–37.

Gray, A. (2005) The changing availability of grandparents as carers and its implications for childcare policy in the UK. *Journal of Social Policy,* **34(4)**, 557–577.

Gray, A. (2006) The time economy of parenting. *Sociological Research,* **11(3).** Online at http://www.socresonline.org.uk/11/3/gray.html

Green, A.E. and Canny, A. (2003) *Geographical mobility: family impacts.* York: Joseph Rowntree Foundation.

Green, H. and Parker, S. (2006) *The other glass ceiling: the domestic politics of parenting.* Online at http://www.relationshipsfoundation.org/download.php?id=98

Gregg, P. and Harkness, S. (2003) Welfare reform and lone parent employment in the UK. CMPO Working Paper Series.

Grossman, K., Grossman, K.E., Fremmer-Bombik, E., Kindler, H., Scheuerer-Englisch, H. and Zimmermann, P. (2002) The uniqueness of the child–father attachment relationship: fathers' sensitive and challenging play as a pivotal variable in a 16-year longitudinal study. *Social Development,* **11(3)**, 307–331.

Grundy, E., Murphy, M. and Shelton, N. (1999) Looking beyond the household: intergenerational perspectives on living kin and contacts with kin in Great Britain. *Population Trends,* **97**, 19–27.

Gudmunson, C., Beutler, I., Israelsen, C., Kelly McCoy, J. and Hill, J. (2007) Linking financial strain to marital instability: examining the roles of emotional distress and marital interaction. *Journal of Family and Economic Issues,* **28(3)**, 357–376.

Gunter, B., Oates, C. and Blades, M. (2005) *Advertising to children on TV: content, impact, and regulation.* Mahwah, NJ: Lawrence Erlbaum Associates.

Haines, L., Chong Wan, K., Lynn, R., Barrett, T.G. and Shield, J.P.H. (2007) Rising incidence of type 2 diabetes in children in the UK. *Diabetes Care,* **30(5)**, 1097–1101.

Hakim, C. (2000) *Work–lifestyle choices in the 21st century: preference theory.* Oxford: Oxford University Press.

Hales, J., Tipping, S. and Lyon, N. (2007) *Mothers' participation in paid work: the role of 'mini-jobs'.* London: Department for Work and Pensions.

Hall, S. (2004) Tories may pay mothers to stay at home. *Guardian,* 19 February. Online at http://www.guardian.co.uk/politics/2004/feb/19/uk.conservatives2/print

Hanley, P. (2002) *Striking a balance: the control of children's media consumption.* London: BBC/Broadcasting Standards Commission/ITC.

Hansen, K., Joshi, H. and Verropoulou, G. (2006) Childcare and mothers' employment: approaching the millennium. *National Institute Economic Review,* **195(1)**, 84–102.

Hantrais, L. (1994) Comparing family policy in Britain, France and Germany. *Journal of Social Policy,* **23(2)**, 135–160.

Hardy, R., Lawlor, D.A., Black, S., Mishra, G.D. and Kuh, D. (2009) Age at parenthood and coronary heart disease risk factors at age 53 years in men and women. *Journal of Epidemiology and Community Health,* **63**, 99–105.

Harrop, A. and Moss, P. (1994) Working parents: trends in the 1980s. *Employment Gazette,* **102(10)**, 343–352.

Hasebrink, U., Livingstone, S. and Haddon, L. (2008) *Comparing children's online opportunities and risks across Europe: cross-national comparisons for EU Kids Online.* London: EU Kids Online.

Haskey, J. (2001) Cohabitation in Great Britain: past, present and future trends and attitudes. *Population Trends,* **103**, 4–25.

Haskey, J. (2005) Living arrangements in contemporary Britain: having a partner who usually lives elsewhere and living apart together (LAT). *Population Trends,* **122**, 35–45.

Hawkes, D. (2008) The UK Millennium Cohort Study: the circumstances of early motherhood. In R. Edwards (Ed.), *Researching families and communities* (pp.147–163). London: Routledge.

Hawkes, D. and Joshi, H. (2007a) The grandparents: what is their role in the family? In K. Hansen and H. Joshi (Eds), *Millennium Cohort Study second survey* (pp.48–51). London: Institute of Education.

Hawkes, D. and Joshi, H. (2007b) *Millennium Cohort Study: grandparents. Briefing 4.* London: Institute of Education.

Hayes, B.C. and Dowds, L. (2006) Social contact, cultural marginality or economic self-interest? Attitudes towards immigrants in Northern Ireland. *Journal of Ethnic and Migration Studies,* **32(3)**, 455–476.

Heath, A. and Tilley, J. (2005) British national identity and attitudes towards immigration. *International Journal of Multicultural Societies,* **7(2)**, 119–132.

Heatherington, E.M., Cox, M. and Cox, R. (1982) Effects of divorce on parents and children. In M.E. Lamb (Ed.), *Non traditional families: parenting and child development* (pp.233–288). Hillsdale, NJ: Erlbaum.

Henderson, M. (2008) NHS denies infertile couples full IVF and offers them just one chance. *The Times,* 24 June. Online at http://www.timesonline.co.uk/tol/life_and_style/health/article4201163.ece

Hensley, W.E. (1977) Probability, personality, age, and risk taking. *Journal of Psychology,* **95(1)**, 139–145.

Herman-Giddens, M.E. (2007) The decline in the age of menarche in the United States: should we be concerned? *Journal of Adolescent Health,* **40(3)**, 201–203.

Higher Education Authority (2008) *Higher education: key facts and figures.* Online at http://www.hea.ie/files/files/file/statistics/2008/HRAfacts06_07.pdf

Hillman, M., Adams, J. and Whitelegg, J. (1990) *One false move.* London: Policy Studies Institute.

Hinds, K. and Jarvis, L. (Eds) (2000) *The gender gap. British Social Attitudes: focusing on diversity – the 17th report.* London: Sage.

HM Treasury (2005) *Leitch Review of Skills. Prosperity for all in the global economy – world class skills.* London: HMSO. Online at http://www.dcsf.gov.uk/furthereducation/uploads/documents/2006-12%20LeitchReview1.pdf

Hobcraft, J. (1998a) *Childhood experiences and the risks of social exclusion in adulthood. CASE briefs.* London: Centre for Analysis of Social Exclusion, London School of Economics.

Hobcraft, J. (1998b) *Intergenerational and life-course transmission of social exclusion: influences of childhood poverty, family disruption, and contact with the police. CASE papers.* London: Centre for Analysis of Social Exclusion, London School of Economics.

Hobcraft, J. and Kiernan, K. (1999) *Childhood poverty, early motherhood and adult social exclusion. CASE paper 28.* London: Centre for Analysis of Social Exclusion.

Home Office (2009) *Class A, B and C drugs: drugs and the law.* Online at http://www.homeoffice.gov.uk/drugs/drugs-law/Class-a-b-c/

Howe, G., Levy, M. and Caplan, R. (2004) Job loss and depressive symptoms in couples: common stressors, stress transmission, or relationship disruption? *Journal of Family Psychology,* **18(4)**, 639–650.

Human Fertilisation Embryology Authority (2007) *A long term analysis of the HFEA register data 1991–2006.* Online at http://www.hfea.gov.uk/docs/Latest_long_term_data_analysis_report_91-06.pdf

Inman, P. (2009) Unemployment will soar above 3 million in 2009, say Chambers of Commerce. *Guardian,* 1 January. Online at http://www.guardian.co.uk/business/2009/jan/01/unhappy-new-year

International Monetary Fund (2009) *Global economic policies and prospects.* Washington, DC: International Monetary Fund.

IpsosMORI (2004) *Public backs equality law change for children.* Online at http://www.ipsos-mori.com/researchpublications/researcharchive/poll.aspx?oItemId=604

IpsosMORI (2007) *A study into the views of parents on the physical punishment of children.* London: Department for Children, Schools and Families.

Ives, J., Draper, H., Pattison, H. and Williams, C. (2008) Becoming a father/refusing fatherhood: an empirical bioethics approach to paternal responsibilities and rights. *Clinical Ethics,* **3(2)**, 75–84.

Jaffee, S.R., Moffitt, T.E., Caspi, A. and Taylor, A. (2003) Life with (or without) father: the benefits of living with two biological parents depends on the father's antisocial behavior. *Child Development,* **74(1)**, 109–126.

Jahoda, M. (1982) *Employment and unemployment: a social-psychological analysis.* Cambridge: Cambridge University Press.

James, C. (2008) *Families and the credit crunch 2008.* London: Family and Parenting Institute.

James, C. and Henricson, C. (2009) *Family policy across Europe: a compendium of comparative studies.* London: Family and Parenting Institute.

Jarvis, M.J., Goddard, E., Higgins, V., Feyerabend, C., Bryant, A. and Cook, D.G. (2000) Children's exposure to passive smoking in England since the 1980s: cotinine evidence from population surveys. *British Medical Journal,* **321(7257)**, 343–345.

Jebb, S.A., Rennie, K.L. and Cole, T.J. (2003) Prevalence of overweight and obesity among young people in Great Britain. *Public Health Nutrition,* **7(3)**, 461–465.

Jefferies, J. (2005) The UK population: past, present and future. In R. Chappell (Ed.), *Focus on people and migration* (pp.1–18). Houndmills: Palgrave Macmillan.

Jodl, K.M., Michael, A., Malanchuk, O., Eccles, J. and Sameroff, A. (2001) Parents' roles in shaping early adolescents' occupational aspirations. *Child Development,* **72(4)**, 1247–1265.

Jones, G. (2002) *The youth divide: diverging paths to adulthood.* York: York Publishing Services/ Joseph Rowntree Foundation.

Joshi, H. (2008) Setting the scene. Paper presented at the Modern motherhood conference, Family and Parenting Institute, London, 2 July.

Joshi, M.S. and MacLean, M. (1995) Parental attitudes to children's journeys to school. *World Transport Policy and Practice,* **1(4)**, 29–36.

Kalil, A. and Ziol-Guest, K. (2004) *Single mothers' employment dynamics and adolescent well-being.* Ann Arbor, MI: National Poverty Center, University of Michigan.

Kan, M.L. (2008) Does gender trump money? Housework hours of husbands and wives in Britain. *Work, Employment and Society,* **22(1)**, 45–66.

Kan, M.Y. (2007) Work orientation and wives' employment careers: an evaluation of Hakim's preference theory. *Work and Occupations,* **34(4)**, 430–462.

Kasperson, R.E., Renn, O., Slovic, P., Brown, H., Emel, J., Goble, R., Kasperson, J. and Ratick, S. (1988) The social amplification of risk: a conceptual framework. *Risk Analysis,* **8(2)**, 177–187.

Kazimirski, A., Smith, R., Butt, S., Ireland, E. and Lloyd, E. (2008) *Childcare and early years survey 2007: parents' use, views and experiences. Research Report RR025.* London: Department for Children, Schools and Families.

Kent, K. (2009) Households, families and work. *Economic and Labour Market Review,* **3(5)**, 17–22.

Kenway, P. and Palmer, G. (2007) *Poverty among ethnic groups: how and why does it differ?* York: Joseph Rowntree Foundation.

Kiernan, K. (1995) *Social backgrounds and post-birth experiences of young parents. Social policy research.* York: Joseph Rowntree Foundation.

Kiernan, K. (1997) Becoming a young parent: a longitudinal study of associated factors. *British Journal of Sociology,* **48(3)**, 406–428.

Kiernan, K. (2006) Non-residential fatherhood and child involvement: evidence from the Millennium Cohort Study. *Journal of Social Policy,* **35(4)**, 651–669.

Kiernan, K. and Pickett, K.E. (2006) Marital status disparities in maternal smoking during pregnancy, breastfeeding and maternal depression. *Social Science Medicine,* **63(2)**, 335–346.

Kiernan, K. and Smith, K. (2003) Unmarried parenthood: new insights from the Millennium Cohort Study. *Population Trends,* **114**, 26–33.

Kinnunen, U. and Feldt, T. (2004) Economic stress and marital adjustment among couples: analyses at the dyadic level. *European Journal of Social Psychology,* **34(5)**, 519–532.

Kipping, R.R., Jago, R. and Lawlor, D.A. (2008) Obesity in children. Part 1: epidemiology, measurement, risk factors, and screening. *British Medical Journal,* **337(7675)**, 922–927.

Klesges, R.C., Stein, R.J., Eck, L.H., Isbell, T.R. and Klesges, L.M. (1991) Parental influence on food selection in young children and its relationships to childhood obesity. *American Clinical Journal of Nutrition,* **53(4)**, 859–864.

Klett-Davies, M. (2002) *Lone mothering in Britain and Germany: balancing choices and constraints.* London: London School of Economics and Political Science.

Klett-Davies, M. (2007) *Going it alone? Lone motherhood in late modernity.* Aldershot: Ashgate.

Kodz, J. (2003) *Working long hours: a review of the evidence. Employment Relations Research series.* London: Department of Trade and Industry.

Koslowski, A.S. (2009) Grandparents and the care of their grandchildren. In J. Stillwell, E. Coast and D. Kneale (Eds), *Fertility, living arrangements, care and mobility,* (pp.177–190). London: Springer.

Krunkel, D., Wilcox, B.L., Cantor, J., Palmer, E., Linn, S. and Dowrick, P. (2004) *Report of the APA task force on advertising and children. Section: psychological issues in the increasing commercialization of childhood.* Washington, DC: American Psychological Association.

La Valle, I., Arthur, S., Millward, C., Scott, J. and Clayden, M. (2002) *Happy families? Atypical work and its influence on family life.* York: Joseph Rowntree Foundation.

Lacey, L. (2007) *Street play opinion poll summary.* Online at http://www.playday.org.uk/docs/street-play-opinion-poll-summary.doc

Lader, D. (2008a) *Non-resident parental contact, 2007/8. Omnibus Survey report.* Newport: Office for National Statistics.

Lader, D. (2008b) *Smoking-related behaviour and attitudes, 2007.* Newport: Office for National Statistics.

Lake, J.K., Power, C. and Cole, T.J. (1997) Child to adult body mass index in the 1958 British birth cohort: associations with parental obesity. *Archives of Disease in Childhood,* **77**, 376–380.

Lamb, M.E. (Ed.) (1981) *The role of the father in child development.* New York: Wiley.

Lamb, M.E. and Lewis, C. (2004) The development and significance of father–child relationships in two-parent families. In M.E. Lamb (Ed.), *The role of the father in child development* (pp.272–306). Hoboken, NJ: John Wiley and Sons.

Lamb, M.E. and Tamis-Lemonda, C.S. (2004) The role of the father: an introduction. In M.E. Lamb (Ed.), *The role of the father in child development* (4th edn) (pp. 1–31). Hoboken, NJ: John Wiley and Sons.

Lamb, M.E., Pleck, J.H., Charnov, E.L. and Levine, J.A. (1987) A biosocial perspective on paternal behaviour and involvement. In J.B. Lancaster, J. Altmann, A.S. Rossi and L.R. Sherrod (Eds), *Parenting across the lifespan: biosocial dimensions* (pp.111–142). Hawthorne, NY: Aldine de Gruyter.

Lampard, R. (1994) An examination of the relationship between marital dissolution and unemployment. In D. Gallie, C. Marsh and C. Vogler (Eds), *Social change and the experience of unemployment* (pp.264–298). Oxford: Oxford University Press.

Larson, J. (1984) The effect of the husband's unemployment on marital and family relations in blue-collar families. *Family Relations,* **33(4)**, 503–511.

Lawler, S. (1999) Children need but mothers only want: the power of 'needs talk' in the constitution of childhood. In P. Bagguley and K. Seymour (Eds), *Relating intimacies: power and resistance* (pp.64–88). New York: St Martin's Press.

Lawlor, D.A. and Shaw, M. (2004) Teenage pregnancy rates: high compared with where and when? *Journal of the Royal Society of Medicine,* **97(3)**, 121–123.

Leak, J. (2004) It's not the fruit it used to be. *Sunday Times,* 8 February. Online at http://women.timesonline.co.uk/tol/life_and_style/women/diet_and_fitness/article1015215.ece

Leaker, D. (2008) The gender pay gap in the UK. *Economic and Labour Market Review,* **2(4)**, 19–24.

Leathard, A. (1980) *The fight for family planning: the development of family planning services in Britain, 1921–1974.* London: Macmillan.

Lee, E., Clements, S., Ingham, R. and Stone, N. (2004) *A matter of choice? Explaining national variation in teenage abortion and motherhood.* York: Joseph Rowntree Foundation.

Lee, K. (2009) *Fatherhoods? Fathers, fathering and family diversity.* Unpublished PhD thesis. City University.

Leinonen, J., Solantaus, T. and Punamäki, R. (2002) The specific mediating paths between economic hardship and the quality of parenting. *International Journal of Behavioral Development,* **26(5)**, 423–435.

Levin, D.E. and Kilbourne, J. (2009) *So sexy so soon: the new sexualized childhood and what parents can do to protect their kids.* New York: Ballantine.

Lewis, C. (1975) Fathers: forgotten contributors to child development. *Human Development,* **18(4)**, 245–266.

Lewis, C. and Lamb, M.E. (2007) *Understanding fatherhood: a review of recent research.* York: Joseph Rowntree Foundation.

Lewis, C. and O'Brien, M. (Eds) (1987) *Reassessing fatherhood: new observations on fathers and the modern family.* London: Sage.

Lewis, J. and Giullari, S. (2005) The adult worker model family, gender equality and care: the search for new policy principles and the possibilities and problems of a capabilities approach. *Economy and Society,* **34(1)**, 76–104.

Lewis, J., Campbell, M. and Huerta, C. (2008) Patterns of paid and unpaid work in Western Europe: gender, commodification, preferences and the implications for policy. *Journal of European and Social Policy,* **18(1)**, 21–37.

Lewis, J., Sarre, S. and Burton, J. (2007) Dependence and independence: perceptions and management of risk in respect of children aged 12–16 in families with working parents. *Community, Work and Family,* **10(1)**, 75–92.

Lewis, M.E. (1987) *Beyond the dyad.* New York: Plenum Press.

Lewis, S., Gambles, R. and Rapoport, R. (2007) The constraints of a 'work–life balance' approach: an international perspective. *International Journal of Human Resource Management,* **18(3)**, 360–373.

Lindley, J. and Dale, A. (2004) Ethnic differences in women's demographic, family characteristics and economic activity profiles, 1992 to 2002, ONS Special Feature: labour market trends.

Livingstone, S. and Helsper, E.J. (2006) Does advertising literacy mediate the effects of advertising on children? A critical examination of two linked research literatures in relation to obesity and food choice. *Journal of Communication,* **56(3)**, 560–584.

Lobo, F. and Watkins, G. (1995) Late career unemployment in the 1990s: its impact on the family. *Journal of Family Studies,* **1(1)**, 103–113.

Local Government Association (2009) One person in twelve now on social housing waiting list. Press release.

Lye, D.N. (1996) Adult child–parent relationships. *Annual Review of Sociology,* **22**, 79–102.

Lynch, S. (2008a) Smoking. In E. Fuller (Ed.), *Drug use, smoking and drinking among young people in England in 2007* (pp.107–122). London: NHS Health and Social Care Information Centre.

Lynch, S. (2008b) Drinking alcohol. In E. Fuller (Ed.), *Drug use, smoking and drinking among young people in England in 2007* (pp.123–146). London: NHS Health and Social Care Information Centre.

Lyonette, C. and Clark, C.M. (2009) Unsocial hours: unsocial families? Cambridge: Relationship Foundation.

Maclean, M. and Eekelaar, J. (1997) *The parental obligation: a study of parenthood across households.* Oxford: Hart.

McAllister, F. and Clarke, L. (1998) *A study of childlessness in Britain.* York: Joseph Rowntree Foundation.

McConnell, H. and Wilson, B. (2007) Families. In S. Smallwood and B. Wilson (Eds.), *Focus on families* (pp.2–17). Houndmills: Palgrave Macmillan.

McLaren, L. and Johnson, M. (2007) Resources, group conflict and symbols: explaining anti-immigration hostility in Britain. *Political Studies,* **55(4)**, 709–732.

McLeod, A. (2001) Changing patterns of teenage pregnancy: population-based study of small areas. *British Medical Journal,* **232(7306)**, 199–203.

McRae, S. (2003) Constraints and choices in mothers' employment careers: a consideration of Hakim's Preference Theory. *British Journal of Sociology,* **54(3)**, 317–338.

Manning, W.D. and Smock, P.J. (1999) New families and nonresident father–child visitation. *Social Forces,* **78(1)**, 87–116.

March, A. and Perry, I. (2003) *Family change, 1999 to 2001. Research report.* London: Department for Work and Pensions.

Meltzer, H. (1994) *Day care services for young children.* London: Department of Health.

Miller, J. and Ridge, T. (2008) Relationships of care: working lone mothers, their children and employment sustainability. *Journal of Social Policy,* **38(1)**, 103–121.

Miller, T. (2005) *Making sense of motherhood: a narrative approach.* Cambridge: Cambridge University Press.

Moses, L.J. and Baldwin, D.A. (2005) What can the study of cognitive development reveal about children's ability to appreciate and cope with advertising? *Journal of Public Policy Marketing,* **24(2)**, 186–201.

Moss, P. (2008) Making parental leave parental: an overview of policies to increase fathers' use of leave. In P. Moss and M. Korintus, *International review of leave policies and related research 2008* (pp.86–91). London: Department for Business Enterprise and Regulatory Reform.

Murphy, M. (2000) The evolution of cohabitation in Britain, 1960–95. *Population Studies,* **54(1)**, 43–56.

Murphy, M., Grundy, E. and Shelton, N. (1999) Looking beyond the household: intergenerational perspectives on living kin and contact with kin in Great Britain. *Population Trends,* **97**, 19–27.

Murrin, K. and Martin, P. (2004) *What worries parents: the most common concerns of parents explored and explained.* London: Vermillion.

Nairn, A., Ormrod, J. and Bottomley, P. (2007) *Watching, wanting and wellbeing: exploring the links.* London: National Consumer Council.

National Family and Parenting Institute (2003) *Hard sell, soft targets?* London: National Family and Parenting Institute.

Nave-Herz, R. (1992) *Frauen zwischen Tradition und Moderne.* Bielefeld: Kleine Verlag.

Nepomnyaschy, L. and Waldfogel, J. (2007) Paternity leave and fathers' involvement with their young children: evidence from the American ECLS-B. *Community, Work and Family,* **10(4)**, 427–453.

Nettleton, S. and Burrows, R. (1999) *Losing the family home: understanding the social consequences of mortgage repossession.* York: Joseph Rowntree Foundation.

Nord, C.W., Brimhall, D. and West, J. (1998) Dads' involvement in their kids' schools. *Education Digest,* **63(7)**, 29–35.

NSPCC (2009) *Equal protection for children under the law on assault.* Online at http://www.nspcc.org.uk/Inform/policyandpublicaffairs/KeyProjects/EqualProtection/equal_ protection_under_law_on_assault_wda48541.html

Nuffield Foundation (2009a) *Parents of teenagers are doing a good job.* Online at http://www.nuffieldfoundation.org/go/news/news_1931.html

Nuffield Foundation (2009b) *Time trends in parenting and outcomes for young people.* London: Nuffield Foundation.

O'Brien, M. (2005) *Sharing caring: bringing fathers into the frame.* Manchester: Equal Opportunities Commission.

O'Brien, M. and Moss, P. (2008) 2.25 United Kingdom. In P. Moss and M. Korintus (Eds), *International review of leave policies and related research 2008* (pp.346–355). London: Department for Business Enterprise and Regulatory Reform.

O'Brien, M. and Shemilt, I. (2003) *Working fathers: earning and caring. Research Discussion Series.* Manchester: Equal Opportunities Commission.

O'Brien, M., Brandth, B. and Knande, E. (2007) Fathers, work and family life: global perspectives and new insights. *Community, Work and Family,* **10(4)**, 375–386.

Oakley, A. (1974a) *The sociology of housework.* Oxford: Martin Robertson.

Oakley, A. (1974b) *Housewife.* London: Penguin.

Office for National Statistics (ONS) (2000) *Social trends 30.* London: The Stationery Office.

ONS (2002a) *Social focus in brief: ethnicity 2002.* London: The Stationery Office.

ONS (2002b) Households and families. In J. Matheson and P. Babb (Eds), *Social trends 32* (pp.39–52). London: The Stationery Office.

ONS (2003a) Population. In C. Summerfield and P. Babb (Eds), *Population trends 33* (pp.29–39). London: The Stationery Office.

ONS (2003b) Households and families. In C. Summerfield and P. Babb (Eds), *Social trends 33* (pp.41–53). London: The Stationery Office.

ONS (2004a) *Fertility: women are having children later.* Online at http://www.statistics.gov.uk/CCI/nugget.asp?ID=762&Pos=1&ColRank=2&Rank=1000

ONS (2004b) Population. In C. Summerfield and P. Babb (Eds), *Social trends 34* (pp. 15–24). London: The Stationery Office.

ONS (2005a) *Ethnicity: 4 in 5 Bangladeshi families have children.* Online at
http://www.statistics.gov.uk/CCI/nugget.asp?ID=1167Pos=1ColRank=1Rank=326

ONS (2005b) *Stepfamilies: 10% of families are stepfamilies.* Online at
http://www.statistics.gov.uk/CCI/nugget.asp?ID=1164&Pos=&ColRank=1&Rank=374

ONS (2006) Households and families. In P. Babb, H. Butcher, J. Church and L. Zealey (Eds), *Social trends 36* (pp. 21–48). Houndmills: Palgrave Macmillan.

ONS (2007) *Overview of families: cohabitation is fastest growing family type.* Online at
http://www.statistics.gov.uk/cci/nugget.asp?id=1865

ONS (2008a) Population. In A. Self and L. Zealey (Eds), *Social trends 38* (pp.2–15). Houndmills: Palgrave Macmillan.

ONS (2008b) Households and families. In A. Self and L. Zealey (Eds), *Social trends 38* (pp.15–28). Houndmills: Palgrave Macmillan.

ONS (2008c) *Population change: UK population increases by 388,000.* Online at
http://www.statistics.gov.uk/CCI/nugget.asp?ID=950&Pos=5&ColRank=2&Rank=1000

ONS (2008d) *Living arrangements: marriage is most common form of partnership.* Online at
http://www.statistics.gov.uk/CCI/nugget.asp?ID=1652&Pos=1&ColRank=2&Rank=1000

ONS (2008f) *Work and family: two-thirds of mums are in employment.* Newport: Office for National Statistics.

ONS (2008g) *Focus on gender.* Online at
http://www.statistics.gov.uk/statbase/product.asp?vlnk=10923

ONS (2008h) *Internet access 2008: household and individuals.* Online at
http://www.statistics.gov.uk/pdfdir/iahi0808.pdf

ONS (2008e) *Lone parents in employment.* Online at
http://www.statistics.gov.uk/cci/nugget_print.asp?ID=409

ONS (2009a) Population Change: UK population increases by 408,000 Office of National Statistics
http://www.statistics.gov.uk/cci/nugget.asp?ID=950

ONS (2009b) *Live births: fertility highest for 35 years.* Online at
http://www.statistics.gov.uk/CCI/nugget.asp?ID=369&Pos=1&ColRank=1&Rank=176

ONS (2009c) *Dependent population by age, United Kingdom.* Online at
http://www.statistics.gov.uk/STATBASE/Expodata/Spreadsheets/D7215.xls

ONS (2009d) *Households by size, Great Britain.* Online at
http://www.statistics.gov.uk/STATBASE/Expodata/Spreadsheets/D4968.xls

ONS (2009e) *Household size by ethnic group of head of household, spring 2002.* Online at
http://www.statistics.gov.uk/STATBASE/Expodata/Spreadsheets/D6208.xls

ONS (2009f) *Resident population by ethnic group, 2001.* Online at
http://www.statistics.gov.uk/STATBASE/Expodata/Spreadsheets/D7666.xls

ONS (2009g) *Projected population by age, sex and legal marital status, England and Wales, 2007–2031.* Online at
http://www.statistics.gov.uk/downloads/theme_population/Marr-proj06/legalsummaryPRINCIPAL.xls

ONS (2009h) *Population: age, sex and legal marital status.* Online at
http://www.statistics.gov.uk/STATBASE/Expodata/Spreadsheets/D9532.xls

ONS (2009i) *Marriage rates fall to lowest on record.* Online at
http://www.statistics.gov.uk/pdfdir/marr0209.pdf

ONS (2009j) *Births: live births outside marriage, age of mother and whether sole or joint registration,
1964–2004.* Online at
http://www.statistics.gov.uk/StatBase/xsdataset.asp?More=Y&vlnk=4192&All=Y&B2.x=50&B2.
y=13

ONS (2009k) *Live births outside marriage: age of mother and type of registration.* Online at
http://www.statistics.gov.uk/StatBase/Expodata/Spreadsheets/D9527.xls

ONS (2009l) *Civil partnerships down 18 per cent in 2008.* Online at
http://www.statistics.gov.uk/pdfdir/cpuknr0809.pdf

ONS (2009m) *Percentage of dependent children living in different family types.* Online at
http://www.statistics.gov.uk/STATBASE/Expodata/Spreadsheets/D7256.xls

ONS (2009n) *Fewer children live in married couple families.* Online at
http://www.statistics.gov.uk/cci/nugget.asp?id=2193

ONS (2009o) Households and families. In H. Hughes, J. Church and L. Zealey (Eds), *Social trends 39*
(pp.13–26). Houndmills: Palgrave Macmillan.

ONS (2009p) *Social trends 39.* Houndmills: Palgrave Macmillan.

ONS (2009q) Table 4: employment rates for working age people by parental status. Online at
http://www.statistics.gov.uk/STATBASE/Product.asp?vlnk=12859

ONS (2009r) Table 4: employment rates for working age people by parental status. Online at
http://www.statistics.gov.uk/StatBase/Product.asp?vlnk=14977&Pos=1&ColRank=1&Rank=240

ONS (2009s) *Workforce jobs by industry.* Online at
http://www.statistics.gov.uk/statbase/product.asp?vlnk=8286

ONS (2009t) Labour Force Survey: employment status by occupation and sex. Online at
http://www.statistics.gov.uk/STATBASE/Product.asp?vlnk=14248

ONS (2009u) Health. In H. Hughes, J. Church and L. Zealey (Eds), *Social trends 39* (pp.95–126).
Houndmills: Palgrave Macmillan.

ONS (2009v) *The impact of the recession on the labour market.* Newport: Office for National
Statistics.

Office of Communications (2006) *Television advertising of food and drink products to children:
statement and further consultation.* London: Office of Communications.

Office of Health Economics (2009) *Growth in UK elderly population and projections as a percentage
of UK population, 1948–2051.* Online at
http://www.ohe.org/lib/liDownload/110/comp2.csv?CFID=976145&CFTOKEN=59925903

Organisation for Economic Cooperation and Development (OECD) (2006) *Starting strong II: early
childhood education and care.* Paris: OECD.

Papp, L., Cummings, E. and Goeke-Morey, M. (2009) For richer, for poorer: money as a topic of marital
conflict in the home. *Family Relations,* **58(1)**, 91–103.

Parsons, J.T., Manor, O. and Power, C. (2005a) Changes in diet and physical activity in the 1990s in a
large British sample (1958 birth cohort). *European Journal of Clinical Nutrition,* **59(1)**, 49–56.

Parsons, J.T., Power, C. and Manor, O. (2005b) Physical activity, television viewing and body mass index: a cross-sectional analysis from childhood to adulthood in the 1958 British cohort. *International Journal of Obesity,* **29(10)**, 1212–1221.

Paton, D. (2002) The economics of family planning and underage conceptions. *Journal of Health Economics,* **21(2)**, 207–225.

Paton, G. (2008) Sex lessons not halting rise in teen pregnancy. *Daily Telegraph,* 31 January. Online at http://www.telegraph.co.uk/news/uknews/1574422/Sex-lessons-not-halting-rise-in-teen-pregnancy.html

Patton, G. and Viner, R. (2007) Pubertal transitions in health. *The Lancet,* **369(9567)**, 1130–1139.

Payne, J. and Range, M. (1998) *Lone parents' lives: an analysis of partnership, fertility, employment and housing histories in the 1958 British birth cohort. DSS research report.* London: HMSO.

Penn, R. and Lambert, P. (2002) Attitudes towards ideal family size of different ethnic/nationality groups in Great Britain, France and Germany. *Population Trends,* **108**, 49–59.

Perez-Pastor, E.M., Metcalf, B.S., Hosking, J., Jeffery, A.N., Voss, L.D. and Wilkin, T.J. (2009) Assortative weight gain in mother–daughter and father–son pairs: an emerging source of childhood obesity. Longitudinal study of trios (EarlyBird 43). *International Journal of Obesity,* **33(7)**, 727–735.

Peters, M., Seeds, K., Goldstein, A. and Coleman, N. (2008) *Parental involvement in children's education 2007.* London: Department for Children, Schools and Families.

Philo, D., Maplethorpe, N., Conolly, A. and Toomse, M. (2009) *Families with children in Britain: findings from the 2007 Families and Children Study (FACS). Research report no. 578.* London: Department for Work and Pensions.

Phoenix, A. (1991) *Young mothers?* Cambridge: Polity Press.

Phoenix, A., Woollett, A. and Lloyd, E. (1991) *Motherhood, meanings, practices and ideologies.* London: Sage.

Portanti, M. and Whitworth, S. (2009) A comparison of the characteristics of childless women and mothers in the ONS longitudinal study. *Population Trends,* **136**, 10–20.

Power, C. and Moynihan, C. (1988) Social class and changes in weight-for-height between childhood and early adulthood. *International Journal of Obesity,* **12(5)**, 445–453.

Prime Minister's Office (2003) *National childcare strategy.* Online at http://www.number10.gov.uk/Page1430

Pryor, J. and Rodgers, B. (2001) *Children in changing families: life after parental separation.* Oxford: Blackwell.

Purvis, A. (2005) It's supposed to be lean cuisine. So why is this chicken fatter than it looks? *Observer Food Monthly,* 15 May. Online at http://www.guardian.co.uk/lifeandstyle/2005/may/15/foodanddrink.shopping3

Pykett, E. (2009) Mothers return to work early as recession eats into family budget. *The Scotsman,* 8 April. Online at http://news.scotsman.com/latestnews/Mothers-return-to-work-.5151191.jp

Ram, B. and Hou, F. (2003) Changes in family structure and child outcomes: roles of economic and familial resources. *Policy Studies Journal,* **31(3)**, 309–330.

Rendall, M. and Salt, J. (2005) The foreign-born population. In R. Chappell (Ed.), *Focus on people and migration* (pp.131–151). Houndmills: Palgrave Macmillan.

Rendall, M.S. and Smallwood, S. (2003) Higher qualifications, first birth timing, and further childbearing in England and Wales. *Population Trends,* **111**, 19–26.

Reynolds, T., Callender, C. and Edwards, R. (2003) *Caring and counting: the impact of mothers' employment on family relationships, family and work.* Bristol: Policy Press/Joseph Rowntree Foundation.

Richins, M.L. and Dawson, S. (1992) A consumer values orientation for materialism and its measurement: scale development and validation. *Journal of Consumer Research,* **19(3)**, 303–316.

Riley, M.W. and Riley, J.W. (1993) Connections: kin and cohort. In V.L. Bengston and W.A. Achenbaum (Eds), *The changing contract across generations* (pp.169–190). Hawthorne, NY: Aldine de Gruyter.

Rindfleisch, A., Burroughs, J. and Denton, F. (1997) Family structure, materialism, and compulsive consumption. *Journal of Consumer Research,* **23(4)**, 312–325.

Roberts, J.A., Manolis, C. and Tanner Jr, J.F. (2003) Family structure, materialism, and compulsive buying: a re-inquiry and extension. *Journal of Academy of Marketing Science,* **13(3)**, 300–311.

Roseneil, S. (2006) On not living with a partner: unpicking coupledom and cohabitation. *Sociological Research*, **11(3)**. Online at http://www.socresonline.org.uk/11/3/roseneil.html

Sainsbury, D. (1996) *Gender, equality and welfare states.* Cambridge: Cambridge University Press.

Sherbert Research (2007) *A study into children's views on physical discipline and punishment.* London: Sherbert Research.

Shrosbree, E. (2009) Conceptions in England and Wales 2007. *Health Statistics Quarterly,* **41**, 66–68.

Sigle-Rushton, W. (2008) England and Wales: stable fertility and pronounced social status differences. *Demographic Research,* **19(15)**, 455–502.

Silverstein, M. and Bengston, V.L. (1997) Intergenerational solidarity and the structure of adult child–parent relationships in American families. *American Journal of Sociology,* **103(2)**, 429–460.

Simons, R.L., Whitbeck, L.B. and Wu, C.-I. (1994) Resilient and vulnerable adolescents. In R.D. Conger and G.H. Elder Jr (Eds), *Families in troubled times: adapting to change in rural America* (pp.223–234). Hawthorne, NY: Aldine de Gruyter.

Simpson, B. and McCarthy, P. (1995) *Being there: fathers after divorce.* Newcastle: Relate Centre of Family Studies.

Simpson, B., Jessop, J. and McCarthy, P. (2003) Fathers after divorce. In A. Bainham, B. Lindley, M. Richards and L. Trinder (Eds), *Children and their families: contact, rights and welfare* (pp.201–222). Oxford: Hart.

Singh, S. and Darroch, J.E. (2000) Adolescent pregnancy and childbearing: levels and trends in developing countries. *Family Planning Perspectives,* **32(1)**, 14–23.

Skaliotis, E. (submitted) Changes in parental involvement in secondary education: an exploration study using the Longitudinal Study of Young People in England. *British Educational Research Journal.*

Sloggett, A. and Joshi, H. (1998) Deprivation indicators as predictors of life events 1981–1992 based in the UK ONS Longitudinal Study. *Journal of Epidemiology and Community Health,* **52**, 228–233.

188

Slovic, P. (2000) What does it mean to know a cumulative risk? Adolescents' perceptions of short-term and long-term consequences of smoking. *Journal of Behavioral Decision Making,* **13(2)**, 259–266.

Slovic, P., Finucane, M., Peters, E. and MacGregor, D.G. (2002) Risk as analysis and risk as feelings: some thoughts about affect, reason, risk, and rationality. *Risk Analysis,* **24(2)**, 1–12.

Slovic, P., Fischhoff, B. and Lichtenstein, S. (1982) Why study risk perception? *Risk Analysis,* **2(2)**, 83–93.

Sly, F. (1994) Mothers in the labour market. *Employment Gazette,* **102(11)**, 403–420.

Smart, C. (2007) *Personal life.* Cambridge: Polity Press.

Smeaton, D. and Marsh, A. (2006) Maternity and paternity rights and benefits: survey of parents 2005. *Employment relations research series No. 50.* London: Department for Work and Pensions.

Social Exclusion Unit (1999) *Teenage pregnancy.* London: The Stationery Office.

Solantaus, T., Leinonen, J. and Punamäki, R.L. (2004) Children's mental health in times of economic recession: replication and extension of the family economic stress model in Finland. *Developmental Psychology,* **40(3)**, 412–429.

South, S.J. (1985) Economic conditions and the divorce rate: a time-series analysis of the postwar United States. *Journal of Marriage and the Family,* **47(1)**, 31–41.

Speake, S., Cameron, S. and Gilroy, R. (1996) *Young single, non-residential fathers: their involvement in fatherhood.* Oxford: Family Policies Centre.

Steele, H., Steele, M., Croft, C. and Fonagy, P. (1999) Infant–mother attachment at one year predicts children's understanding of mixed emotions at six years. *Social Development,* **8(2)**, 161–178.

Strategy Unit (2008a) *Food: an analysis of the issues.* London: Cabinet Office.

Strategy Unit (2008b) *Food matters: towards a strategy for the 21st century.* London: Cabinet Office.

Sullivan, O. (2000) The division of domestic labour: twenty years of change. *Sociology,* **34(3)**, 437–456.

Sun, Y. and Li, Y. (2001) Marital disruption, parental investment and children's academic achievement: a prospective analysis. *Journal of Family Issues,* **22(1)**, 27–62.

Tanaka, S. and Waldfogel, J. (2007) Effects of parental leave and work hours on fathers' involvement with their babies: evidence from the Millennium Cohort Study. *Community, Work and Family,* **4(10)**, 409–426.

Taylor, M., Pevalin, D. and Todd, J. (2007) The psychological costs of unsustainable housing commitments. *Psychological Medicine,* **37(7)**, 1027–1036.

Thomas, M.C., Hardoon, S.L., Papacosta, A.O., Morris, R.W., Wannamethee, S.G., Sloggett, A. and Whincup, P.H. (2009) Evidence of an accelerating increase in prevalence of diagnosed type 2 diabetes in British men, 1978–2005. *Diabetic Medicine,* **26(8)**, 766–772.

Thomson, R., Kehily, M.J., Hadfield, L. and Sharpe, S. (2008) *The making of modern motherhood: memories, representations, practices.* Milton Keynes: Open University Press.

Townsend, J., Roderick, P. and Cooper, J. (1994) Cigarette smoking by socio-economic group, sex, and age: effects of price, income, and health publicity. *British Medical Journal,* **309(6959)**, 923–927.

Travis, A. (2009) Eastern Europeans seeking work in UK down 47%. *Guardian,* 25 February. Online at http://www.guardian.co.uk/uk/2009/feb/25/eastern-european-migrants-fall/print

TUC (2008) *Closing the gender pay gap: an update report for TUC women's conference 2008.* London: TUC. Online at http://www.tuc.org.uk/equality/tuc-14435-f0.pdf

TUC (2009) *Women and recession.* Online at http://www.tuc.org.uk/extras/womenandrecession.pdf

Twomey, B. (2002) *Women in the labour market: results from the spring 2001 LFS.* Online at http://www.statistics.gov.uk/articles/labour_market_trends/Women_in_the_labour_market_mar2002.pdf

Unicef (2001) *A league table of teenage births in rich nations. Innocenti report card 3: Innocenti report.* Florence: Unicef.

Uren, Z., Sheers, D. and Dattani, N. (2007) Teenage conceptions by small area deprivation in England and Wales, 2001–2002. *Health Statistics Quarterly,* **33**, 34–39.

Variyam, J.N., Blaylock, J., Lin, B.-H., Ralston, K. and Smallwood, D. (1999) Mother's nutritional knowledge and children's dietary intakes. *American Journal of Agricultural Economics,* **81(2)**, 373–384.

Verropoulou, G., Joshi, H. and Wiggins, R.D. (2002) Migration, family structure and children's well-being: a multi-level analysis of the second generation of the 1958 Birth Cohort Study. *Children and Society,* **16(4)**, 219–231.

Viner, R.M. and Cole, T.J. (2005) Television viewing in early childhood predicts adult body mass index. *Journal of Pediatrics,* **147(4)**, 429–435.

Viner, R.M. and Cole, T.J. (2006) Who changes body mass between adolescence and adulthood? Factors predicting change in BMI between 16 and 30 years in the 1970 British Birth Cohort. *International Journal of Obesity,* **30(9)**, 1368–1374.

Walling, A. (2005) *Families and work. Labour market trends.* Cardiff: Office for National Statistics.

Wang, Y.Q., Thomas, B., Ghebremeskel, K. and Crawford, M.A. (2004) Changes in protein and fat balance of primary foods: implications for obesity – abstract. Paper presented at the 6th Congress of the International Society for the Study of Fatty Acids and Lipids, Brighton, 27 June–1 July.

Ward, K. and Dex, S. (2007) *Millennium Cohort Study: employment and education, briefing 9.* London: Institute of Education.

Wardle, J., Parmenter, K. and Waller, J. (2000) Nutrition knowledge and food intake. *Appetite,* **34(3)**, 269–275.

Warr, P., Jackson, P. and Banks, M. (1988) Unemployment and mental health: some British studies. *Journal of Social Issues,* **44(4)**, 47–68.

Washbrook, E. (2007) Fathers, childcare and children's readiness to learn. *Working Paper.* Bristol: Centre for Market and Public Organisation, University of Bristol.

Webster, C., MacDonald, R., Shildrick, T. and Simpson, M. (2005) *Social exclusion, young adults, and extended youth transitions. Lost in transition: a report of the Barrow Cadbury Commission on young adults and the criminal justice system.* London: Barrow Cadbury Trust.

Weinstein, N.D. (1980) Unrealistic optimism about future life events. *Journal of Personality and Social Psychology,* **39(5)**, 806–820.

Weiss, Y. and Willis, R.J. (2007) Match quality, new information and marital dissolution. *Journal of Labor Economics,* **15(1)**, S293–S329.

Which? (2007) TV ad rules continue to fail children. Online at
http://www.which.co.uk/news/2007/11/tv-ad-rules-continue-to-fail-children-125160.jsp

Whincup, P.H., Gilg, J.A., Odoki, K., Taylor, S.J.C. and Cook, D.G. (2001) Age of menarche in
contemporary British teenagers: survey of girls born between 1982 and 1986. *British Medical
Journal,* **322(7294)**, 1095–1096.

Whitehead, J. (2007) *Can parents smack their children? Protecting children.* Online at
http://www.teachingexpertise.com/articles/can-parents-smack-their-children-2931

Williams, F. (2005) *Rethinking families.* London: Galouste Gulbenkian Foundation.

Williams, Z. (2007) *Commercialisation of childhood.* London: Compass.

Wilson, B. (2009) Estimating the cohabiting population. *Population Trends,* **136**, 21–27.

Women and Work Commission (2009) Shaping a fairer future: a review of the recommendations of the
Women and Work Commission three years on. London: Government Equalities Office.

Woodroffe, J. (2009) *Not having it all: how motherhood reduces women's pay and employment
prospects.* London: Fawcett Society.

Woods, R. (2009) Briefing. Internet access: broadband Britain. *Sunday Times,* 21 June. Online at
http://technology.timesonline.co.uk/tol/news/tech_and_web/article6543780.ece

Working Families (2006) *Working Families policy paper on flexible working.* Online at
http://www.workingfamilies.org.uk/asp/main_downloads/Working_Families_Policy_on_Flexible_
Working.doc

Yeandle, S. (2006) Local labour markets and the gender pay gap: new evidence from the GELLM
programme on factors constraining progress towards pay equality in England. Paper presented at
the European Sociological Association Interim Conference, University of Leeds, September.

Yeo, A. (2007) Experience of work and job retention among lone parents: an evidence review. *Working
Paper.* London: Department for Work and Pensions.

Zaninotto, P., Wardle, H., Stamatakis, E., Mindell, J. and Head, J. (2006) *Forecasting obesity to 2010.*
London: Joint Health Surveys Unit.

Zurbriggen, E.L., Collins, R.L., Lamb, S., Roberts, T.-A., Tolman, L.M., Ward, L.M. and Blake, J. (2007)
Report of the APA task force on the sexualisation of girls. Washington, DC: American Psychological
Association.

Index